Library of
Davidson College

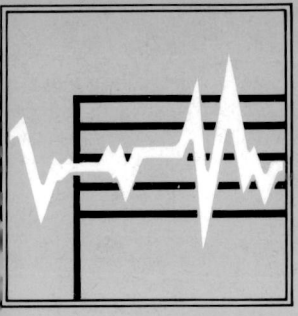

CONTEMPORARY MUSIC REVIEW
Editor-in-Chief **Nigel Osborne**

Music, Mind and Structure

Issue Editors **Eric Clarke**
Simon Emmerson

Volume 3, Part 1

Preface

Formal structures and psychological processes in music

Mind the gap: formal structures and psychological processes in music Eric F. CLARKE	1
Modelling musical cognition H. Christopher LONGUET-HIGGINS and Edward R. LISLE	15
Modelling musical cognition as a community of experts Alan MARSDEN and Anthony POPLE	29
An artificial intelligence approach to musical grouping analysis Michael BAKER	43
A computational model of rubato Neil TODD	69

Continued on back cover

 **harwood academic publishers**
chur • london • paris • new york • melbourne

CONTEMPORARY MUSIC REVIEW

Editor-in-Chief
Nigel Osborne (UK)

Regional Editors
Fred Lerdahl (USA)   Takemitsu Tōru (Japan)

Editorial Boards

UK	USA	JAPAN
Paul Driver	John Adams	Joaquim M Benitez, S.J.
Alexander Goehr	Jacob Druckman	Kondō Jō
Oliver Knussen	John Harbison	Shōno Susumu
Peter Nelson	Tod Machover	Tokumaru Yoshihiko
Bayan Northcott		
Anthony Payne		

Aims and scope: Contemporary Music Review is a contemporary musicians' journal. It provides a forum where new tendencies in composition can be discussed in both breadth and depth. Each issue will focus on a specific topic. The main concern of the journal will be composition today in all its aspects — its techniques, aesthetics and technology and its relationship with other disciplines and currents of thought. The publication may also serve as a vehicle to communicate actual musical materials.

Notes for contributors can be found at the back of the journal.

Subscription rates: Each volume is comprised of approximately 400 pages with an irregular number of issues scheduled. Issues are available individually as well as by subscription.

Subscription rates per volume:
Corporate subscription rate per volume $138.00 (including postage)
Institutional subscription rate per volume: $96.00 (including postage)
Individual subscription rate per volume: $48.00* (including postage)
*Individual subscription rates are available only to individuals who subscribe directly from the publisher and who pay through personal checks or credit cards.

This price applies in North America only. All other countries will be invoiced at our current conversion rate. The subscription rates include a distribution charge of $20.00 for postage and handling. Send your order to your usual supplier or direct to Harwood Academic Publishers GmbH, c/o STBS Ltd, 1 Bedford Street, London WC2E 9PP, England. Claims for non-receipt of issues should be made within three months of publication of the issue or they will not be honoured without charge. Subscriptions are available for the microform editions. Please write for details.

LICENCE TO PHOTOCOPY. Photocopying is only permitted by license, obtainable from the Publisher (P.O. Box 161, 1820 Montreux 2, Switzerland) and payment of relevant fee. This publication is registered for copyright in the United States of America under the Universal Copyright Convention, and is protected under United States copyright law worldwide. The Publisher is not a member of the Copyright Clearance Center, and has not entered into agreement with any other copyright payment centers in any part of the world. Accordingly the license from the Publisher includes the right to photocopy beyond the fair use provisions of the US and most other copyright laws. Please note however that the license does not extend to other kinds of copying, such as copying for general distribution, for advertising or promotion purposes, for creating new collective works, or for resale. It is also expressly forbidden to any individual or company to copy any article as agent, either express or implied of another individual or company.

REPRINTS OF INDIVIDUAL ARTICLES. Copies of individual articles may be obtained from the Publisher's own document delivery service, On-Demand Publishing, at appropriate fees. Write to: P.O. Box 786 Cooper Station, New York, NY 10276, USA, or P.O. Box 197, London WC2E 9PX, U.K.

©1989 Harwood Academic Publishers GmbH

All rights reserved. No part of this publication may be reproduced or utilized in any form or by any means, electronic or mechanical, including photocopying and recording, or by any information storage retrieval system, without permission in writing from the publisher.

Distributed by STBS Ltd, 1 Bedford Street, London WC2E 9PP, England.
Printed in Great Britain by Bell and Bain Ltd.
April 1989

Preface

The papers in this volume are a selection from the Second Conference on Science and Music, held at City University, London in September 1987. The double sub-title of this conference was "Formal Structures and Psychological Processes in Music" and "New Approaches to the Composition and Analysis of Electroacoustic Music", and the papers presented here are intended to represent some aspects of the wide range of approaches included in the conference. The manner in which this issue of the *Contemporary Music Review* is organised reflects this division, the issue being in two roughly equal halves corresponding to the two subject areas, each of which opens with a paper by the appropriate organiser and editor. We have not attempted to introduce explicit links between the two halves, but it is evident that there are certain strong connections between the concerns of the two — a feature that the conference was designed to explore. Some of these are: the concern with temporal organisation, and our perception of it (papers by David Clarke, Baker, D'Escrivan, and Alvarez); the use of generative theory to model musical structure (papers by Jones, Longuet-Higgins, Todd, Sundberg *et al.*, and Marsden & Pople); the interest in developing rule-based approaches to musical expression that have important implications for electroacoustic music that incorporates live electronics (papers by Sundberg *et al.*, Todd, and Longuet-Higgins & Lisle); and the quest for new ways of representing musical knowledge that may facilitate more powerful compositional tools (papers by Marsden & Pople, Longuet-Higgins & Lisle, and Baker). Within this area of common ground, the theoretical approaches are about as diverse as one could imagine, including semiotics, artificial intelligence, cognitive psychology, generative theory, literary criticism, educational theory and compositional practice. Our hope is that this collection of papers will demonstrate the tremendous potential for exchange between the multi-disciplinary approaches to music exemplified in this volume, and will stimulate composers, psychologists, analysts and performers to find out more about their colleagues' activities.

Eric Clarke
Simon Emmerson

Formal structures and psychological processes in music

Mind the gap: formal structures and psychological processes in music

Eric F. Clarke

Music Department, City University, Northampton Square, London, UK

While there are increasing links between musicology and the psychology of music, the two disciplines nonetheless remain distinct in terms of their aims and hence their evaluation of different findings. This paper is concerned with the gap between formal treatments of musical structure and the approach of cognitive psychology, concentrating on the problems that are a consequence of both the failure to establish a rapport between the two approaches, and the somewhat unstructured conceptual leakage that can also be observed between the two. By means of a single concrete musical example, some general characteristics of cognitive and analytical approaches are examined, and certain recommendations made, concluding with the proposal that we need a description of musical events and the way they are performed, perceived and created by performers, listeners and composers which gives greater recognition to the mutual relationship that characterises an organism and its environment.

KEY WORDS musical structure, psychological process, mutualism, cognition, analysis.

Introduction

As you come into Embankment station on the London underground, an authoritative voice repeatedly warns travellers in stentorian tones to "Mind the gap" as they leave the train — a message reproduced in large white letters on the edge of the offending gap between the station platform and the train[1]. It is a piece of advice which summarises rather succinctly the subject of this paper, since it is a 'gap' of a disciplinary kind and the manner in which it should be handled with which I am concerned. The gap in question is one which is encapsulated in the title of the conference from which these papers come — "*Formal structures and psychological processes* in music".
It is important to recognise at the outset that the formal approach to musical structure undertaken by composers and musicologists has a rather different aim from the approach of psychologists of music, and that it is in part these differences of aim that lead to some of the difficulties discussed here. Broadly speaking, the aim of musicologists and composers in tackling issues of musical structure can be characterised as

the attempt to formulate theories of the structural relations within and between musical works, and their origins, development and effectiveness as formal devices. A correspondingly brief summary of the aim of psychologists of music is the development of theories of the mental processing of musical events, or the relationship between the listener, performer or composer and the musical environment. In a number of respects these aims are quite complementary, but the different disciplines that they represent come into conflict in the way in which they describe their material, and in what they extract and evaluate as significant findings. To the psychologist it may, for instance, be very significant to demonstrate the existence of categorical perception for pitch, since this may contribute in an important way to a more general theory of perceptual processes; but the finding is of little or no value to a composer or analyst in the Western classical tradition who has almost certainly been treating pitch categorically as a matter of course. Similarly it may be of considerable interest to a musicologist or composer to give a detailed account of a complex number formalism (like the Fibonacci series, or magic squares) that underlies a composition or series of works, since it may suggest a useful compositional strategy, or indicate a significant aspect of stylistic development or identity; but it may be of marginal interest to a psychologist if there is no evidence either that the game itself can be perceived, or that it contributes significantly to the shaping and projection of those parameters of the musical structure that can be perceived[2] (see also Emmerson, this volume, for further discussion).

There is, of course, no sense in which any one of these different kinds of aim can claim priority over another, and I do not intend to try to debate their various merits and drawbacks. Rather, the problem raised by the state of affairs described here is that while the disciplines involved have the potential for considerable mutual benefit, the situation at present contains a good deal of misunderstanding, and some rather unstructured 'leakage' between the disciplines. This 'leakage' is apparent both in the way in which analytical writing on music appeals to psychological criteria in one way or another (gestalt theory in Meyer, 1973, or Lerdahl & Jackendoff, 1983, for example), and in the increasing reference to music theory concepts in work on the psychology of music (the circle of fifths in work on tonality, such as Shepard (1982), is an obvious example). The problem here is a sometimes rather indiscriminate use of these different kinds of criteria, enabling authors to slip around tricky problems by changing their terms of reference. There is therefore some ambivalence in what I am proposing: on the one hand the separation between different disciplines concerned with musical knowledge and understanding is a limitation and impediment; and on the other an indiscriminate and uncontrolled borrowing of bits and pieces sometimes seems to be little more than an attempt to grasp at anything that will bolster up inadequate theories, with scant concern for the compatibility or otherwise of their theoretical origins.

In order to examine these matters in a little more detail, it is useful to anchor the discussion to a concrete example, and since one of the purposes of this paper is to compare different approaches, there can hardly be a better short musical extract on which to focus than that overexposed analytical object — the theme of the first movement of Mozart's piano sonata in A major, K.331 (Figure 1).

Figure 1 The theme of the first movement of Mozart's paino sonata in A major, K.331.

Psychological processes in Mozart's K.331

Let us start by considering the kind of approach to the theme of this Mozart piano sonata movement that might typically be found within the psychology of music. There are of course different approaches within the discipline, but the prevailing model has the following components.

(1) *The absent work*. It is a characteristic of the psychology of music that it is primarily *not* concerned with individual pieces of music. There is some research that has made use of an individual work as its subject matter (e.g. Clarke, 1985; Krumhansl & Schmuckler, 1987), but in virtually every case this is only to provide a focus, or the material, for

an investigation of more general matters. Once again this takes us back to the issue of aims: it is perfectly reaonable within musical analysis to concentrate on a single movement of music, since the aim is to understand how particular pieces are constructed. In the psychology of music, however, as also in psychology more generally, the aim is virtually without exception to explore general processes that have a variety of manifestations and applications.

(2) *The paraphernalia of modern cognitive psychology.* The psychology of music is still primarily a part of psychology in general, and cognitive psychology in particular. Thus it has made use of theories of memory, attention, perceptual organisation and information pick-up, mental representation, motor control, skill acquisition and so on that have been developed in relation to a variety of human activities. Added to these are certain special music features, such as the hierarchically organised perceptual frameworks of tonality and metre.

(3) *Separate musical parameters.* Although there is increasing interest in the perceptual relations between different parameters of musical structure (e.g. Monahan & Carterette, 1985), it is still very much the norm to treat music perception as if individual musical parameters are processed relatively independently by specialised psychological mechanisms. It may be no accident that musical analysis is also dominated by the same 'parametric separatism'.

(4) *Organising and abstracting processes in each parameter.* The most widely presented view within music perception is that for each parameter, the ear takes in relatively unstructured, or at least ambiguous, perceptual information and 'makes sense' of it by assembling mental representations of one sort or another that accumulate and integrate individual notes of a performance or score into successively more abstract and global representations. Higher levels of these hierarchically organised representations capture higher order features of the music, and whilst there may be feedback from higher to lower levels, the general direction in which these representations are constructed is from the bottom up (i.e. from atomic to global).

The processes which give rise to these abstract representations can be briefly summarised as follows. For durational organisation in music we have:

(i) "Raw" duration judgements made on the basis of clock-like mechanisms coupled with a measure of information content, which are then subject to a categorical decision process that transforms durational information into a set of relative proportions organised into a hierarchical metrical structure, frequently represented as a tree diagram (e.g. Longuet-Higgins, 1987).

(ii) Boundary detection processes which segment musical sequences into groups or chunks at a number of different levels, ranging from the immediate musical surface to large scale formal organisation, again structured hierarchically (e.g. Lerdahl & Jackendoff, 1983).

For pitch structure in music the corresponding outline has the following elements:

(i) A well-developed psychophysics, which deals with the transformation of continuously variable frequency into the sense of pitch. Pitch is characterised by essentially discrete values, and by a sense of singularity even though the signal may be described as consisting of a number of Fourier components. A good deal of this psychophysical theory is closely related to the operation of relatively well established physiological mechanisms, though there is also some work that adopts a more abstract algorithmic approach (e.g. Patterson, 1986).

(ii) Once these supposedly primary pitch qualities have been formed, they act as the input to a whole range of cognitive processes responsible for the construction and elaboration of higher level pitch structures. While there is a certain separation between theories that are primarily melodic in orientation (e.g. Cuddy, Cohen & Miller, 1979; Deutsch, 1982; Dowling, 1978) and those that are primarily scalar or harmonic (e.g. Cross, Howell & West, 1985; Krumhansl & Kessler, 1982; Bharucha, 1987) there is an increasing recognition of the importance of interactions between particular melodic configurations and more abstract pitch frameworks (e.g. Dowling & Harwood, 1986; Sloboda & Parker, 1985).

(iii) The highest level, and in some sense the 'net result' of the series of stages that the information processing approach to pitch perception embodies, is an abstract tonal framework within which pitch events of all types and levels are contained, and from which they derive their functional significance. A variety of such global frames have been proposed, in some cases as the outcome of empirical work (e.g. the multidimensional scaling work of Krumhansl, 1979 and Shepard, 1982) and in others as formal models (e.g. Balzano, 1980; Longuet-Higgins, 1987). The format in which these models are presented frequently employs a geometrical metaphor to convey relationships of similarity or functional proximity between pitch components: Krumhansl's scaling solution is shown as a conical surface on which pitches are arranged in three levels; Shepard develops a "double helix wrapped around a helical cylinder in five dimensions" (Shepard, 1982, p. 364) — which looks something like a thick hose twisted around in a helical manner; Balzano and Longuet-Higgins present cyclical and two- or three-dimensional matrix representations (see Longuet-Higgins, this volume).

It is these abstract representations, and their equivalents in the domain of duration, that highlight the primary question of this paper: are these models of the formal constraints of the pitch system to be viewed as mental representations that are the end result of perceptual and cognitive processes (the information processing position), or as a set of environmental constraints within which perceptual processes operate, the perceptual processes themselves being still largely unexplained? Many of the authors cited above make it clear that they do not regard their representations as mental structures, but as descriptions of data (in the case of those derived from multidimensional scaling studies), or theoretical frameworks. However there is a strong sense in much of this work that these descriptions or formalisms are regarded as being very close to truly mental structures – not least because they are presented as contributions to the cognitive psychology of music. Just what the mental structures themselves might be like, and how they may differ from their formal counterparts is left unclear.

If the alternative position of regarding these models as descriptions of the environmental constraints within which music perception operates, a different kind of problem remains: a constraint of this kind is only psychologically significant if it can be picked up, attuned to, or (in the language of information processing) internally represented. Any number of environmental constraints can be described, but unless the constraint has the potential to become a part of the mental life of the organism (i.e. if the organism in question has the ability to respond to the constraint), there is very little of psychological significance to be said. As yet we still know too little about the real perceptual processes involved in picking up musical information from the environment to be clear on this.

These are the general characteristics of a cognitive approach to a piece of music, concentrating primarily on listening. As remarked at the outset of this section, the psychology of musical listening has almost entirely avoided detailed analysis of individual pieces of music, reflected in the fact that this account of the psychological processes involved in listening to Mozart's K.331 has so far not even mentioned the piece. An undertaking that might generate some interesting insights would be to apply as many of the principles of current music cognition as possible to a single piece (such as K.331) in order to see how these general listening principles interact with a concrete musical instance. Such a project might allow some evaluation of the extent to which the intuitions and experiences of listeners are reflected in the application of current theory (both empirical and formal) in the psychology of music, which could be important for at least two different reasons: first, it might reveal strengths, weaknesses and perhaps undiscovered goldmines or pitfalls in the theory itself; and second, it might help to convince a wider body of musicians (and non-musicians) than at present that the psychology of music is an important source of insight and understanding.

Turning briefly to psychological approaches to the composition and performance of a piece, it is evident that a rather more detailed consideration of the individual piece itself is almost inevitable. A compositional approach to K.331 actually raises some pretty thorny problems, since a reasonably rigorous cognitive approach to composition (e.g. Sloboda, 1985) relies on the existence of either sketches of the music at various stages of working, or some record of the compositional protocols of the composer. In the case of Mozart, who is often cited as the prime example of an almost magically intuitive and immediate composer[3] who had no need for sketching or the explicit and laborious working out of ideas, there is therefore virtually nothing on which to base a reconstruction of compositional processes other than the finished work. Any attempt to understand the psychological processes in composition seems at present to be restricted to composers such as Beethoven or Chopin, who left substantial amounts of sketching, or to current living and working composers who are prepared to cooperate by providing a detailed record of their thoughts and activities at the time of composing. Clearly, material of this kind, while providing the opportunity to extract general principles, will initially be closely tied to individual works and their special characteristics.

Empirical performance research is also closely tied to individual works for the simple reason that a performer must play some particular piece. However, as noted earlier, empirical approaches to performance data usually use the piece as a particular case of a more general issue with which the research is primarily concerned. For example, the Chopin étude used in Shaffer (1981) represents a particularly striking and consistent example of polyrhythm between the hands, allowing the control of hand independence and coordination to be analysed; and the piano piece by Satie in Clarke (1985), which combines considerable rhythmic diversity in the right hand with a simple metrical left hand, provides a setting within which to investigate how a variety of rhythmic transitions are structured in a metrical framework. In both cases the piece simply represents a particular context in which to explore a general issue. Gabrielsson (1987) has actually analysed some performances of the theme of K.331, and coupled his data analysis with a reasonably detailed consideration of structural characteristics of the piece, providing an example where a genuine rapport between formal structure and psychological processes can be observed. Once again a part of Gabrielsson's interest in using this piece is connected with a general issue (the extent to which different performers agree on an interpretation) as well as specific matters concerned with the structure of the Mozart theme and the most appropriate way to phrase it.

To finish this brief view of psychological issues in performance, let us consider its parallels with the characterisation of listening given above. We have already seen that while there is some consideration of the particularities of the individual pieces whose performance is analysed, the individual work is nonetheless primarily regarded as a vehicle for the investigation of general processes. The other three features discussed above (the paraphernalia of cognitive psychology, parametric specialisation, and processes of abstraction) all apply equally to performance, though with modifications to the latter two. Parametric specialisation is rather less pronounced in considering music performance because the observed behaviour consists of a single class of events – timed movements. This minimises the distinction between different parameters (such as pitch and rhythm) since the combination of movement and timing is used to control pitch, rhythm, tone quality, and dynamic level. The unitary nature of the observed behaviour helps to

8 *Eric F. Clarke*

reintegrate the separate features that listening research tends to emphasise.

Finally, the abstracting and organising processes referred to in connection with listening are largely viewed in reverse when considering performance. A primary question in this field is how it is that an abstract representation of some kind is transformed into the controlled sequence of movements that constitutes a performance. This is a conversion from a symbolic representation to a concrete manifestation, while listening is essentially the converse. Some consideration has been given to the way in which the symbolic representation that constitutes the performer's information source is structured and built up in various different circumstances (e.g. Clarke, 1988; Sloboda 1984; Todd, this volume), but a good deal of performance research takes the representation as given, modelling it along the lines of established analytical or cognitive theory, and concentrates on the production rules that convert the representation into action. An important approach to this issue is the attempt to devise formal descriptions, or rules, that take an abstract musical representation as input, and give a flexible and expressive performance as output (e.g. Sundberg, Friberg and Fryden, this volume). Once again this is an area where formal structures and psychological processes meet and interpenetrate, since the production rules are clearly intended as descriptions of, or at least metaphors for, the psychological processes taking place within a performing musician — though whether the musician is really *following* the rules or simply behaving in manner that can be *described* by the rules remains unclear.

Formal structure in Mozart's K.331

Let us now turn briefly to a consideration of formal structural approaches to music, with the theme of the first movement of K.331 as our example. The theme is, as Narmour has remarked, "one of the most overanalyzed pieces in the history of music theory" (Narmour 1983, p. 160), and all that will be attempted here is a sketch of the general nature of two of these analyses (Figures 2 and 3). Schenker (1979) analyses the theme as a three-part form, based on voice-leading properties of the music (Figure 2). The rationale for this is his identification of two outer sections (bars 1 to 8 and 13 to 18) which consist of a descending fifth in the upper voice coupled with a tonic prolongation in the lower voice, and a middle section (bars 9 to 12) which consists of a descending fourth in the upper voice coupled with a tonic to dominant progression in the lower voice. While it is these reductional features which motivate Schenker's identification of a tripartite form, notice that he does also recognise that the structure is reflected in motivic changes, as indicated by the a_1, b, and a_2 labels below the beginning of each of the three sections.

By contrast Meyer (1973) analyses the same theme as a two-part form (Figure 3). His criteria are primarily those of overall symmetry (the theme is divided into 8 + 10 bars), large scale rhythmic balance (a high level iamb

Mind the gap: formal structures and psychological processes in music 9

Figure 2 Schenker's analysis of the theme of the first movement of Mozart's piano sonato in A major, K.331, from Schenker (1979). Copyright Schirmer Books, a division of Macmillan Publishers, reproduced with their kind consent.

in each of the repeated halves, each of which is an iamb, as the 'summary' in figure 3 shows), and motivic differentiation and parallelism.

The two analyses illustrate the general pattern for structural analysis of this kind: a theory is developed which is then applied to a particular piece for some specific purpose. Meyer's purpose is to discuss the relationship between structure and performance, and in particular the relative merits of two different editions of the music which indicate different ways of phrasing the theme. Schenker uses the theme as an example of a three-part form that acts as the theme in a variation movement — in other words as part of a formal typology that is used to support his theory that form is the reflection or consequence of voice-leading.

However if we look a little more closely at analyses of the kind presented here, the formal nature of the theory starts to look a little dubious. It must be said that Schenker's analyses are some of the more formal in the analytical literature, based as they are on strict principles of counterpoint and voice-leading. But even these are far from being rigorously formal as is evident from the discrepancies between different Schenkerian analysts' interpretations of the same piece of music, and the failure of anyone to produce an algorithmic version of Schenker's theory — one in which these supposedly strict principles can be automatically applied. Meyer's analysis is less formal than Schenker's and is quite explicit about employing a mixture of criteria from different disciplinary sources to form the analysis: some are essentially psychological criteria, based around gestalt principles such as proximity in time and pitch, or good continuation, and others are more formal, such as symmetry, hierarchical simplicity, or formal regularity. A more recent and more

Figure 3 Meyer's analysis of the theme of the first movement of Mozart's piano sonato in A major, K.331, from Meyer (1973). Copyright University of Chicago Press, reproduced with their kind consent.

pronounced example of this kind of disciplinary mixture in an analytical framework is Lerdahl and Jackendoff's generative theory of tonal music (1983), which mixes gestalt principles of perception with more abstract criteria in developing a set of formal rules for understanding musical structures.

There is nothing intrinsically objectionable in adopting an eclectic approach of this kind, but there are certain problems associated with the way the mixture is handled, and the inferences drawn from the resulting analyses. First, an indiscriminate disciplinary mixture implies that formal and perceptual properties function in the same way, and are equally perceptible. This is a highly dubious assumption as a more extreme example of the same phenomenon, such as an analysis that contains findings based on the Fibonacci series or the Golden Section, illustrates. A notorious example of this kind of confusion or sleight of hand is Stockhausen's attempt in "How time passes . . ." (1959) to take a psychophysical perceptual principle from one domain (the logarithmic nature of pitch perception), apply it to another (duration), and then extend and elaborate it into a formal principle for compositional purposes. The perceptual *origin* of the principle is then used to justify the perceptibility of the resulting compositional structures.

A second problem with the mixing of psychological and formal principles is that most psychological processes are rather subjectively variable, and appealing to them as if they had the fixity and objectivity of formal principles can be misleading. It is in part this problem which has led to some of the critical reaction to Lerdahl and Jackendoff's theory. Though presented as a formal theory, it turns out in practice to rely on a large amount of subjective decision making on the part of the individual analyst, based on his/her particular (and variable) perception of the relative importance of a number of different musical factors. It is this contrast between the formal presentation of the theory as a whole and the strict nature of some of the individual rules, with the subjective variability that is encountered when the theory is put into practice, which has provoked critical response.

Third, there is a tendency to confuse *cultural norms* (such as the norms of formal design) which are established by convention, with *perceptual norms* which are the consequence of the characteristics and limitations of perceptual systems. This is one consequence of a fairly general failure to acknowledge historical factors in the "strict" analytical tradition, and the almost complete rejection of a historical perspective in cognitive psychology. It potentially leads to the absurd situation in which attempts are made to account for socio-historical conventions in terms of innate perceptual characteristics (for example, accounts of Western tonality based solely, or heavily, on psychoacoustics or auditory physiology). It seems certain that most human cultural systems reflect fundamental biological and perceptual capacities at some very deep level, but so extensively mediated by the developments and ramifications of these cultural systems themselves as to make an appeal to such "origins" for an explanation of phenomena here and now senseless. Without rejecting the human nature of cultural systems, and hence the stamp of human biological and psychological capacities at some level on their products and manifestations, it is important to be careful about the *kind* of explanatory framework that is appropriate given the enormous weight of cultural history that lies between us and these primary qualities.

I will conclude by making two apparently contradictory recommendations.

(1) On the one hand it is important to maintain a clear separation between the aims, concepts and criteria of different approaches to the structure, function, and psychology of musical events if we are to avoid sinking into a morass of inconsistency and incompatibility.

(2) On the other hand an attempt should be made to establish a rapport between these different kinds of approach — not through the rather sterile exercise of simply identifying mapping relationships between the terms of one and the terms of another, but by developing a different kind of description that recognises the mutual relationship between a perceiver and its environment. The aim of such an approach would be to describe musical events for a particular kind of perceiver, taking account of the stimulus material, the perceptual systems that exist, and the cultural systems within which evaluations of musical function are made. This is in essence an argument for an ecological description, since it proposes that while there is an indefinite number of possible descriptions of the same state of affairs from a variety of different perspectives, and at a number of different levels, the kind of description that is of primary interest to us will be at a level, and of a breadth appropriate to human beings, their musical artifacts and activities, and the natural and cultural environment within which they are situated.

Notes

1. I am grateful to Alan Marsden for reminding me of this.
2. It may not, of course, be easy to decide what is or is not perceivable in a piece of music, or to be sure that an apparently abstruse compositional feature does not subtly influence directly perceivable events on the surface of the music.
3. These remarks are not intended to add support to this rather starry-eyed view of Mozart's genius, but only to point out the difficulties of attempting research into the creative processes of a composer whose working style appears to have been so internalised.

References

Balzano, G.J. (1980) The group-theoretic description of 12-fold and microtonal pitch systems. *Computer Music Journal*, **4**, 66–84
Bharucha, J.J. (1987) Music cognition and perceptual facilitation: a connectionist framework. *Music Perception*, **5**, 1–30
Clarke, E.F. (1985) Some aspects of rhythm and expression in performances of Erik Satie's "Gnossienne No. 5". *Music Perception*, **2**, 299–328
Clarke, E.F. (1988) Generative principles in music performance. In J. Sloboda (Ed) *Generative Processes in Music* Oxford: The Clarendon Press
Cross, I., Howell, P. & West, R. (1985) Structural relationships in the perception of musical pitch. In P. Howell, I. Cross, & R. West (Ed) *Musical Structure and Cognition* London: Academic Press
Cuddy, L.L., Cohen, A.J., & Miller, J. (1979) Melody recognition: the experimental application of musical rules. *Canadian Journal of Psychology*, **33**, 148–156
Deutsch, D. (1982) The processing of pitch combinations. In D. Deutsch (Ed) *The Psychology of Music* New York: Academic Press

Dowling, J. (1978) Scale and contour: two components of a theory of memory for melodies. *Psychological Review,* **85,** 341–354

Dowling, J. & Harwood, D. (1986) *Music Cognition.* New York: Academic Press

Gabrielsson, A. (1987) Once again: the theme from Mozart's piano sonata in A. Major (K.331). In Gabrielsson (Ed) *Action and Perception in Rhythm and Music* Publications issued by the Royal Swedish Academy of Music no 55, Stockholm

Krumhansl, C.L. (1979) The psychological representation of musical pitch in a tonal context. *Cognitive Psychology,* **11,** 346–374

Krumhansl, C.L. & Kessler, E.J. (1982) Tracing the dynamic changes in perceived tonal organisation in a spatial representation of musical keys. *Psychological Review,* **89,** 334–368

Krumhansl, C.L. & Schmuckler, M.A. (1987) The *Petroushka* chord: a perceptual investigation. *Music Perception,* **4,** 153–184

Lerdahl, F. & Jackendoff, R. (1983) *A Generative Theory of Tonal Music* Cambridge, Mass: MIT Press

Longuet-Higgins, H.C. (1987) *Mental Processes* Cambridge, Mass: MIT Press

Meyer, L.B. (1973) *Explaining music* Berkeley: University of California Press

Monahan, C.B. & Carterette, E.C. (1985) Pitch and duration as determinants of musical space. *Music Perception,* **3,** 1–32

Narmour, E. (1983) Some major theoretical problems concerning the concept of hierarchy in the analysis of tonal music *Music Perception,* **1,** 129–199

Patterson, R.D. (1986) Spiral detection of periodicity and the spiral form of musical scales. *Psychology of Music,* **14,** 44–61

Schenker, H. (1979) *Free Composition* (trans. E Oster). New York: Longman

Shaffer, L.H. (1981) Performances of Chopin Bach and Bartok: studies in motor programming. *Cognitive Psychology,* **13,** 326–376

Shepard, R.N. (1982) Structural representations of musical pitch. In D. Deutsch (Ed) *The Psychology of Music* New York: Academic Press

Sloboda, J.A. (1984) Experimental studies of music reading: a review. *Music Perception,* **2,** 222–236

Sloboda, J.A. (1985) *The Musical Mind.* Oxford: The Clarendon Press

Sloboda, J.A. & Parker, D.H.H. (1985) Immediate recall of melodies. In P. Howell, I. Cross & R. West (Ed): *Musical Structure and Cognition* London: Academic Press

Stockhausen, K. (1959) How time passes . . . *Die Reihe,* **3,** 10–41. London: Universal Edition

Modelling musical cognition

H. Christopher Longuet-Higgins and
Edward R. Lisle
Centre for Research on Perception and Cognition, Laboratory of Experimental Psychology, University of Sussex

The intelligent appreciation of classical music requires a listener to recreate in his mind the rhythmic and tonal structures originally conceived by the composer and realised in sound by the performer. The present paper reviews the theory of rhythm and tonality, and shows how it can be used to construct working models of the perception and production of real-time keyboard performances.

KEY WORDS computer modelling, rhythm, tonality, perception, production, cognition.

1. The modelling of musical cognition

Twelve years ago (Longuet-Higgins, 1976) one of us described in the columns of *Nature* a computer program that could transcribe the Prelude to Act III of *Tristan und Isolde* from a live keyboard performance into the equivalent of standard musical notation. The program was intended not as a nine-day wonder but as a computational model of how musicians perform the task. Since then the idea of modelling cognitive processes by computer programs has come into its own in musical as well as psychological circles, and in this paper we describe some more recent work on the computer modelling of musical perception and production, and the theoretical foundations on which it is based.

1.1 Music and language

There is a close analogy between music and poetry (see Figure 1).

Like a poem, a piece of music can be realised in sound or represented in symbols, and subsequently recreated in the mind of the listener or the reader. But a particular piece of music, or a poem, is neither a sequence of sounds nor a series of marks on paper; it is an entity of an altogether more

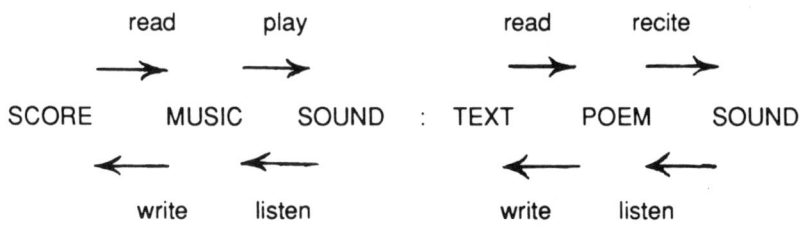

Figure 1   The analogy between music and natural language

abstract kind. Just as a poem is made up of words in certain grammatical relations, so a piece of music is composed of notes linked by rhythmic and tonal relationships. In order to understand the processes of musical cognition one must be absolutely clear about the nature of these relationships, and for this purpose the Chomskian idea of a generative grammar is eminently suitable (Sundberg & Lindblom, 1976; Longuet-Higgins, 1978).

1.2 Generative music theory

A generative grammar, as originally conceived by Chomsky (1965), is a formal specification of the set of utterances that belong to a particular language. In the course of "generating" a particular utterance the grammar assigns it a structure, upon which the meaning of the utterance largely depends. Regarded as a theory of the language, the most satisfactory grammar will be that which accomplishes its task most effectively and economically, and explains in the most natural way the linguistic intuitions of the native speaker.

(For those unfamiliar with Chomskian terminology, grammars "generate" utterances only in the sense in which recipes generate cakes; actually producing them is quite another matter.)

The application of these ideas to music is surprisingly direct, if one allows the word *language* to encompass a particular musical idiom such as that of Bach or Mozart, takes the term *utterance* to embrace any composition in that idiom, and understands the word *meaning* in an affective rather than a logical sense. The analogy has been made much of in *A Generative Theory of Tonal Music* (Lerdahl & Jackendoff, 1983), but the generative theory we outline below, developed over the last 25 years (Longuet-Higgins, 1962, 1987), is rather different from that of Lerdahl & Jackendoff and closer, in our opinion, both to the Chomskian paradigm (Chomsky, 1957, 1965) and to the ways of thinking of the active musician

(Tovey, 1949; Meyer, 1956, Cooke, 1959). An important question about any such theory is whether it lends itself to the faithful representation of the structures by which pieces of music are represented in the human mind, and the processes by which they are expressed by performers and recreated by listeners. But before considering this question it is necessary briefly to review the theory itself.

1.3 The generation of tonal intervals

A basic problem in the theory of tonality is that of enumerating all the intervals of tonal music — all the tonal relations in which any two notes of a composition may stand. The first necessity is to recognise the problem as non-trivial: is not every tonal interval simply a whole number of twelfths of an octave? The pitiful inadequacy of this suggestion is evident from its failure to explain (i) the fact that tonally distinct intervals such as the major 3rd and the diminished 4th span equal numbers of keyboard semitones or (ii) why the octave should be divided into 12 parts rather than 13, or (iii) why these parts should be equal, or (iv) how the process of division is to be performed *musically* rather than acoustically (we challenge the reader divide an octave into 5 equal parts without the help of a frequency meter), or (v) why it is the octave, rather than anything else, that is to be submitted to this act of duodecimation.

An altogether different picture emerges from the realisation that tonal intervals are constructed, not by division of the octave or multiplication of the semitone, but by the *addition* and *subtraction* of more primitive intervals such as octaves and perfect 5ths. (No reasonable musician would wish to deny that, for example, the perfect 4th is an octave minus a perfect 5th.) Remarkably enough, this simple thought can be developed into a formally precise theory of tonality, using the mathematical theory of groups.

A group is, in essence, a set of elements which may be combined in pairs to produce further elements that also belong to the group. If the order in which two elements are combined makes no difference to the result, the group is called Abelian. As we shall see immediately, the set of all tonal intervals, regarded as upward or downward *transitions* between notes, constitutes an Abelian group.

First, any pair of tonal intervals can be combined in either order to give another tonal interval; thus an upward octave plus a downward 5th gives an upward 4th — another tonal interval — and so does a downward 5th plus and upward octave. Secondly, to be a group a set of elements must contain a special element U with the property that the result of combining U with any element R is R itself. The repertoire of tonal intervals does indeed include such an element, namely the *unison* — the interval from any note to the same note. Thirdly, every element of a group must possess a unique *inverse:* when the element is combined with its inverse the result must be the element U. Just so, every tonal interval has an inverse with which it combines to give the unison; for example the upward octave is the inverse of the downward octave, and *vice versa*. Finally, in order to constitute a group, a set of elements must obey the axiom of *associativity:* for any 3 elements R, S and T the combinations (RS)T and R(ST) must yield the same element. So if the intervals of tonal music are to form a group, then the result of combining any three intervals R, S and T should be independent of the order in which they are combined. (This axiom is also satisfied: thus if R is a major 3rd, S is a minor 3rd and T is a perfect 4th, RS will be a perfect 5th and ST will be a minor 6th; combining a perfect 5th with a perfect 4th gives the same interval — the octave — as combining a major 3rd with a minor 6th.) The intervals of tonal music therefore do indeed constitute an Abelian group — a conclusion that rests on purely *musical* axioms and is equally invulnerable to discoveries in acoustics, psychophysics or auditory physiology.

The received theory of tonality implicitly adopts a further axiom — we may call it the Pythagorean axiom — namely that *all* the intervals of tonal music can be formed from octaves and perfect 5ths *alone*. The only recommendation for this axiom is the use to which the "circle of fifths" can be put in transposing written music from one key to another. It is not, however, suitable for adoption as an axiom of tonal theory, as it undermines many of the conceptual distinctions that such a theory ought to illuminate. Its most blatant clash with musical intuition is in mistaking the major 3rd — one of the most self-explanatory intervals in all music — for a Pythagorean 3rd — a combination of four upward 5ths and two downward octaves! (In describing the major 3rd as "self-explanatory" we are implicitly contrasting it with intervals such as the augmented 4th, which out of context is equally likely to suggest a diminished 5th; or with the major 2nd, which might be perceived, with equal likelihood, as the interval from tonic to supertonic or as the interval from supertonic to mediant). The theory reviewed here rejects the Pythagorean axiom and assumes instead that the octave, the perfect 5th and the major 3rd are *independent* generators of the group of all tonal intervals and, furthermore, that the group so generated comprises all the intervals of classical tonal music.

This assumption leads directly to a number of interesting conclusions. First, that the group of all tonal intervals has an infinite number of elements. Secondly, that every interval in the group can be assigned a unique set of indices (x,y,z) specifying the numbers of (upward) perfect 5ths, major 3rds and octaves of which it is composed; the minor 3rd, for example, has indices (1, -1, 0), while the indices of the imperfect 3rd are (-3, 0, 2). Such distinctions are obliterated by any tonal model, such as the circle of fifths, that invokes the Pythagorean axiom.

The structure of the tonal group can most easily be exhibited by using its generators to construct a lattice of notes from an arbitrary initial note. On such a lattice (Longuet-Higgins, 1962) every tonal interval is a *vector*, i.e. a 3-dimensional displacement in the space of the perfect 5th, the major 3rd and the octave, rather than a mere increment in pitch, measurable in keyboard semitones (Davies, 1978). In drawing the lattice it will often be convenient to suppress the octave dimension, and to use oblique rather than rectangular axes. Thus in Figure 1, due to Mark Steedman (private communication), every triad appears as an equilateral triangle — either "the right way up" if it is a major triad, or "upside down" if it is a minor triad:

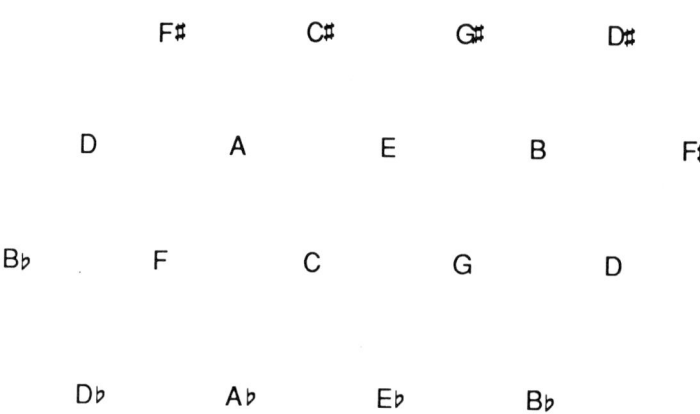

Figure 2 The Steedman representation of tonal space

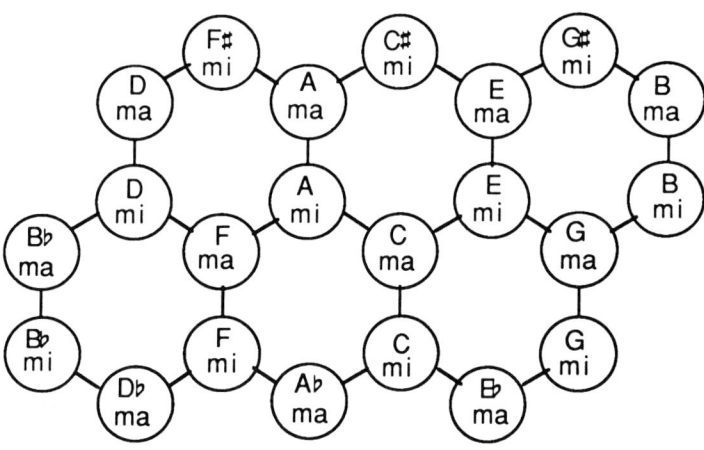

Figure 3 The tonal connections between major and minor triads

Figure 3 is the dual of Figure 2, obtained by writing inside each triangle the name of the major or minor triad defined by its vertices. In this figure the two triads of every pair joined by a line have two notes in common, and each set of parallel links corresponds to a particular type of relation between the triads involved.

The generative theory of tonal intervals is, of course, no substitute for a manual of composition; like a generative grammar of a natural language it merely lays out the choices that are open to the language user without in any sense preferring one to another. The same applies to the rhythmic component of the grammar, to which we now turn.

1.4 The generation of rhythms from metres

The way in which grammars generate structures could hardly be better illustrated than by the musical concept of a time signature. The metre specified by a time signature such as 6/8 is nothing less than a generative grammar for the rhythms of the succeeding measures — a set of rules for realising a measure as a sequence of note values and rests. Here the essential concept is that of a *metrical unit*, of which a 6/8 measure is a typical instance. (The term *time span* is, we submit, insufficiently abstract in its implications; it belies the fact that the first line of "God Save the Queen" is not something that can be measured in seconds.) In generative terminology, a 6/8 unit may be "realised" either as a single note (or rest) or as a sequence of two 3/8 units; each of these, in turn, may be realised as either a single note or a rest, or as a sequence of three 1/8 units; and so on. In contrast, the metre specified by the time signature 3/4 requires a measure to be divided, if at all, into three metrical units of value 1/4; each of these, if not realised as a note or a rest, is to be further broken up into two 1/8 units; and so on.

The significance of such statements is to be sought, not in their validity, which is almost embarrassingly obvious, but in the formal precision of the theory in which they are embedded. Without such a theory it would be hopeless to attempt to construct a computational model of the perception of musical rhythms. What, for example, should such a program do when supplied with a succession of 6 equal notes — assuming that there were grounds for supposing them to occupy a complete measure? As soon as the question is asked, the musician realises that its answer must depend on the metre that the listener has in mind (and on the tempo, but this we ignore for the moment). If this metre is 3/4, notes 3 and 5 will be heard as falling on beats 2 and 3 of the measure, which is therefore to be divided into three metrical units of value 1/4; these in turn will be interrupted by the onsets of notes 2, 4 and 6, and the measure will ultimately be perceived to consist of three pairs of (1/8)–notes. But if the listener has a 6/8 metre in mind, he will naturally tend to hear the six notes as a pair of triplets. Without the apparatus of generative grammar — in particular the concept of realisation rules — it would be impossible even to recognise such ambiguities, let alone make proposals as to how musicians might resolve them.

2. The representation of polyphonic music

In the early model of the perception of melodies (Longuet-Higgins 1976) no difficulties seemed to arise from the assumption that every note or rest is to be attached to a terminal node of the rhythmic tree. A further assumption of the model was that a measure or a subunit thereof is perceived to be divided if and only if it is interrupted by the onset of a note; the offset times of notes were not allowed to affect the rhythm, only the perceived articulation. Thus if (within a certain tolerance) a note lasted for as little as half its metrical unit, the note was classified as *staccato*; if it lasted for the full unit, as *legato*, and if for an intermediate time, as *tenuto*; but if it continued into the following metrical unit, then that unit was deemed to be initiated by a *tied* note. Tied notes were (and still are) represented by pointers to the notes of which they are extensions, rather than to separate data tokens; grace notes were represented as notes sharing a terminal node with the principal note; but more elaborate types of ornament such as trills were not allowed for.

In extending the model to polyphonic music we have found it necessary to increase its representational power in a number of ways; some of these will now be described.

2.1 Vocal multiplicity

In pure counterpoint such as fugue one may wish to respect the individuality of the different voices by assigning each a separate melodic line. But if as often happens the metre is the same for all the voices, and particularly if the parts vary in number, it may be appropriate to represent more than one part on the same rhythmic tree, just as a composer will often write two or more parts on the same stave. A good example is the C major Prelude from Book I of *Das Wohltemperierte Klavier* (see Figure 4).

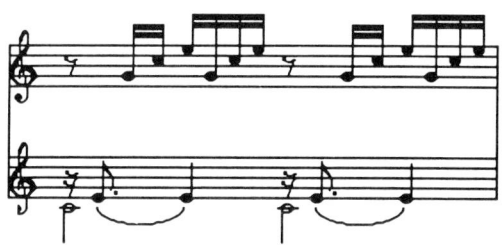

Figure 4 The first measure of the First Prelude of *Das Wohltemperierte Klavier*

Though the piece has a strong polyphonic undercurrent, the number of parts is of little consequence; what must be represented is the fact that the first note occupies the whole of the first half-measure, while the second note initiates the second half of the first half of the first half of the first half-measure, and survives through the second half of its first half and the whole of its second half. The devastating clumsiness of such indisputable statements is more than enough of a reason for expressing the relevant relations in the precise medium of a computational data structure!

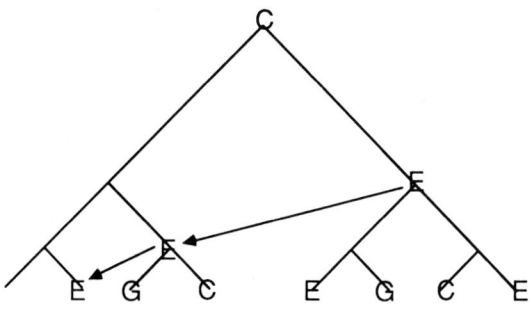

Figure 5 The first half-measure of the First Prelude

Figure 5 illustrates how the earlier concept of a rhythmic tree can be modified to accommodate such relationships. The new feature is that notes (and indeed rests) can be associated not only with terminal nodes (units) but with higher nodes as well. The topmost node represents the first half-measure of the First Prelude, and the note directly attached to it is the C that lasts throughout that unit. The second note (the leftmost E) is sounded at the beginning of the second 1/16 unit, but is subsequently tied over a 1/8 unit and a 1/4 unit, neither of which is a terminal node. The arrows in Figure 5 represent pointers from the corresponding nodes to the note in question. The subsequent notes of the first half-measure are all 1/16 notes, associated with terminal nodes. (Any resemblance between Figure 5 and a Schenkerian "pitch reduction" scheme or a Lerdahl-Jackendoff "prolongational reduction" diagram is quite coincidental; the only relations implied by the diagram are the purely rhythmic relations specified in the first half-measure of Figure 4.)

2.2. Note clusters

Though the notes of a rhythmic figure are closely related, there are other important ways in which notes may be grouped — in chords, trills and ornaments of other sorts. The present model recognizes this by introducing the concept of a *cluster* — a group of notes that are sounded either simultaneously or in rapid succession, and whose offset times are similarly constrained; the type of cluster depends on the precise nature of these constraints. Clusters exhibit many of the properties of individual notes: a chord may be *staccato*, for example; a trill may be tied over from one measure into the next. (It will occasion no surprise, though, that the reliable parsing of trills and other ornaments is nowhere yet in sight!)

2.3 Phrasing and tempo

In listening to a piece of harpsichord music, say, the experienced musician will not merely perceive the finer points of timing and articulation but will interpret them as indications of both tempo and phrase structure. Though the details of this process are still largely obscure, there is no corresponding representational problem: if a particular sequence of notes or note clusters is deemed to constitute a phrase, one may form them into a list as freely as one can enter a slur into a musical score. (Logically there is no need even to respect their temporal order, but this particular freedom has no obvious musical counterpart.)

A challenging problem, hitherto unsolved, is that of representing in formally precise terms the manner of performance of a classical composition, where this term is used to cover the tempo, the dynamics and their variations, both local and global. A linguist might take the view that such "suprasegmental" information is to be clearly distinguished from the structural information embodied in the rhythmic and tonal relations between the notes; that it is the latter that ultimately dictate the acceptability of a given manner of performance. In accordance with this view the present edition of our computational model excludes from the structural representation of a piece of music any information that we would have no idea how to translate into performance rules. An indication such as *appassionato*, though clear enough to a human performer, is, needless to say, beyond the comprehension of our present model!

3. The Computational Model

It is now time to describe in concrete terms the system that we have developed for implementing these ideas. It comprises an electronic music synthesiser that can be used as either an input or an output device, being connected *via* a Midi interface and a BBC micro to a Vax minicomputer. The heart of the system is a suite of three programs: a parser, an editor and a performer. All three are under active development — a state of affairs that reflects the highly provisional state of our ideas about musical cognition. But this does not apply to the overall architecture of the system, which is dictated by the cognitive tasks that it is designed to carry out, namely to construct a faithful representation of a straightforward piece of keyboard music, and to convert such a representation into a workmanlike if uninspired performance.

3.1 The parser

The function of the parser is to convert a sequence of real-time keyboard events into a list of data structures corresponding to the measures in a musical score — a notoriously hazardous task. As already indicated, each measure is represented by a tree whose nodes represent metrical units. Each unit has a time of onset and a duration (observed or estimated) and can accommodate a cluster of sounded notes and/or a cluster of tied notes if required; there is also a pointer to the (possibly null) list of daughter units.

A cluster of notes, as already explained, carries a descriptor such as "chord" or "trill", a list (possibly abbreviated) of the notes involved and a word such as "staccato" indicating the manner of release. An individual note has pointers to its keyboard position, loudness, times of onset and offset and tonal index (0 for a C, 1 for a G, -1 for an F and so on — the quantity that was referred to as the "q value" in the 1976 paper).

Since the parser relies on a knowledge of the metre, the tempo and the key, it requires the performance to be preceded by a measure's worth of beats sounded on one of the keynotes. (The task of inferring the key and the metre from the first few notes of a piece is one that often defeats even a skilled musician!) Each measure is parsed, essentially, in three stages: in the first stage the note onset times are used for establishing the rhythmic structure, the notes themselves being attached temporarily to the terminal nodes of the tree; in the second stage, which involves the offset times, notes that are tied across all the daughters of a given node are promoted to the mother node, and (after the recursive application of this routine) grouped into clusters of appropriate type and manner of release. In the final stage the tonality of each note is inferred from its relation to the keynote.

Experience has proved the value of being able to keep track of the parser's operations measure by measure, so that if it goes off the rails as a result of the player's incompetence or the complexity of the music the operator can intervene and steer it back on to the right track. In its present state of development the parser is able to handle straightforward keyboard music without too much difficulty, but is defeated by all but the simplest ornaments.

3.2 The editor

The output of the parser is an elaborate data structure that usually needs extensive amendment before it can be accepted as a faithful representation of the music and used for the production of a score or a new performance. For making such amendments a musically sophisticated editing program is an almost essential requirement. One might envisage an "artificially intelligent" program that would, on its own initiative, correct wrong notes, infelicites of phrasing and so on, but such pipe dreams are not our concern. The existing editor adopts the "passive" role of an amanuensis: it permits the display of any chosen measure, and offers the operator a range of facilities for altering the parameters of individual notes or clusters and even modifying the structure itself by the insertion or deletion of whole units.

There are two essentially different uses to which one can put an editor of this kind: the correction of minor blemishes in an otherwise acceptable performance, or the creation of a minimal representation of the music itself, akin to an unedited musical score. The "corrective" use of the editor requires a reasonably competent performance to work on; in the "perceptive" application there is no such requirement: the different parts of a fugue, for example, or the different hands of a technically difficult piece can be played in at different times and at arbitrary *tempi*. After parsing (and only then) the various parts can be combined into an overall representation of the piece, and one can (in principle) use this for producing a score or an entirely fresh performance.

3.3 The performer

The "outer shell" of this program simply consults the information associated with the individual notes — their onset times, loudnesses and offset times — and translates these parameters into a sequence of instructions to the music synthesizer. The heart of the program is a set of functions that modify the parameters in accordance with whatever rules the operator cares to specify. The simplest possible rule of this sort is the Rule of Metronomy — that every metrical unit occupy, in performance, the same time span as its sister units. (The foregoing sentence demonstrates the unwisdom — see section 1.4 — of using the words "time span" to refer to a metrical unit.) An equally simple dynamic rule would make the loudness of each note a function of its weight (the value of the highest metrical unit that the note initiates) but the effect would soon become monotonous.

More subtle rules, such as those discussed by Shaffer (1981, 1984) Clarke (1982, 1984), Bengtsson & Gabrielsson (1983), Sundberg, Askenfelt & Fryden (1983) and Todd (1985), can also be put into effect once the relevant structural information is available. Another task the program can be set is that of finding all the (real or virtual) repetitions of a given phrase and realising them in the same way or in similar ways. The development of such structure-dependent rules and their evaluation from synthetic performances, are active growth points of our work. But for the moment we are mainly concerned with the form such rules should take, and with the rhythmic and tonal contexts in which they would be expected to apply.

4. Applications

We conclude by listing some of the possible uses of a reasonably reliable system of this kind.

4.1 The automatic production of musical scores from keyboard input

The state of this art is far from satisfactory, partly because of the lack, until recently, of any formally precise theory of musical structure.

4.2 Musical archiving

The same obstacle has hindered the transcription of classical compositions into computer-accessible representations.

4.3 Musical stylistics

Once a computer archive has been established the stylist will be able to search it for occurrences of particular rhythmic figures or tonal intervals that might be characteristic of a composer's style.

Acknowledgements

Our thanks are due to Eric Clarke for helpful comments and to the Royal Society of London and the Science and Engineering Research Council for financial and research support.

References

Bengtsson, I. & Gabrielsson, A. (1983) Analysis and synthesis of musical rhythm. In J. Sundberg (Ed.) *Studies of music performance*. Stockholm: Publication number 39 of the Royal Swedish Academy of Music
Chomsky, N.A. (1957) *Syntactic Structures* The Hague: Mouton
Chomsky, N.A. (1965) *Aspects of the Theory of Syntax*. Cambridge, Mass: M.I.T. Press
Clarke, E.F. (1982) Timing in the performance of Erik Satie's "Vexations". *Acta Psychologica*, **50**, 1–19

Clarke, E.F. (1984) Structure and expression in the rhythm of piano performance. Unpublished Ph.D. thesis, University of Exeter
Cooke, D. (1959) *The Language of Music*. London: Oxford University Press
Davies, J. Booth (1978) *The Psychology of Music*. London: Hutchinson
Lerdahl, F. & Jackendoff, R. (1983) *A Generative Theory of Tonal Music*. Cambridge, Mass: M.I.T. Press
Longuet-Higgins, H.C. (1962) Two letters to a musical friend. *Music Review* pp. 244–248, 271–280 (reprinted in Longuet-Higgins 1987, q.v.)
Longuet-Higgins, H.C. (1976) The perception of melodies. *Nature* 263, 646–653 (reprinted in Longuet-Higgins 1987, q.v.)
Longuet-Higgins, H.C. (1978) The perception of music. *Interdisciplinary Science Reviews* **3**, 148–156 (reprinted as *The Grammar of Music* in Longuet-Higgins 1987, q.v.)
Longuet-Higgins, H.C. (1987) *Mental Processes: Studies in Cognitive Science*. Cambridge Mass: M.I.T. Press
Meyer, L.B. (1956) *Emotion and Meaning in Music*. Chicago: Chicago University Press
Shaffer, L.H. (1981) Performances of Chopin, Bach and Bartok: studies in motor programming. *Cognitive Psychology*, **13**, 326–376
Shaffer, L.H. (1984) Timing in solo and duet piano performances. *Quarterly Journal of Experimental Psychology*, **36A**, 577–595
Sundberg, J., Askenfelt, A. & Fryden, L. (1983) Musical performance: a synthesis-by-rule approach. *Computer Music Journal* **7**, 37–43
Sundberg, J. & Lindblom, B. (1976) Generative theories in language and music description. *Cognition* **4**, 99–122
Todd, N.P. (1985) A model of expressive timing in tonal music. *Music Perception* **3**, 33–57
Tovey, D.F. (1949) *Essays in Musical Analysis*. London: Oxford University Press

Modelling musical cognition as a community of experts

Alan Marsden and Anthony Pople
University of Lancaster, UK

A consistent deficiency in past modelling of musical cognition has been the failure to take account of the flexibility and adaptability of musicians' behaviour. This flexibility, most evident when dealing with music of a 'transitional' nature, as illustrated in discussion of a piece by Skryabin, suggests that, while existing music-theoretic concepts continue to provide a basis, models must break down the monoliths of music theory into a pluralistic interaction. Similar concerns have exercised researchers in other cognitive domains, leading to proposals for novel modelling frameworks. The potential of one of these 'constraint systems', is explored through a preliminary model of the recognition of harmonies and the interpretation of dissonant notes.

KEY WORDS   musical cognition, AI, constraint systems

Introduction: Plurality and flexibility in music theory

The discussion in this paper draws in more or less equal measure on the disciplines of music theory and cognitive modelling. Our concern is not to propose any single model of musical cognition, but rather to discuss issues fundamental to research in this area. We hope, on the one hand, to contribute to the promotion of a cognitive-psychological context for the development of music theory, and thereby to reorientate the tradition of music analysis, in the conviction that such a reorientation would both allow and encourage a fruitful re-reading of earlier work. On the other hand, we wish also to promote musical cognition as a field sufficiently rich in research potential to claim the interest of the AI community generally.

The development of formal models of musical cognition, both on paper and in computer implementations, has by now a fairly substantial history. A common feature of much of this work — perhaps starting with Winograd's (1968) model of harmonic analysis — is its dependence to some degree on psycholinguistic concepts of grammar. In Winograd's case, the grammatical concepts are Halliday's; Lerdahl & Jackendoff's work (1983) draws similarly on Chomsky: the rule-based nature of such classes of grammar lends itself both to paper formalism and to computer implementation in Lisp or Prolog. The discipline of psycholinguistics has always depended upon a concept of intuition, giving introspection an important role in its methodology. A notable characteristic of such introspection is that it is conducted among experts rather than laypeople, and has thus extended to include a number of technical concepts, such as 'deep structure', which have no everyday meaning. Among existing musicological disciplines, music analysis has for many years provided a framework for introspective expert work similar to that which one can see in the psycholinguistic field, but written music analyses are seldom explicitly concerned with the explication of cognitive processes. Nor is there a fully worked-out cognitive dimension to those theories (such as Schenker's theory of tonal structure) which support the practice of music analysis.

Nevertheless, studies such as those of Winograd, and Lerdahl & Jackendoff, may be said to rely heavily on music theory. Winograd's study is based on functional harmonic theory of a kind that most musicians learn at an early stage of their education: indeed, the psychological claims of his work might be thought to rest largely on the principle that a theory with such a privileged place in musical pedagogy should inevitably underpin behaviour that is regarded as musically competent. Lerdahl & Jackendoff, on the other hand, rely more heavily on Schenker's theory, which, though well established in analytical musicology, is not learned explicitly by trainee musicians prior to undergraduate level. Thus the psychological status of the formalisms they develop is — as their alignment with Chomsky suggests — that of a model. The limitations of this model, in terms of its repertoire-orientation and the kind of listening mode it models, are well recognised, and we have seen a number of less fully developed models to which such criticism is yet more pertinent. While we would agree with the basic premise that the existing body of music theory is essentially a non-formalised cognitive theory, we think it important to recognise the wide range of music theory that is available. A model of musical cognition, if its psychological claims are to be taken seriously, must reflect this range in its incorporation of formal systems derived from music theory.

The principal failing of existing work, in our view, is a lack of flexibility, which originates in the excessive repertoire-specialisation of conventional music theories. The problem is not simply that individual theories are small in scope — that the repertoire they describe is more restricted than they intend — but that music is fundamentally flexible and multi-faceted. This aspect of musical cognition has been tackled by a number of authors (e.g. Leman, 1986). Kunst (1978), whose penchant for formalism is not in doubt, has modelled the flexibility of musical thought in terms of the listener's ability to tolerate continual changes in the 'law-likeness' of a piece of music. He suggests that, as a piece proceeds, the listener will tend to infer norms ('about' the piece) from regularities he perceives, and will formulate these in the manner of grammatical laws or propositions. But when these laws break down — as, by introspection, they frequently do — the mind is able to jump to a new set of propositions which will both make sense of what has gone before and accommodate the irregularity that has triggered the breakdown. Such 'unlearning-plus-learning' processes are, he suggests, very frequent in actual listening situations (see also Kunst & Van den Bergh, 1984).

The idea that grammar, if it is to model the behaviour of individuals, should be flexible even to the point of volatility, is also found in sociolinguistics. Here the principle of codes is the means by which the supposed integrity of language may be broken down, as Roger Bell (1976) suggests:

In place of the view of language as a homogeneous object, we must put forward some notion of language as a set of role-related, and in part role-defining, codes, grouped together as the repertoire of an individual, the combined repertoires of a group and perhaps as the sets of repertoires of formally or functionally related languages. In short, the individual user is to be seen as a chooser amongst codes and it little matters, in terms of pure description, whether the codes are styles, dialects or what are normally thought of as autonomous languages, since any or all of these can be involved in the code-switching behaviour of the language user. (:110)

In other words, the 'language' used by any individual is compounded of a number of 'codes', each of which is appropriate under certain sociologically-definable conditions; for a bilingual speaker the range of these codes may actually cover more than one so-called language. For obvious reasons, it is indeed full bilingualism which provides the richest insights into the 'code-switching' behaviour that is thought to be available at all times to all language users, and the suggestion that 'sandwich words' are crucial to the psychology of the switching process is reminiscent of Kunst's theory.

We would argue similarly that a model of musical cognition ought to proceed initially from a plurality of formalisms, each confined to a small unit of music theory and concerned with specific kinds of recognition rather than with generating descriptions that have claims to completeness. If the necessary degree of flexibility is to be achieved it is of great importance, for example, that one should break down the 'monoliths' of 'tonal theory' and 'rhythmic theory' which are so frequently invoked in the literature. In conventional music analysis the problem of flexibility comes most clearly into focus when discussing music whose style may informally be described as 'transitional'. Much music of the late nineteenth and early twentieth centuries may be said to lie in this category: Richard Strauss' *Salome* and *Elektra*, Mahler's later symphonies, most of Debussy's music, and Stravinsky's famous early ballets *The Firebird, Petrushka* and *The Rite of Spring* are all examples which spring to mind. This music is not fully susceptible to tonal theory, and yet to treat it as atonal (as Forte (1978) does *The Rite of Spring*) would seem to bypass aspects crucial to the understanding of a vast majority of listeners. The response of music theorists and analysts to such music has sometimes entailed the breaking down of previous boundaries, but this development has been largely resisted or overlooked by those committed to even a loose formalisation of specific theories, and a tone of dogmatism is evident even in a number of ostensibly open-minded conventional studies (e.g. Forte 1978, Baker 1986).

The following discussion of Skryabin's *Feuillet d'Album*, Op. 58 (1910) is not intended to be read as a music analysis, although it owes much to post-Schenkerian work, and in particular to that strand of theory which allows the conception of non-triadic configurations as consonant. This line was initiated by Salzer (1962) and Travis (1959), and has been continued by, for example, Morgan (1976) and Ayrey (1982). Of these, Morgan's article is perhaps the most important inasmuch as it makes explicit the historicisation of theory that is involved. The specific point being made here, however, is that a comprehension of this piece (and others: see Pople, in press) may be described with elegance if it is acknowledged that the definition, *in sound*, of 'consonance' may not be the same for all music, even if at the same time the *concept* of 'consonance' — and other concepts appertaining to it — are retained. In so far as it draws on set-theoretic concepts (developed most notably in Forte, 1973), this description might be thought to embody a theoretical synthesis: we would argue, however, that such apparent 'syntheses' are frequently encountered in discussions of works from the 'transitional' repertoire. The methods of achieving such 'synthesis' have differed widely, depending, we are inclined to think, on the pieces under consideration; it may also be observed that despite many years of work in this specialised field (since Travis) no single recognised theory of this kind of music has emerged. We feel that this phenomenon actually offers strong anecdotal evidence in support of the idea of a flexible, even volatile, response to music generally.

Skryabin's *Feuillet* was written while the composer was working on *Prometheus*, a tone poem for orchestra with solo piano and colour-keyboard which is notorious for its introduction of the so-called 'mystic chord'. Although the harmonic style of the *Feuillet* excludes the triadic formations familiar in earlier tonal music it is not difficult to recognise in it a series of 'mystic chords' — at various levels of transposition, and prolonged, in the Schenkerian sense, by arpeggiation and other forms of motion-within-a-chord. As an example, consider bars 5-8 (Figure 1): the mystic chord may here be considered as a pc set (0,2,5,6,8,10), since it is continually recognisable despite being heard in a number of distinct vertical orderings. This pc set is not a literal aggregate of the pc content of bars 5-8, but rather is conceived as a normative collection: notes lying outside it may be heard as neighbour-notes or passing-notes in a manner familiar from Schenkerian thought.

Thus, the A natural in bar 7, and the first two E naturals in bar 8, are heard as neighbour-notes to adjacent consonant pitches, while the E natural and E flat at the end of bar 8 are heard as passing-notes between the consonant F natural and a D natural at the downbeat of bar 9. Similar readings may be made throughout the 22-bar span of the piece in

Figure 1 Skryabin — *Feuillet d'Album*, Op. 58, bars 5–8. Copyright 1968 by Edition Peters, Leipzig. Reproduced by permission of Peters Edition Ltd., London.

connection with each of the prolonged forms of the 'mystic chord'. This result suggests how the concept of 'consonance' must remain fluid in the mind of any listener who may wish on some occasions to play at listening to Mozart, on others to play at listening to Skryabin — or to Wagner (. . . the 'Tristan' chord).

An illustrative constraint model

It is clearly not a simple matter to design, let alone construct and test, a model of such flexible behaviour. Similar problems to those we have outlined in musical terms have exercised workers in other domains of cognitive modelling and artificial intelligence. It is generally recognised that, in contrast to the old computing dictum, 'garbage in, garbage out', humans are superbly equipped to make 'sense' of ill-formed, incomplete, variable and even totally unexpected input. The algorithmic approach, which copes so effectively with well-formed input to a closely defined and delimited task, is hopelessly inadequate here: when faced wth input even slightly different from that for which it was designed, such process models behave badly, producing error messages or other inappropriate output, at best. Furthermore, the task of adapting an algorithmic system to cope with new kinds of input is generally one of rewriting rather than fine tuning. The fundamental problem is that the designer of an algorithmic system must envisage in advance all possible types of input and specifically allow for their proper processing. In many domains — among which musical cognition is just one — this is simply not feasible.

The representation of knowledge in a complex modelling system is also, inevitably, an issue that demands careful judgement. The well-established distinction between declarative and procedural knowledge-representations is a useful basis from which to proceed: in the musical domain, the difference between knowing something and knowing how to use it is shown clearly by the long research into modelling the perception of metre, which has so far, arguably, failed to put into practice the basic categorical knowledge (such as that which distinguishes between duple and triple metre) which is possessed (in some sense) by children from a very early stage of their musical training, and which — more to the point — can be expressed declaratively with great conciseness. Among general work on modelling, the development of constraint systems promises much, in that these both allow a declarative knowledge representation — the model consists of a set of statements of constraint which match well the concise representation of knowledge that is normal in human discourse — and also provide multiple and dynamic (i.e. flexible) paths for the flow of control and information — for a constraint has neither predefined input nor output, and information may flow in both directions. When gathered into a network, these constraints are said to constitutes a constraint system (a well-developed example is described in Steels, 1985; for a musical application, see Levitt, 1984).

As an illustration of this type of model, we present here a simple system dealing with the recognition of harmonies and the interpretation of dissonant notes. Neither the model itself nor the musical concepts used are particularly well developed; our concern is with the aptness of the overall modelling framework.

The main part of the model is the set of constraints in Table 1. Each of these is a logical statement defining a relation between items of information. The various logical symbols have the following meanings: =>, implications; <=>, logical equivalence (implication in both directions); ∧, and; ∨, or. Each item of information refers to a specific time and is represented as 'Time : Information'. Words beginning with an upper case letter, occurring either as times or as parameters to information, are variables. The statements following the backslash (\), where present, which we call 'conditions', specify the range and interrelation of variables over which the constraint applies. The second part of the model is the definition of these conditions in Prolog, the underlying language of the system. These statements of constraint, together with the definition of conditions, constitute the actual 'program' for the underlying system, achieving the sort of declarative representation of knowledge referred to above. Each of the constraints is easily rendered into an English sentence whose meaning is readily apparent to a musician. Constraint number 16 for example is equivalent to 'a passing-note is a note immediately preceded by a note one step above or below and immediately followed by a note one step in the same direction'. From the initial input of information corresponding to the sounding information in a piece of music, recognitions of harmony notes, dissonant notes etc. are made through the spreading activation of constraints. There is no predefined output, nor predefined processing path for input information to follow.

The manner of operation of the system is as follows. A database of items of information is maintained, but in contrast to a standard Prolog database, where all items present are deemed true and any item not

Table 1 Constraints in illustrative model.

1. Time1 : sounding (Note) $\wedge$ Time2 : sounding (Note) < = >
   Time3 : sounding (Note) \
   {time_add (Time1, Time2, Time3)}.
2. not Time1 : sounding (Note) $\wedge$ Time2 : sounding (Note) $\wedge$
   note Time3 : sounding (Note) < = > Time2 : note (Note) \
   {time_sequence (Time1, Time2, Time3)}.
3. Time : sounding (Note) < = > Time : harmony_note (Note) V
   Time : dissonant_note (Note).
4. Time : harmony_note (Note) < = > Time : sounding (Note) $\wedge$
   Time : harmony_pcs ([Pc])\{pitch_class (Pc, Note)}.
5. Time : harmony_pcs (Pcs1) $\wedge$ Time : harmony_pcs (Pcs2) < = >
   Time : harmony_pcs (Pcs3) \
   {no_intersect_union (Pcs1, Pcs2, Pcs3)}.
6. Time : harmony_pcs (Pcs) = >
   always : possible_harmony_pcs (Pcs).
7. always : possible_harmony_pcs 2cs) < = >
   always : possible_harmony (H)\{subset (Pcs, H)}.
8. always : possible_harmony (H) < = >
   always : possible_harmony_type (Ht)\
   {transpose (H, Ht)}.
9. always : possible_harmony_type ([0,3,7]).
10. always : possible_harmony_type ([0,4,7]).
11. Time : harmony_pcs (Pcs)$\wedge$
    always : possible_harmony (Pcs) < = > Time : harmony (Pcs).
12. Time2 : change_in_harmony < = > note Time1 : harmony (H) $\wedge$
    Time2 : harmony (H)\{time_ sequence (Time1, Time2)}.
13. Time1 : dissonant_note (Note) $\wedge$
    Time2 : dissonant_note (Note) < = >
    Time3 : dissonant_note (Note) \
    {time_add (Time1, Time2, Time3)}.
14. Time : dissonant_note (Note) $\wedge$ Time : note (Note) = >
    Time : passing_note (Note) V
    Time : neighbour_note (Note).
15. Time1 : dissonant_note (Note) = >
    not Time1 : change_in_harmony V
    not Time2 : change_in_harmony \
    {time_sequence (Time1, Time2)}.
16. Time1 : passing_note (Note2) = >
    Time1 : step (Note1, Note2, Direction)$\wedge$
    Time2 : step (Note2, Note3, Direction).
17. Time1 : neighbour_note (Note2) = >
    Time1 : step (Note1, Note2, Direction1)$\wedge$
    Time2 : step (Note2, Note3, Direction2) \
    {same_pitch (Note1, Note3)}.
18. Time1 : note (Note1) $\wedge$ Time2 : sounding (Note2) < = >
    Time1 : step (Note1, Note2, Direction) \
    {time_sequence (Time1, Time2),
    step_interval (Note1, Note2, Direction)}.

present is assumed false (the 'closed-world' assumption), each item is marked as true or false and no assumption is made about the truth of an item not included in the database, except for a few specified types of information where the 'closed-world' assumption of a standard Prolog database applies. In the version of the model presently under discussion, information on sounding notes is assumed closed (otherwise the database would have to be cluttered with specific statements that notes not present in the music are not sounding) and so also is information about the available types of harmony — here triads. Essentially, these closed-world assumptions are working interfaces with what, in a full model, would be phonological (i.e. concerning the derivation of primitive musical concepts such as 'notes' from the incoming sound stream) and style recognition components respectively. Whenever new information known to be true or false is established, either through the operation of constraints within the system or as input to the system, specific instances of constraint are made from the general constraints above through the instantiation of variables and the application of conditions. From these it may be possible to establish further new items of information. For example, given the new information that a certain note 'a' is sounding at a certain time 't', a specific constraint can be made from the general constraint number 3:

t : sounding (a) < = > t : dissonant_note (a) V t : harmony note (a).[1]

If it is already known that 'a' cannot be a harmony note at time t, then it must be a dissonant note, and so the new item of information 't : dissonant_note (a)' can be established. If, however, in this case, it is not yet known whether or not note 'a' is a harmony note at time 't', it cannot be established from this constraint whether or not 'a' is a dissonant note. The system then aims to find out by other means the truth of these two items of information by setting up 'queries' about them. These lead to the generation of other specific instances of constraint pertaining to the required information, and possibly yet further instances of constraint through queries arising from those, etc., until the truth of one or both of these items can finally be established. It is here that the importance of the flow of information along multiple paths, and the dynamic nature of those paths, coming into being as circumstances dictate, are most clearly illustrated.

Given the constraints above and information about sounding notes (in the form of items in the pattern 'Time : sounding (Note)'), the system is able to recognise most harmony notes and dissonant notes (with the exception of suspensions and anticipatory notes which are excluded from the present discussion in the interests of brevity) in simple chorale-like music. This is illustrated by a consideration of the behaviour of the model in response to the opening of the first chorale in Riemenschneider's collection of Bach chorale harmonisations (Figure 2). The initial information that the four notes of the first chord are sounding leads to instances of constraint number 3, and hence queries as to whether these

Modelling musical cognition as a community of experts 37

are harmony notes or dissonant notes. The latter queries lead, through constraint number 14, to queries as to whether the notes are passing-notes or neighbour-notes. From these it is established that they are neither passing-notes nor neighbour-notes because, among other reasons, there are no suitable preceding notes, and, passing back through constraints numbers 14 and 3, that they are therefore not dissonant notes, so must be harmony notes. Similar behaviour causes the recognition of the notes of the next chord as also all harmony notes.

Figure 2 Bach—chorale *Aus meines Herzens Grunde*, bars 1–7. Copyright 1941 by G. Schirmer, Inc., New York. Reproduced by permission of G. Schirmer Ltd., London.

At the next crotchet beat the C and alto E both participate in neighbour-note configurations, and thereby are not ruled out as dissonant notes. However, the bass E must be a harmony note, and through constraint number 4 the alto E is also recognised as a harmony note. The situation of the C, on the other hand, remains undecided. It is not ruled out as a harmony note (unlike the B and D on the second quaver of the third bar) because it could form an acceptable triadic harmony. Furthermore, the system cannot decide between recognising the following B as a passing-note or again as a harmony note. Three possible interpretations are thus entertained: that the C and B are both harmony notes, with a change of harmony on the quaver; that the C is a neighbour-note and B a harmony note, with no change of harmony; and that B is a passing-note and C a harmony note, again with no change of harmony. Each of these remains as queries on the database. This reflects a genuine ambiguity in the music here (with respect to the musical concepts underlying the constraints of this model) and illustrates the flexibility of a constraint system: the system does not balk at ambiguous input but makes an appropriate response.

There is an ambiguity under the constraints above also at the next crotchet beat: the syetem cannot decide whether the F sharp and A are passing-notes or not. The previous ambiguity is perhaps acceptable in a model of musical cognition, but a musician is unlikely to entertain the interpretation of these as passing-notes. Here another aspect of the flexibility of constraint systems is illustrated. The model has failed to mimic expert behaviour adequately (note that the failure is not in making a wrong decision but the incapability of making the right decision), but it can be repaired simply by the addition of a further constraint or constraints to embody the expert's reason for making his or her decision. In this case one such reason is that a change in harmony is expected at the beginning of the bar. A change in harmony on the last crotchet beat of the first complete bar is already established from the soprano D; thus changes in harmony at both the beginning and end of the F sharp and A are implied, and hence through constraint 15 they cannot be dissonant notes. To cause the model to behave in accordance with this reasoning, it is only necessary to add the constraint:

19. Time1 : change_of_harmony => Time2 : change_of_harmony \
    {next_stronger_beat (Time1, Time1)}[2]

This causes the identification of a change of harmony on the last crotchet of the first bar to establish a change of harmony at the beginning of the following bar, the next beat stronger than this.

Further specialisation and adaptation of the model is possible simply through the addition of further constraints. For example, it is a simple matter to restrict the interpretation of harmonies to triads within a particular key by the addition of the following constraints (together with appropriate conditions) and information as to the appropriate key.

20. always : collection (C) <=>
    always : possible_harmony_pcs ([Pc]) \
    {member (Pc, C)}.

21. always : key (K) <=> always : collection (C) \
    {key_collection (K, C)}.

Similarly the model could be adapted to cope with music in a less chordal, arpeggiated style by the addition of the constraint:

22. not Time2 : change_in_harmony $\wedge$
    Time2 : harmony_pcs ([Pc]) =>
    Time1 : harmony_pcs ([Pc]) \
    {time_sequence (Time1, Time2)}.

In a fuller model this constraint would be derived from constraint number 12 through the application of 'meta-knowledge' on the constraints, or it could be rendered unnecessary by a capacity to deal with the partial instantiation of variables into constrained or multiple values, e.g. that the harmony at a particular time is one of a few possible alternatives.

Adaptation to cope with a repertoire more distant, such as that to which the Skryabin piece discussed earlier belongs, requires not only the addition of new constraints but the removal of some old ones. The adaptations necessary for the model to arrive at the same recognitions as in our discussion earlier are: (i) the addition of constraint number 22 above, (ii) a new constraint preventing interpretations of changes in harmony while the sustain pedal remains depressed:

23. Time : pedal_down => not Time : change_of_harmony.

and (iii) the replacement of constraints numbers 9 and 10 by:

24. always : possible_harmony_type ([0,3,4,6,8,10]).

This adaptation conforms precisely to the adaptations of music-theoretic concepts used in the earlier discussion: the general notions of consonance and dissonance remain unchanged except for a redefinition of the pitch-class configurations considered consonant.

A full model of musical cognition would make these adaptations spontaneously, just as listeners spontaneously adapt their listening to the music they hear. This arises not only from the recognition of a *known* style; listeners also spontaneously learn to make appropriate recognitions in a *novel* style (the role of learning in listening is explored in Marsden, in press). A degree of learning behaviour is displayed by the present model, again arising from the ability of information to flow in all directions. When the original model is given the Skryabin piece as input, the need for adaptation is indicated by conflict between constraints, with items of information being constrained to be both true and false: some notes are recognised as not being dissonant notes because they do not occur in suitable passing- or neighbour-note configurations, but at the same time they cannot be harmony notes because they do not form suitable triadic harmonies. This conflict motivates either a rejection of the piece as unmusical (modelling the response of some musicians) or (as for others) a relaxation of some constraints so as to remove the conflict and promote an attempt to rebuild a constraint system suitable for this piece. The appropriate relaxation here is to remove the closed-world assumption on acceptable harmony types. (As indicated above, in a fuller model this decision would be made in interaction with a style-recognition component.) In other words the system acknowledges that it does not have complete information about what constitutes a harmony in Skryabin's music. Now the system functions without conflict and begins to recognise, through the working of the existing constraints, collections of harmony notes, i.e. candidates for the status of acceptable harmony, hence beginning to learn how to interpret Skryabin's music. Full learning behaviour would also require the selection of appropriate harmonies from among the candidates, which in turn would require constraints defining the notion of consistently observable set-class used above in the discussion of the Skryabin piece.

Towards a more flexible model

As stated earlier, our intention is to explore appropriate modelling frameworks, and it is important to acknowledge and discuss the shortcomings of the framework employed in this illustrative model. An important issue arises, for example, in connection with constraint number 19, which refers to changes of harmony at the beginnings of bars. The constraint reflects a 'rule' in the pedagogical theory of harmonisation stating that a harmony initiated on a weak beat should not be carried over onto the following strong beat, but, as is so often the case, the 'rule' does not always apply. There are two cases later in the Bach chorale harmonisation discussed above where the harmony changes on the last beat of a bar and that same harmony is carried over into the next bar. What music teachers really mean by the rule is that the constraint should apply 'other things being equal', i.e. there is the possibility of a constraint being overruled by other constraints. This could be achieved by *competition* among constraints, requiring constraints to have degrees of strength, and items of information to have truth values in a range of likelihood rather than simply true, false or unknown. Such competition could also lead to the resolution of ambiguities, such as that between C major and E minor triads in the first bar of the Bach chorale, towards 'preferred' interpretations, thereby more closely modelling the behaviour of musicians. (Such mechanisms are essential in 'connectionist' models, which have many similarities with constraint systems but lack their conceptual clarity (Rumelhart & McLelland, 1986; Leman, in press.) This proposal echoes the 'preference rule' notion of Lerdahl & Jackendoff (1983), towards which much of the criticism of their work has been directed. Our own view is that the notion is along the right lines, but incomplete. In particular, they fail to specify what is meant by 'other things being equal', specifying no general mechanism for the interaction of preference rules and the resolution of conflicts. Furthermore, we believe that the flexibility implied in the preference rule notion does not sit comfortably with the authors' notion of a fixed style system called 'tonal music'.

An alternative to conflict resolved by competing strengths is to introduce an explicit control mechanism. Steels (1985) proposes a system of constraints and managers, hierarchically organised, with units behaving as constraints in relation to units higher in the hierarchy and as managers in relation to lower units. A manager will decide on a constraint to consult, pass to it certain information, and receive back certain advice, which might be new information, a request to find out further information, whether or not the information supplied is consistent under the constraint, and so on. Thus constraints act as *expert consultants* whose advice may be used in a variety of ways, including being disregarded. In a musical application of such a system, we might see a manager at a low level of the hierarchy choosing to ignore the advice of a constraint that the harmony must change at the beginning of the bar because other constraints advise otherwise. Higher up the hierarchy a manager might receive advice from an expert on tonal harmony (which at this level would be a manager controlling a whole system of constraints) that the information supplied does not match its constraints. It would then consult a number of alternative experts, perhaps in parallel, until it received advice from one whose constraints were matched by the available information, hence 'recognising' the style of the piece.

This system of management promises to enable a model to adapt its behaviour according to its input, but only to the degree of selection among alternative behaviours. Altogether more difficult to achieve is full adaptation through the acquisition of new behaviours, i.e. learning. One promising framework, however, is provided by the PI ('processes of induction') system of Thagard & Holyoak (Holland, Holyoak, Nisbett & Thagard, 1986). This is not a constraint system, though it shares characteristics of behaviour with such systems, but rather a system of production rules competing on the basis of their strength (a measure of their past usefulness), the strength of their inputs (a measure of their appropriateness), and their degree of activation (a measure of their relevance). The system also includes mechanisms for the revision of the strength of rules on the basis of their usefulness in achieving the system's goals, and mechanisms for the creation of new rules, generally from the components of existing rules. The system thus learns in an evolutionary manner, with new rules proving their right to survive in competition with existing rules. (The promise of modelling musical cognition within the PI framework is discussed further in Marsden & Pople, in press.)

Clearly a great deal of ground remains to be covered in finding the appropriate framework for models of musical cognition. However, on the basis of the arguments and illustrations above, it is our firm belief that any successful framework must have the following characteristics. Firstly it must be *modular:* there are a variety of ways of hearing music, and new ways of hearing often involve a re-working of old ways, i.e. a rearrangement of modules; furthermore modularity enables clarity of knowledge representation. Secondly it must be *distributed:* crucial decisions cannot be localised at any one stage of processing but instead different modules must be free to respond to the information available to them. Thirdly it must be *connected:* decision will depend on the interaction of modules, and information must be able to flow in both directions between modules. Finally it must *learn:* listeners spontaneously adapt their hearing to the music they hear, and so a model of musical cognition must also spontaneously adapt itself. A model with the first three of these is best characterised as a *community of experts* (Roads, 1984, pp. 30–32), and it appears that learning too is best achieved among such a community, just as advances in science, or for that matter music theory, are best achieved in expert communities.

Acknowledgement

The authors would like to acknowledge the financial support of the Levenhulme Trust.

Notes

1. The statements of constraint are actually compiled into statements of logical disjunction (i.e. A *or* B *or* C . . . etc.) which are then indexed

according to the items referred to. The specific constraint illustrated here, for example, is actually represented as 'not t : sounding (a) V t : dissonant-note (a) V t: harmony-note (a)' together with another disjunction to represent the implication in the opposite direction. Whenever an item is established as true or false, the disjunctions embodying constraints involving that item are checked. If an item in the disjunction is true, the disjunction is of no more potential use and it is removed from the database. If all items are found to be false, an inconsistency has been discovered. If all items except one are found to be false, that item is established as true.

2. The constraint is expressed in these terms rather than simply that the beginning of a bar implies a change in harmony in order to cope adequately with the opening two chords. (This problem is discussed below.) The input times are already structured metrically; obviously a more complete model would include constraints enabling metrical recognitions from less structured input.

References

Ayrey, C. (1982) Berg's 'Scheideweg': Analytical Issues in Op. 2/ii. *Music Analysis*, **1**, 189–202
Baker, J. (1986) *The Music of Alexander Scriabin*. New Haven: Yale University Press
Bell, R. (1976) *Sociolinguistics: Goals, Approaches and Problems*. London: Batsford
Forte, A. (1973) *The Structure of Atonal Music*. New Haven: Yale University Press
Forte, A. (1978) *The Harmonic Organization of The Rite of Spring*. New Haven: Yale University Press
Holland, J.H. Holyoak, K.J., Nisbett, R.E. & Thagard, P.R. (1986) *Induction*. Cambridge Mass.: M.I.T. Press
Kunst, J. (1978) *Making Sense in Music: an Enquiry into the Formal Pragmatics of Art*. Ghent: Communication and Cognition, Ghent University
Kunst, J. & Van den Bergh, H. (1984) The analysis of musical meaning: a theory and an experiment. *Interface*, **13**, 75–106
Leman, M. (1986) A process model for musical listening based on DH-networks. *CC–AI*, 3(3), 225–239
Leman, M. (in press) Symbolic and sub-symbolic processing in models of musical communication and cognition. *Interface*
Lerdahl, F. & Jackendoff, R. (1983) *A Generative Theory of Tonal Music*. Cambridge, Mass.: M.I.T. Press
Levitt, D. (1984) Machine tongues X: constraint languages. *Computer Music Journal*, 8(1), 9–21
Marsden, A. (in press) Listening as discovery learning. *Contemporary Music Review*
Marsden, A. & Pople, A. (in press) Towards a connected distributed model of musical listening. *Interface*
Morgan, R. (1976) Dissonant prolongation: theoretical and compositional precedents. *Journal of Music Theory*, **20**(1), 49–91
Pople, A. (in press) *Skryabin and Stravinsky 1980–1914: Studies in Theory and Analysis*. New York: Garland
Roads, (1984) An overview of music representations. In *Musical Grammars and Computer Analysis*, M. Baroni and L. Callegari (eds.) pp. 7–37. Florence: Olschki
Salzer, F. (1962) *Structural Hearing*. New York: Dover
Steels, L. (1985) Constraints as consultants. In *Progress in Artificial Intelligence*, L. Steels and J.A. Campbell (eds.) pp. 146–165. Chichester: Ellis Horwood
Travis, R. (1959) Towards a new concept of tonality? *Journal of Music Theory*, 3(2), 257–284
Winograd, T. (1968) Linguistics and the computer analysis of tonal harmony. *Journal of Music Theory*, **12**(1), 2–49

An artificial intelligence approach to musical grouping analysis

Michael Baker

Institute of Educational Technology, The Open University, Milton Keynes, UK

Work on modelling music cognition now seems to be at the stage where theories concerning the ongoing processes of musical understanding are required. This paper describes and critically assesses algorithms for two possible approaches to modelling how listeners process the 'musical surface' of discrete pitches to produce high level grouping structures in memory, being (i) *syntactic processing* using a grammar of chord function, and (ii) *knowledge-based recognition* of stereotypical phrase-level structures, using a system of *frames* (Minsky 1977). An integrated and *resource limited* system is described, which combines a parser of musical chord function with schema-based expectations concerning grouping structures. Major problems include describing how real-world knowledge of musical context is brought to bear on the listening experience, and integrating the processing of grouping structure within a broader theory of musical cognition.

KEYWORDS AI and music, cognitive modelling, music cognition, music grammars, schema theory, musical form, musical grouping structure

> "We have not developed a theory of the algorithms used in the processing of music . . ."
>
> (Jackendoff 1987, §11.9)

Introduction

Grouping is arguably the most important level of musical understanding. It performs the function of extending the scope of the piece of music which can be available for processing at any given time by 'chunking' pitches into higher level units. Modelling how listeners 'understand' melodies is restricted here to the problem of how listeners assign grouping structures to tonal melodies by processing discrete serially input pitches, in combination with their knowledge of other pieces. Since we take the view that any approach to modelling grouping perception must do justice to how a number of processes interact, studying melodies (rather than fully harmonised pieces) forces us to specify these interacting processes — such as the unconscious inference of harmony — in conjunction with grouping perception. Furthermore, we agree with Lerdahl & Jackendoff (1983) that separate grouping analyses are probably required for each polyphonic line, so the study of grouping in single melodic lines is a necessary precursor to this wider problem.

Extensive use has been made of the analogy between musical listening and the comprehension of natural languages. A significant difference exists, however, in the extent of our present knowledge of natural language processing mechanisms and analogous mechanisms for musical processing. In the former case, a substantial literature exists, whereas in the latter

"... theories of the course of active musical processing are at the moment based more on considerations of plausibility than on empirical evidence."

(Jackendoff 1987, §11.9).

Precise algorithms for processing grouping structure are therefore presented, inspired by two main strands of work in natural language processing ('NLP'), which have converged on those who assign a predominant role to *syntactic* processing, and those who assign that role to *semantics*. In musical terms the syntactic approach is exemplified by the AGA system (Baker 1989, in press), where knowledge in the form of *processing heuristics* is used to guide a parser using a context-free grammar of chord function towards the most musically acceptable phrase-level grouping structures. We explore the 'semantic' approach by describing the problems facing design of a system for grouping analysis (the GRAF system — "Grouping Analysis with Frames") based on the use of knowledge stored in the form of *frames* (Minsky, 1977), within a very limited musical domain. Our aim is to present psychological evidence drawn largely from studies of NLP concerning processing mechanisms, and known constraints on human memory capacity, to establish the relative claims of each approach to be the best research program for developing a cognitive model for understanding musical grouping structure, implemented as a computer program.

The paper has a three-part structure:

(i) Existing approaches to grouping analysis are critically reviewed. They mostly embody substantially correct insights which are couched in terms of unworkable theoretical formats.

(ii) The syntactic processing approach is reviewed (the AGA system, Baker 1988) in terms of its psychological plausibility. The approach suffers from the dilemma of either combinatorial explosion of possible assigned structures, thus violating psychological processing and memory restrictions, or else use of heuristic knowledge which overconstrains solutions.

(iii) The knowledge-based approach is described with reference to a specification for a frame-based system (GRAF) to assign grouping structures to English nursery rhyme melodies. The approach is based on the psychological theory of *schemata* (Bartlett, 1932), and faces the problems of restricted application, selection from a very large number of schemata, and determination of musical context.

We conclude with prospects for further research to develop a cognitive model for grouping analysis within an overall model of musical cognition.

Some existing approaches to grouping analysis

In reviewing possible approaches to modelling music cognition we use the following criteria of assessment[1]: C1: *explanatory power;* C2: *completeness;* C3: *combinatorial constraint;* and C4: *psychological validity,* amongst other more informal observations. 'Explanatory power' refers to the ability of a scientific theory to produce a model or theory of the processes which underlie and explain empirically determined qualitative or quantitative behaviour, as opposed to merely restating that behaviour in a numerical or probabilistic form. 'Completeness' describes the extent to which the role of theoretical terms and constructs is fully specified, 'combinatorial constraint' refers to the extent to which processing demands are practically manageable[2], and 'psychological validity' refers to the extent to which the theory violates known psychological constraints and evidence.

Musical alphabets and patterns

Our musical intuitions concerning grouping structure relate in some way to recurring patterns in melodic contour, harmony, rhythm and (possibly) reductional structure. A well-defined research program has attempted to formalise these intuitions, initially inspired by theories of encoding based on sequences of letters, from Simon and Sumner's classic paper "Pattern in Music" (1968), to work on recursion in encoding rules for melodies (Deutsch & Feroe, 1981). Some recent research may suggest that symmetry and phenomenal accent may be more important than these rules in encoding melodies (Boltz & Reiss Jones, 1986), but our main criticism concerns combinatorial constraint [C3]. Since we are given no description of the mechanisms by which a melody is encoded [C1], we do not know how a system could be developed which could apply a set of rules to produce 'cognitively economical' encodings without the ability to look ahead to the complete melody. For a melody of only a few bars, the number of possible ways of applying a rule-set would produce a very large number of possible encodings, and a combinatorial explosion [C3] for any reasonably lengthy melody. Applying straightforward pattern-matching techniques to sequences of integers representing intervals or durations produces *combinatorial debris:* without the knowledge possessed by musical intuition, unguided pattern-matching will fail to select those patterns which human intuition would select as musically relevant. The objections to embracing such combinatorial debris are that they make demands on memory and processing capacity which are psychologically unrealistic [C4], and that it is implausible to suggest that listeners could remember these possible encodings in order to subsequently select the one which finally turned out to be most economical.

The preference rule approach

The approach of assigning numerical 'strength' weightings to rules which predict grouping boundaries has been suggested in various forms by a number of workers (Tenney & Polanski, 1980; Lerdahl & Jackendoff, 1983; Heefer & Leman, 1986). In Tenney and Polanski's work this takes the form of deriving a 'distance metric' to relate strengths of rules which initiate possible group boundaries ("clang initiation"). Numerical measures of this kind tell us little about the underlying processes of grouping perception [C1], or about the psychological reality of metrics. Most workers in AI recognise that a resort to numerical or statistical solutions represents a relatively shallow level of understanding of the problem (such models are termed "black box" models). For example, initial use of probablistic 'certainly factors' in expert systems research, has given way to the realisation that deeper level knowledge representations are required to increase our understanding of decisions achieved by such 'black boxes' (Steels, 1987).

Lerdahl & Jackendoff eschew assigning numerical weightings to their preference rules which mark possible group boundaries, citing Winston's (1975) recognition that a resort to numerical weightings in a program designed to learn structural descriptions from examples was mere computational expediency, which did not further our understanding. There is a more fundamental reason why the assignment of numerical weightings would be inappropriate for their theory: since the musical parameters referred to in the rules such as dynamics and articulation are not themselves precisely quantified (this would need to be done at the acoustic level), the erection of a system of numerically based decision procedures on this foundation would be a kind of spurious accuracy.

As the authors themselves clearly state, the system of well-formedness and preference rules which comprises Lerdahl and Jackendoff's theory does not constitute an algorithm for performing grouping analyses[3], and is to that extent incomplete [C2]. It does not do so mostly because of a lack of specification of the concept of 'parallelism' and because we are given no means of rule conflict resolution. Finally, in terms of C1 (explanatory power) and C4 (psychological validity) the theory provides no psychologically plausible mechanisms for controlling the interaction between processing in the areas of musical understanding which the theory describes, and it is not clear how the psychological reality of required intermediary representations could be determined. Nevertheless, the theory does encapsulate many insights into grouping intuitions: it simply appears that these insights are contained within an unworkable theoretical framework.

Possible frameworks from artificial intelligence

Characterising the problem of grouping analysis in terms of a number of interacting processes relates closely to a number of AI approaches to 'reasoning under uncertainty': given that there are possibly a number of 'well-formed' grouping structures for a given piece, uncertainty arises as to which is musically preferred. Cohen (1985) identifies four approaches to resolving uncertainty — *engineering, diversification, parallel certainty* and *control*. The engineering approach simply redefines the problem so as to exclude uncertainty, and 'parallel certainty' is an example of the probabilistic approaches (the probability of one assertion is used to estimate that of another) which we reject here as involving a 'black box' [C1]. Diversification involves something akin to 'spreading your bets': the classic example is found in the medical expert system MYCIN (Shortcliffe, 1976), where, given a number of candidate diagnoses, this uncertainty was discounted by choosing the diagnosis with the smallest number of well-recommended drugs (to avoid undue side-effects).

The control approach involves specifying some set of procedures which tells a problem-solver 'what to do next', rather than explicitly representing and reasoning about the state of uncertainty. The classic example is the *blackboard architecture* of the HEARSAY-II speech recognition system (Erman, Hayes-Roth, Lesser & Reddy, 1980), where the 'blackboard' is a partitioned database upon which hypotheses or expectations concerning the speech input are placed by a number of knowledge sources. A scheduling program processes according to 'islands of certainty' on the blackboard, without which the whole system would be subject to an uncontrolled combinatorial explosion of hypotheses. As a candidate cognitive model, the blackboard approach thus suffers from problems of explanatory power [C1] (certainty factors are used to limit hypothesis generation, and flow of control constitutes a 'black box') and psychological validity [C4] (the system relies too heavily on top-down constraints). Importing the blackboard approach to musical processing would involve specifying a set of independent processes for grouping, metre, harmony and reductions. Whilst it is clear, however, that a hypothesis concerning a syntactic linguistic boundary such as a sentence ending relates to and is constrained by hypotheses concerning the meaningfulness of that unit, we do not yet understand how independent processes for analogous musical factors could be specified, nor how such processes interact with each other. Nevertheless, the blackboard approach does seem a promising long-term research project for modelling musical processing (although not necessarily the human processor), which awaits greater understanding of component processes.

One further possible approach should be mentioned, derived from the virtually self-contained subfield of AI called *connectionism*, which has been used to model low-level aspects of perception, such as vision (see Hinton & Anderson, 1981), but may be less appropriate for higher level cognitive processes. Musical applications of connectionism include Bharucha's (1987) model of musical harmony, and Lischka's (1987) model for harmonisation of Bach chorales. We would maintain that for modelling high-level cognition ('chunking') in the auditory domain, the connectionist approach is at the wrong level of explanatory description [C1].[4]

What can we learn from existing work?

Pattern perception clearly plays a role in grouping perception, but must be heavily constrained by expectancy-based knowledge in order to indicate where such processing should take place. Recent empirical research (Deliege, 1987) has shown that Lerdahl & Jackendoff's grouping preference rules do accord with segmentation by certain listeners, but it is clear that the rules are not sufficient to form an algorithm for grouping analysis. With respect to AI-based methods, we retain the principle that a system should have the explanatory power which control methods of resolving uncertainty often lack: we need an approach which is essentially *symbolic* and 'transparent'.

The syntactic processing approach

The Automated Grouping Analysis system ('AGA', Baker, 1989, in press) is a computational model of how listeners process discrete pitches to chunk tonal melodies at the level of the phase[5]. AGA can be viewed as a combination of syntactic processing of harmony with the 'diversification' approach to resolving uncertainty, which involves specifying a set of decision criteria for ranking a set of possible solutions. In AGA, the set of possible solutions is the set of well-formed syntactic parses according to a context-free grammar of chord function, which identify possible grouping boundaries at the level of the phrase. The principal decision criterion used is to rank the possibilities according to the maximal extent of matching in melodic contour between phrase groups, at the highest reductional level. Since the overall system is described in detail elsewhere (Baker, 1989, in press), we restrict ourselves to a critical assessment of fundamental principles.

The automated grouping analysis system

AGA was motivated by a desire to do justice to the way in which harmony, melody, rhythm and grouping *constrain* each other. AGA exploits one such interrelationship, between grouping and time-span reductions (TSR's). For Lerdahl & Jackendoff, grouping analysis is required as input to TSRs, and in turn, stability in the TSR is a criterion for assigning preferred grouping structures (grouping preference rule 7). At present we have no algorithm for generating grouping structures in the first place, so AGA inverts this situation by using TSRs in order to *generate* sets of well-formed grouping structures and specify their relative stability from the parallelism exhibited at successive reductional levels.

Grouping and TSRs relate principally via the "normal forms" of TSRs, these being 'templates' or fundamental structures to which they must conform. For example, the normal form for the interrupted form is <I V> <I V-I>, (Lerdahl & Jackendoff 1983, p. 139). We use normal forms as the higest level rules of a context-free grammar of chord function[6] which can be abstracted from the TSR theory as a notational equivalent to their parse trees. The general theory is that parsing according to the normal form will identify possible positions for the phrase-level groups identified in the normal form. The grammar implicit in Lerdahl and Jackendoff's TSR simply encapsulates the way in which chords function according to traditional tonal harmony. For example, the normal form for the interrupted form is represented by the grammar rules

interrupted_form → L R
L → I V
R → I V I;

examples of rules extending an initial opening towards a cadence are

I → I IV
x → x x (any chord can be extended by repetition);

and examples of rules which extend a cadence backwards are

V → ii V,
ii → vi ii, and so on.

In addition, any number of 'trivial' substitution rules — such as I → vi, V → V7 — can be specified, depending on the "musical sub-language" (Steedman, 1984) being modelled[7].

The system works according to a 'linear process model' of the kind commonly used in natural language parsers, where the major component processes are the *harmoniser, parser, reductions analyser* and *evaluation mechanism*. **Figure 1** summarises the model, which can be viewed as analogous to a natural language processor with stages for lexical analysis, syntactic parsing, and application of semantic constraints.

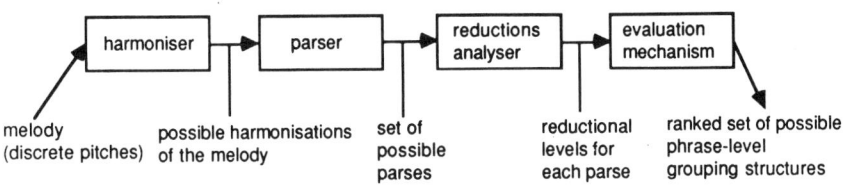

Figure 1 The linear process model of the Automated Grouping Analysis system (Baker, 1989, in press).

The melody input to the harmoniser is represented as a list of notes. The harmoniser performs a simple matching procedure between groups of notes and a 'chord vocabulary', for metric units for each bar, down to the half-bar and beat (making no assumptions about harmonic rhythm), under a set of *melodic viewpoints*. Melodic viewpoints simply express the fact that a group of pitches, considered in isolation, can be construed as having different harmonisations, depending upon which tones are selected as harmonically 'essential'. **Figure 2** shows just two such melodic viewpoints and their harmonisations: 'arpeggio' simply attempts to match tones which leap an interval greater than a 2nd, and 'appoggiatura' views the note one scale step below a note which is quit by step as a harmony note, along with the note leapt from.

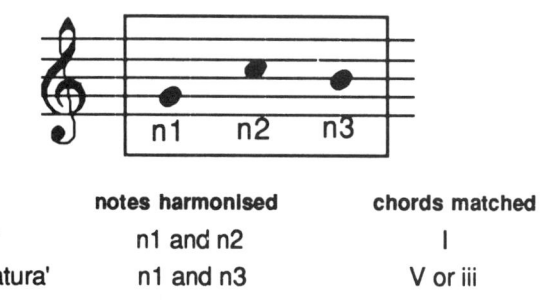

viewpoint	notes harmonised	chords matched
'arpeggio'	n1 and n2	I
'appoggiatura'	n1 and n3	V or iii

Figure 2 Harmonisation of three pitches in C major, under two melodic viewpoints, with a chord vocabulary restricted to **I, ii, iii, IV, V** and **vi**.

The output of the harmoniser is a set of all alternative possible chord functions attached to each harmonised metric unit, and is passed to a *chart parser* (Kay 1980)[8], which uses a data structure for recording well-formed 'partial parses' ("substrings" of possible complete parses) created in the course of the parse. For example, suppose the first bar is harmonised by **iii** or **I**, and the next bar by **V**. According to the rule **I → I V**, the chord **V** is a possible continuation to a chord **I**, and so a new substring of a possibly complete parse is stored in the chart according to the left-hand side of the rule; i.e. a substring with label "**I**", spanning the first two bars. The parsing process terminates when there are no more substrings to process, and returns the set of strings which span the whole chart. With a normal form of <**I V**><**I V – I**>, the output corresponds to possible ways of rewriting the melody into two phrases, the first with a cadence on **V**, and the second on **I**, with indication of the metric positions of the boundaries.

During the course of the parse, additional 'book-keeping' is necessary to record the 'children' of each 'parent' substring as it is created. When the possible parses are passed to the reductions analyser, this information enables the program to extract complete parse trees from the chart datastructure similar to the Lerdahl and Jackendoff TSR trees, by simply recursively looking for the children of each parent substring. A full set of reductional levels is generated by a combination of removing harmonically 'inessential' tones in a 'bottom-up' fashion, and the 'top-down' reduction of individual tones according to the 'subordination' relation (Lerdahl & Jackendoff 1983, p. 113) specified by the parse tree. In essence, this process depends on the assumption that if the grammar has correctly encapsulated the functional role of harmonies, parse trees built from the grammar will express hierarchical and reductional relationships between time-spans and the harmonies ascribed to them. For example, if in an antecedent phrase, two adjacent time-spans have chords **I** and **V** assigned (in that order from left to right), then the 'parent' chord in some parse tree could be chord **I**, from the rule **I** → **I V**. Since **I** is the chord which therefore dominates this pair of chords, then the notes within the compass of chord **I** are retained in the next reductional level, rather than those falling within the compass of chord **V** (see Baker, 1989, in press, for fuller treatment).

Thus far, the system has generated a set of reductional levels for each of the well-formed phrases predicted by the parser. The evaluation mechanism utilises and theoretically defines Lerdahl and Jackendoff's notion of 'parallelism', postulating a second way in which our perceptions of grouping and reductions are related. The criterion of 'stability' used is to prefer the parse which shows the greatest extent of matching in rhythm or melodic contour. It is clear that in our perception of such patterns, decorative figures are disregarded, and furthermore, it seems that the property of 'deep reductional parallelism' often emerges when a reduction co-exists with an intuitively correct grouping analysis (Lerdahl & Jackendoff, 1983, p. 145). AGA therfore performs pattern matching between well-formed phrase groups at successive reduction levels, which encapsulates the notion of 'decorative' or inessential notes, and in any case makes the problem of *where* to search for parallelism simpler and computationally tractable. Since a match which is closer to the musical surface is more exact and 'obvious', we use the further criterion of preferring matches at higher reductional levels (i.e. those closer to the 'musical surface', or the actual notes of the melody). The final output is a set (of possibly one or nil members) of possible phrase-level grouping structures, ranked in order of preference.

AGA was intended as a prototype system to test the viability of the theory which it implements, and to that extent has not been empirically evaluated. For simple tonal melodies — such as nursery rhyme tunes — it is able to constrain the problem of identifying phrase boundaries within very restricted musical domains.

Psychology and syntactic processing of music

The unidirectional nature of processing in the AGA prototype is probably untenable as a model of musical grouping cognition. As Jackendoff puts it,

> In musical perception one clearly cannot derive each level of representation in its entirety before going on to process the next level up since that would require listening to the entire piece before even beginning to derive grouping, let alone reductions.

(1987, §11.9).

It is not difficult to see how the component processes of AGA could be reformulated to produce a model of musical cognition which was more *integrated* into a single unilinear act of processing, by making the parser the central mechanism of control, invoking dependent harmonisation, reduction and evaluation processes when appropriate. To integrate the parser and harmoniser all that is required is to call the harmonisation process when examining a substring's conditions for continuation. To return to our earlier example, supposing the first bar is harmonised by **iii** or **I**, matching with grammar rules **I** → **I IV** and **I** → **I V** (supposing no rule for **iii**) would narrow down the harmoniser's task to simply determining whether **I** or **IV** was the best candidate for harmonisation of that metric unit. This would make harmonisation *expectancy based*, proceeding in parallel with parsing from left-to-right. Given the possibility for some degree of mental rehearsal in working memory, the harmoniser would be able to revise its conclusions if no satisfactory continuation was found. Since the bottom-up element of performing reductions involves removing harmonically inessential notes, this implicitly assumes some set of possible harmonisations against which to assess whether a note is essential or not. It would therefore be logical to integrate the reductional process via the harmoniser, so that once the harmoniser decided that a group of notes were to be harmonised with a certain chord, these 'essential notes' would be stored in memory as the parse/harmonisation proceeds. Performing reductions in this way does not imply a greater cognitive memory load, since harmonically essential notes are identified by the harmonisation process.

Analogical evidence from NLP suggests that musical processing may *not* involve a single unilinear act of processing through time, and may involve some degree of mental rehearsal and *retrospective hearing*. Processing does not wait until the piece is finally over before assigning a structure, but does so through time on the basis of available 'evidence', subsequently restructuring the interpretation if those expectations turn out to be unfulfilled. The top-down element of reductions, and evaluation processes, can therefore operate on the well-formed substrings stored in working memory (the chart) as the parse proceeds, building parse trees and rejecting subtrees which display little reductional parallelism in favour of those which do. Again, this evaluation mechanism is likely to be highly sensitive to the specific properties of the genre concerned, and could easily lead to either over or under constraint, in combination with the set of heuristics derived from grouping preference rules.

Given such an *integrated processing* model of musical cognition, the chart data-structure leaves the choice of parsing strategy completely open[9]. AGA uses a combination of top-down and bottom-up methods called a 'left-corner parse' (Johnson-Laird's term), which seems to be psychologically preferred (Johnson-Laird 1983, pp. 338–355). Tonal music is quite dissimilar to natural languages such as English in terms of local 'lexical ambiguities' — four or five chord functions could possibly be assigned to each metric unit, and furthermore, we don't even know which metric units should be harmonised. This means that in the parsing of even a simple two phrase fragment of a melody, literally *thousands* of substrings are built, which is not at all psychologically plausible.

A solution adopted in AGA was to incorporate knowledge into the system in the form of *processing heuristics*, to limit the building of substrings to those which were likely to lead to musically preferable results, and *genre-specific constraints* on the kinds of melodic figuration and harmonic rhythms which need to be considered by the harmoniser. The latter were based on conventional theory of tonal harmony, and the specification of processing heuristics was derived from a new theoretical alignment of Lerdahl and Jackendoff's grouping preference rules. Although the preference rules predict many redundant boundaries, it is nevertheless true that the boundaries which would accord with musical intuition are usually contained within the total set predicted. Accordingly, we can use the boundaries predicted by the rules as a weak set of heuristics, to prevent the building of a new edge by the parser which would predict a phrase boundary at a point which was not indicated by the preference rules. Four of the rules (GPR2a, GPR2b, GPR3a, GPR3d)[10] are implemented as 'demons' which fire if a grouping boundary is predicted. There may well be other stronger heuristics which could be specified, but a major problem is to specify heuristics which are 'strong' enough to restrict substrings stored in the chart within human memory constraints, without being so constrained that no suitable parse is found at all. Such heuristics would have to be very strong indeed — in fact, so strong as to virtually constitute the kind of *expectancy-based* knowledge of grouping structures which we discuss in the next section concerning frame-based processing.

The major limitation of the whole approach concerns the 'closed world hypothesis', which restricts the applicability of the system to a "musical sub-language" (Steedman 1984). AGA only attempts to answer the question

> *given* that we know the melody will be of a particular ('normal') form, how can the system process pitches in order to determine the position of possible boundaries?

This raises the problem of how the listener *knows* that the piece will be of a certain form in the first place. If the parser were to consider several possible top-level rules simultaneously, then a combinatorial explosion of sub-strings would again emerge. As will be discussed in the next section, this is a problem which faces any natural language processing strategy, concerning how the perceiver obtains sufficient knowledge from long-term memory and the real world to determine the *context* of an utterance. We offer no solution to this general problem here, but merely describe how it arises in the area of processing musical grouping structures.

It does seem possible to argue for the psychological plausibility of this integrated processing model of grouping perception, in terms of its adherence to constraints on the direction and amount of processing, and to limitations on intermediary representations stored in working memory.

A frame-based approach to grouping analysis

In AGA, the contextual knowledge required for musical understanding was represented in the form of *processing heuristics*, to constrain search for appropriate combinations of well-formed substrings of chord-progressions. A number of writers (Stoffer, 1985; McAdams, 1987; Jackendoff, 1987; West, Cross & Howell, 1987) have suggested that *schema theory*[11] may provide an alternative approach to understanding how a listener's knowledge of stereotypical metrical, harmonic and grouping structures is utilised in musical listening. Their proposals do not, however, include details of how a computable cognitive model of musical recognition based on schemata could be developed. We describe how schema-based knowledge in the form of *frames* (Minsky, 1977) could be used to guide processing as part of a cognitive model of chunking in the auditory domain.

Recognition in frame-based systems proceeds by *matching* the contents of working memory at any one time to a set of frames/schemata in long-term memory which are (unconsciously) viewed as relevant to the context of the act of recognition. There are a number of systems which demonstrate such processing mechanisms, two examples being the PIP system (Pauker, Gorry, Kassirer & Schwartz, 1984), which used frames to form diagnoses from patient case-studies in a medical subfield, and the GUS system (Bobrow, Kaplan, Kay, Norman, Thompson & Winograd, 1977), which generated (restricted) natural language dialogues. GUS used frames with slots for dialogue topics as the final representation at the end of a unilinear process model of language comprehension, analogous to the first AGA prototype. Its most interesting feature was in the use of two forms of procedural attachment to frames, being 'demons', which are activated automatically when a slot receives a value and 'servants', which are activated on demand from the central control mechanism. We incorporate both these features in the implementation design for the frame-based parser *GRAF* (Grouping Analyser with Frames). GRAF also uses processing mechanisms which are very similar to PIP[12], with a much greater degree of procedural attachment. In PIP information about the patient's symptoms are organised in terms of desriptors which may or may not match with the values of 'trigger' slots in the set of frames in long-term memory. "Triggers" are findings which clinicians view as especially relevant, from the mass of data presented to them, to sparking off a particular working hypothesis (a frame representing a disease) which they use to request further data. PIP entertains a small set of such hypotheses at any one time, using probabilistic criteria to select the most likely hypothesis to use in guiding selection of new material. In addition, each frame has an associated set of logical decision criteria which specify necessary and sufficient conditions for the truth of the hypothesis, and conditions which imply its falsehood. The GRAF system differs from PIP in that any input information to activate, confirm or disconfirm a hypothesis requires some processing to be done on the input pitches (via procedural attachment), and that several hypotheses drive expectancy-based processing simultaneously.

Design for a frame-based parser: the GRAF system

The GRAF system is a prototype designed to explore the completeness, consistency and psychological plausibility of using the 'integrated processing' version of AGA within a system of frames which represent the kind of stereotypical grouping structures described by Lerdahl & Jackendoff's (1983) 'normal forms'. The first prototype will be implemented to recognise the grouping structure of a limited class of *English nursery tunes*[13]. These melodies exhibit a small number of possible forms, where the kinds of frame-based knowledge required — such as harmonic vocabulary and melodic figurations — can be easily specified. Furthermore, we have good reason to assume that the kind of melodies which children find easy to remember will be highly stereotypical of many tonal genres.

To model phrase structures in these songs, only *four* 'harmonic formats'[14] are required, corresponding to schema-based knowledge of phrase-level grouping structures. The formats combine two phrase structures, which do not represent the chords which are literally used to harmonise the melody (unconsciously), but which act as 'templates' for the grammar rules described for AGA:

<I x I> (='**C**', or 'Circular'; **x** is a variable);
<I V>   (='**O**', 'Opening' phrase).

Figure 3 lists the harmonic formats required, together with example songs and their chord progressions.

Harmonic formats do not correspond directly to chord progressions in the tunes themselves, but are abstractions from them, which relate via the context-free harmonic grammar described for AGA. For example **Figure 4** shows how they relate via just two grammar rules for the last phrase of "Jack and Jill".

(1) C C C C (<l x l > <l x l > <l x l > <l x l >):
    example:
    "The Farmer's in his den"; actual chords: <l   V   l> <l   V   l> <l   V   l> <l   V   l>
(2) O O O C (<l   V> <l   V> <l   V> <l   x   l>):
    example:
    "Jack and Jill", actual chords: <l   V> <l   V> <l   V> <vi ii V l>
(3) O C (<l   V> <l   x   l>):
    example:
    "Looby lou", actual chords: <l   V> <l   V   l>
(4) C C O C (<l   x   l> <l   x   l> <l   V> <l   x   l>):
    example:
    "Baa baa black sheep"; actual chords: <l   IV l> <IV l V l> <l   V> <l ii V l>

Figure 3 Harmonic formats for English nursery rhyme melodies, with examples and their chord progressions.

Fourth phrase of "Jack and Jill" = <vi ii V l> ;
harmonic format = <l x l>

grammar rules required: R1: vi → l
                        R2: V → ii V

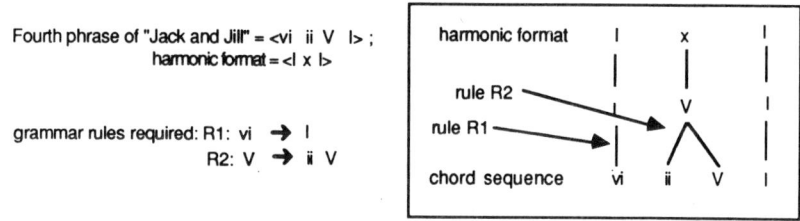

Figure 4 An example of how harmonic fomats and actual chord sequences interrelate via grammar rules.

In order to explain how the knowledge required for the recognition of this relationship is derived, we need to introduce the notion of *context-spaces* (Grosz, 1979). For our purposes, a context-space is simply an area of long-term memory which encapsulates all the generalised knowledge specific to a musical genre, which is implemented as the *parent* frame to subframes for possible grouping and metrical structures. **Figure 5** gives a picture (oversimplified) of tonal music as a very large set of related context spaces, of which our nursery rhyme tunes constitute just one.

Just as in the PIP system described earlier, where each disease frame has pointers to related frames, the nursery rhyme frame will have pointers to other closely related genres, such as simple hymn tunes. At any point in the frame recognition process, matching with a particular stereotypical grouping frame can call on the knowledge contained in the

An AI approach to grouping analysis 57

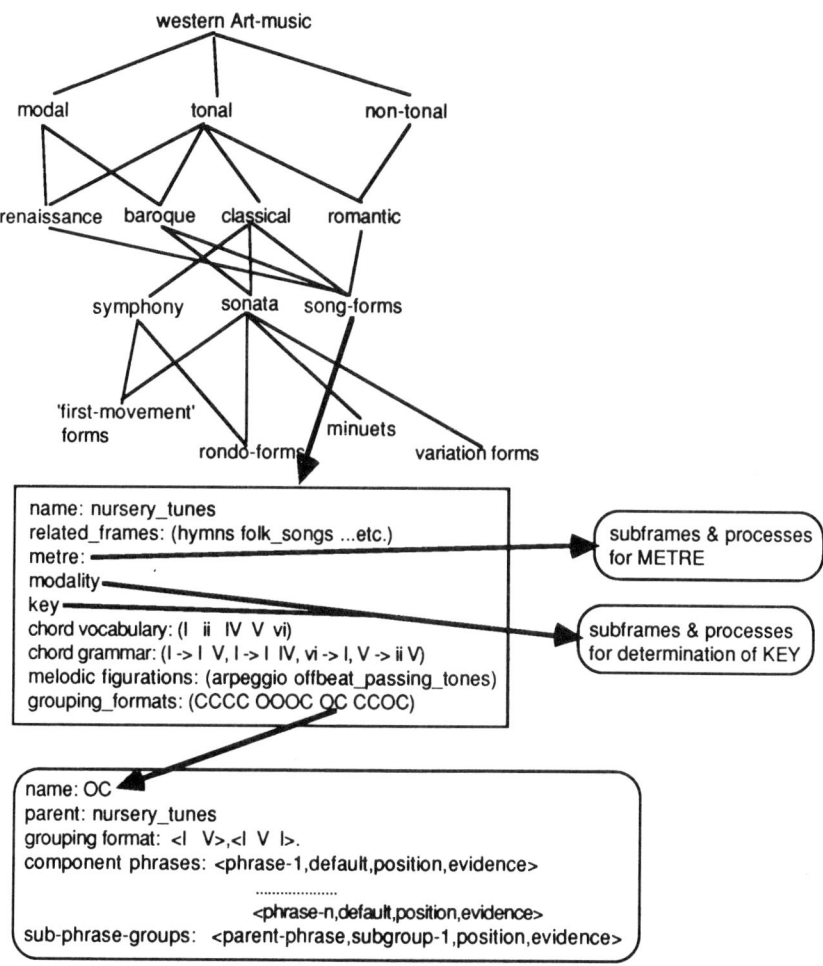

Figure 5 A system of interrelated 'context spaces' for Western Art music, with parent and children frames for English nursery rhyme melodies.

parent grouping frame. In GRAF we assume that the key and metre of the piece being recognised is known. For a 'complete' model of music cognition, key and metre would need to be derived from separate systems of subframes and recognition processes, which could build on existing work in this field (Steedman, 1972; Longuet-Higgins, 1976; Longuet-

Higgins & Steedman, 1970; Longuet-Higgins & Lee, 1983).

We explain the process of how GRAF will recognise a melody by working top-down through the simplified algorithm shown in **Figure 6**. The system steps through the melody from left to right, responding to significant 'clues' on the musical surface (potential phrase boundaries) by invoking the revised AGA harmonic processor, and subsequently generating expectations concerning the positions of boundaries by activating hypotheses (frames) concerning the likely form of the melody. Several hypotheses are retained in working memory, and are 'filled in' when expectations are confirmed, and rejected when discomforted or if working memory limitations are exceeded. The algorithm reads as follows (italicised functions are explained subsequently). The function 'frame_recogniser' takes a melody represented as a list of notes, and a set

```
function: frame_recogniser
inputs:   melody (a list structure)
          *context_space* (a system of frames relevant to the genre of the melody)
algorithm:

   initialisations:
   *wm* <-- nil
   *expectations* <-- nil
   *current_position* <-- 0

   do
      exit_when *current_position* is the last note of the melody;
                return the value (contents) of *wm*
      if  trigger_clue? at *current_position* in melody
      and
          matches?  ( invoke_harmonic_processing
                     <*current_position* in melody> each member of *context_space*  )
      then  push matched frame(s) into *wm*

      if  *current_position* is at a position which corresponds to one or more expectation in *wm*
      then   fill in the slot which has been confirmed for each matched frame, and
             generate_expectations  for the next slot to be filled for each frame in *wm*
      otherwise  remove each frame from *wm* whose expectations were disconfirmed

      generate_expectations  for each matched frame added to *wm* on this cycle

      if   *wm* limits exceeded
      then  forget *wm*

      *current_position* <-- next note in the melody
   loop
```

Figure 6 A simplified algorithm for the top-level control structure of the frame-based musical grouping structure recogniser 'GRAF' (GRouping Analysis using Frames).

of frames (a 'context space') relevant to understanding that melody as inputs. Initially, there is nothing in working memory, no expectations have been generated as to likely phrase-boundary positions, and we start at the first note of the melody. The function executes the following series of steps in order, repeatedly until we reach the end of the melody, when it returns a list of its hypothesised grouping structures (frames with values in the slots). It checks whether the current position is a **trigger_clue?** (a position where grouping preference rules strongly suggest a possible phrase boundary). If it is, then it checks each frame in the context space to see if the phrase boundary could be construed as matching (**matches?**) one or more of its slots for phrase boundary positions, by applying the AGA parser to check to which of the formats (O or C) the section of music could be rewritten (**invoke_harmonic_processing**). For any that are matched, it puts the frames into working memory as current hypotheses. If the current position is one for which one or more frames have generated some expectation, then it fills in values for frames whose expectations were confirmed, removes those which were disconfirmed from working memory, and generates expectations for those confirmed frames. For all new frames added this cycle, the function generates their expected phrase boundary positions in working memory. If the limits on the number of hypotheses which can be simultaneously worked on have been exceeded, it **forgets** those which have the least confirmatory evidence. The function then moves on to the next note in the melody.

Triggering processing
The predicate **trigger_clue?** calls the set of Lerdahl and Jackendoff grouping preference rules described for AGA, implemented as functions rather than data structures. Just as a clinician does not attempt to form a clinical diagnosis from a single observation, but waits for some kind of key finding or 'trigger' (*re* the PIP system), the idea is that the listener waits for an especially significant 'clue' or indication as to a phrase boundary before matching with phrase-boundary schemata. Depending on the genre concerned, this involves the assumption that possible boundaries which are reinforced by several rule applications (Lerdahl & Jackendoff's grouping preference rule 4, 'Intensification') are better candidates to trigger processing, since processing on every single preference rule indication would invoke far more processing than is psychologically plausible.

The matching process
The **matches?** predicate checks which of the two possible 'harmonic formats' ('O' and 'C') the possible phrase unit can be construed as, which involves calling the harmonic parser (**invoke_harmonic_processing**) used in AGA with the proposed amendments. This represents a limited departure from the strictly left-to-right processing of the melody in time, and depends on the extent to which working memory can support mental rehearsal and retrospective hearing. Given an elapsed section of the

melody on which to work, the function can call on the knowledge residing in the parent frame (see Figure 5) to constrain the task, so minimising memory and processing demands. In the case of our nursery tunes, we need to consider only two simple melodic figurations, a very limited chord vocabulary, and just four grammar rules. This should lead to a clear decision as to which of the two phrase formats (O or C) is appropriate (or neither) and hence which of the four larger level combinations (see Figure 3) will be matched at this point. For example, if the phrase can be rewritten as 'O', and the previous phrase was C, then the format is number 4, CCOC. If a slot gains a value in this way, then rather than the overall control process pushing the frame hypothesis into working memory, a procedure which is attached to that particular slot (called a 'demon') is invoked automatically, so that it sends a particular instance of the frame into working memory[15].

The matching process is in fact a little more complicated than this, in a way which has important implications for the psychological plausibility of the GRAF system. As described so far the process of matching frames in the context space implies that a frame would take more time to recall (hypothesis formation) the further along the list of frames it is. In fact, this is nothing like the recall process in humans, who, for example, take the same time to recall any word in a list which they "know" (i.e. have overlearned), regardless of its position in the list, assuming that the items are independent in the sense of not being known on the basis of some rule-set which generates one item from another. A better (although still problematic — see Johnson-Laird, 1988, pp. 151 ff) model of recall is to use a *discrimination net* (Feigenbaum, 1963), which is in fact used in PIP (see Alpay, 1987). A discrimination net is a way of structuring data in memory in a tree structure so that recall time is very fast by the method of "divide and conquer". If each phrase format (consisting of perhaps four subphrases) was represented individually, and stored in a simple unstructured list, then the matching process would have to search this list serially, which would be very inefficient, slow, and psychologically implausible. In a discrimination net, each component phrase of the formats is represented as a node in a decision tree, so that recognition of a complete phrase format would involve simple and more efficient binary search through a network which represented all phrase formats relevant to the current musical context. In GRAF this network would take the form of each phrase format having 'pointers' (the name in a slot) to other frames which could continue the phrase format found so far, so that each of the four phrase formats represented in **Figure 3** would have a unique recognition path in the tree. **Figure 7** shows this discrimination net, from which it is not difficult to see that if our domain is limited to just four possible phrase structures, with the matching (**matches?**) predicate performing a test at each node, then not only is this process greatly speeded up, but once we are past the point marked with a dotted line in **Figure 7**, only a single hypothesis need be maintained.

An AI approach to grouping analysis 61

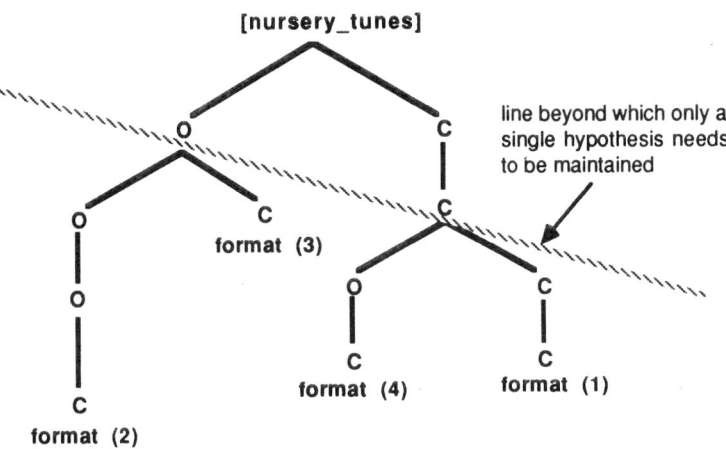

Figure 7 A discrimination net for the four possible phrase-formats in the musical context of English nursery rhyme melodies. Each format traces a unique path through the network (see Figure 3 for descriptions of the formats).

By restricting the context and structuring hypotheses in this way, we may be able to account for the way in which grouping expectations may be initially unclear and require a great deal of processing (the space of possible phrase formats which could initially match is large), but that the amount of processing required may shrink to a passive monitoring of a single hypothesis, which could of course turn out to be disconfirmed[16]. In the final section of this paper, the problem of premature commitment to solutions which turn out to be falsified is discussed in relation to issues of 'plausible reasoning'.

Generating expectations
Expectations are generated by the *default values* for the remaining unfilled slots in a frame. Default values are simply those which are initially assigned unless we receive some information to the contrary. For example, if the first phrase boundary occurs after the first two bars, then we may assume as a 'default' that the second boundary will occur after the next two bars, assuming even-sized groups, unless there is some indication of another phrase boundary in that vicinity, which invokes harmonic processing leading to the diconfirmation of that default value. Again, we believe that the nature of these 'default grouping structures' is encapsulated within an area of Lerdahl and Jackendoff's theory

(grouping preference rule 5) which prefers symmetrical and even-sized groups. Although this is not always the case, we feel that it captures the notion of default grouping positions, which can be simply calculated from units of the phrase-groups recognised so far by the system at any point. Where this is not the case, the boundary should be detected by the triggering of significant surface boundary clues.

Forgetting hypotheses in working memory
In the restricted domain which we have described, it would be possible to retain *all* the possible hypotheses in working memory. When the system is extended to larger contexts this becomes more and more psychologically unrealistic, and we need to find some kind of criterion for deciding which currently active hypotheses should be lost from working memory. The PIP system used probabilistic measures of the relative likelihood of diseases represented by frames. At present we have no firm answers to this problem, but it is likely that recency effects, and a measure of confirmatory support may play a role. In any case, structuring the context-space in the form of a discrimination net greatly ameliorates these problems in its use of just two phrase formats ('O' and 'C'). In addition to forgetting frame hypotheses themselves, only recently assigned slot values should remain in working memory at the end of the recognition process.

Limitations of knowledge-based approaches

The major limitations of this approach concern
(i) the process of determining the context of the current listening situation (which frames are relevant?);
(ii) the matching process;
(iii) extensibility and generality of frame-based systems; and
(iv) the issue of 'informal reasoning'.
(i) The algorithms described for the GRAF system considered the problem of how we recognise the grouping structure of a melody, given that we know the context of the listening situation, i.e. a hierarchical set of frames relevant to English nursery rhyme melodies. As Charniak (1982) points out, we don't really know how people combine 'low-level' cues in an environment to activate knowledge stored in long-term memory which is relevant to that context[17]. Given that there are no known limitations on long-term memory, this is a non-trivial problem.
(ii) the problem of matching arises from the diversity of the objects subsumed under a particular schema, where the detailed properties of one object may be carried over to another for which they are not appropriate. As Winograd & Flores (1986) point out with respect to this problem, ". . . if we look at the literature of frame systems, we find a mixture of hand waving and silence." (p.117).

An AI approach to grouping analysis   63

(iii) It is clear that to the extent to which a system (organism) relies on prestored knowledge of what to expect as input from an environment, its competence can not extend beyond that finite domain of prestored knowledge. This problem of the highly knowledge intensive nature of many cognitive skills is termed the "real world knowledge" problem in AI research, which is that intelligent human agents are able to draw on the kind of extensive real-world knowledge — from memory and dynamically processed from the environment — which essentially 'closed world' computer-based models are not able to do. We do not at present understand how the vast knowledge of tonal music which most individuals unconsciously acquire in the course of their lifetimes, could be adequately represented in a frame system. Research over the past decade in knowledge-based systems has indicated that to do this it would represent an enormous feat of knowledge-engineering.

(iv) "The frame intuition can be implemented only in a system that does informal reasoning — one that comes to conclusions based on partial evidence." (Winograd & Flores, 1986, p. 117). GRAF would need to use informal reasoning of this kind both to specify reasons for preferring one possible hypothesis over another under conditions where working memory is overloaded, and in the assumption that once a hypothesis has been disconfirmed at *one* position in the melody, it will not turn out to be confirmed at some subsequent point. It is possible to amend the design of GRAF to avoid this, by retaining hypotheses which have their expectations disconfirmed in case they turn out to be satisfied later, but at the cost of additional memory. The problem is to achieve the right balance in the trade-off between conserving memory and processing resources, and committing the system to conclusions too early, which may subsequently turn out to be disconfirmed. It seems quite plausible that this accurately represents the state of affairs with human musical cognition, where the grouping of a piece may turn out to be fully understood only on *rehearing*, even though we may gain an initial and sketchy conception of locations of group boundaries on first hearing alone.

Finally, we need to account for perception of grouping at levels below that of the phrase. In terms of our description of GRAF we hypothesise that these levels are most likely to be decided by retrospective hearing and mental rehearsal, once the larger-level phrase unit has been confirmed. It also seems likely that at such level, pattern-matching under 'limited transformations', such as inversion and transposition, and at successive reductional levels, plays a larger role than exclusively harmonic factors. Given that the area over which pattern matching is performed is constrained in this way, it is easy to see how the algorithm of Figure 6 could be augmented to include this additional processing as part of the **invoke_harmonic processing** function, in a way which did not make inordinate memory and processing demands (as described for the integrated processing version of AGA).

Conclusions and further work

The syntactic processing (AGA) and frame-based recognition (GRAF) approaches to musical grouping perception face precisely the dilemma which has been identified for language understanding models. Judith Greene (1986) succinctly expresses the dilemma as follows:

> ... *language understanding models are faced with a dilemma: either to specify detailed rules for selecting syntactic categories and word meanings or to rely on world knowledge for resolving ambiguities. In the former case, there are too many sentence interpretations to choose from; in the latter there is the danger of going for only the most probable interpretation. In either case, there is an explosion to deal with, making it difficult to select from many possible word senses and grammatical constructions or from a vast number of knowledge-based inferences.* (p. 144).

In the GRAF system we have argued that the best response to this dilemma is an *integrated processing* approach, which is resource limited, and where the syntactic processing approach is guided by knowledge represented as frames. Given sufficient effort, it would clearly be possible to represent the extensive amount of knowledge required for understanding musical grouping structures either in the form of processing *heuristics* (the syntactic approach) or as *frames*. Both theories have support in the psychological literature. In the former case, unified theories of cognition (such as the SOAR architecture, Laird, Newell & Rosenbloom, 1987) are being developed where a theory of learning predicts that intelligent behaviour may acquire sufficient knowledge to yield *direct* paths to solutions, without requiring search at all. In the latter case, schema theory is well established and pervasive in the literature. One conclusion which both approaches share, and which merits re-emphasis is that *intelligent musical cognition requires a great deal of knowledge on the part of the perceiver*. In our discussion of GRAF we have discussed a first prototype model which aims to increase our understanding of the role of that knowledge in human grouping perception. In the course of doing so we have generated a fresh set of problems, probably the most important of which concerns the role of contextual knowledge in musical cognition. Given the analogy with natural language processing which we have made throughout, this is hardly surprising given the current focus of research in this area on questions concerning how we use knowledge of pragmatics and context in understanding dialogue.

Finally, we may mention a danger which is inherent in pursuing separate lines of enquiry into music cognition. A unified model for music cognition would involve the detailed specification of how individual processes — grouping, metre, harmony — interact, and precisely what kinds of knowledge would be required to manage the balance between cognitive constraints on memory and processing. If we posit separate 'grammars' for each process, then a set of intermediary representations are required between perception on the 'musical surface' and the understanding of musical form residing in memory. Existing evidence (Johnson-Laird, 1983) does not support the psychological reality of these representations. We need to produce a model which does justice to the way in which analytically separable processes constrain each other, which is at the same time integrated within a single representation. With our present state of knowledge of these processes, such a larger enterprise would probably be premature.

Acknowledgements

In writing this paper I have received more general support than I am able to quantify from the members of the Intelligent Computer-Aided Instruction research group in the Open University, without which this work could not have been produced in the time available to me. Thanks to my supervisor, Mark Elsom-Cook, for inspiration, intelligent comment and for guiding my research in this direction. Thanks to Simon Holland for his time, his ideas, for many discussions about the contents of this paper, for reading the final draft and for making many useful comments. Thanks to Fiona Spensely for reading the final draft and augmenting my knowledge of psychology, to Claire O'Malley and Richard Joiner for pointing me to the literature on connectionism and schema theory, and to Laurence Alpay for explaining her work on implementing frame-based systems. Finally, many thanks to Dr P.N. Johnson-Laird of the Cambridge Applied Psychology Unit, for giving freely of his time, informed criticism and good ideas.

Notes

1. We assume that these are in fact reasonable criteria of assessment, but will not argue for them here.
2. We implicitly assume the more stringent criterion of computability of mental models, as described by Johnson-Laird, 1983.
3. Heefer and Leman (1986) have implemented a number of these rules in Prolog.
4. The issue is a contentious one. See Broadbent 1985, and replies in Rumelhart & McClelland 1985, on the issue of connectionism and the reductional thesis concerning levels of theoretical explanation.
5. It is implemented in Common lisp and the object-oriented extension 'flavors' on an Apollo Domain AI workstation, interfaced to a Yamaha KX88 touch-sensitive keyboard.
6. This is closely related to Steedman's (1984) use of a high-level rule which served the function of a template into which other rules were substituted, in a grammar of twelve-bar blues chord progressions.
7. For restricted genres such as simple nursery rhyme melodies, the full power of a recursive context-free grammar of this kind would probably not be required. Given that for other genres it probably would be required, we use this overpowerful grammar to avoid having separate grammars for separate genres. We are not identifying these grammar rules with psychological processes since, as McAdams points out (1987) no single grammar is unique to the language which it purports to model, nor ar all grammars equally learnable.
8. A more physically accessible account is in Winograd 1983, §3.6.

9. Formal properties of the grammar used would, however, preclude a purely top-down mechanism, since the grammar contains left and right recursive rules (such as I → I V, and V → ii V, respectively), which would cause the parser to go into an infinite loop (see Baker, 1989, in press; Winograd, 1983, p. 101, 112).
10. The rules are inspired by Gestalt principles, and relate to interval leaps, rests between notes, and differences in attack points.
11. Schema theory has been used to explain phenomena as diverse as story understanding (Schank & Abelson, 1977), concept representation (Rosch, 1975) and as a general theory of memory (Rumelhart & Ortony, 1977). See Alba & Hasher, 1983 for an influential critique. This very breadth of application has resulted in the criticism that the theory is so vague that it can be used — vacuously — to explain anything. Minsky's (1977) notion of *frames* gave new formal rigour to the schema theory.
12. I am indebted to Laurence Alpay for explaining her re-implementation and extension of the PIP system to me (Alpay, 1987).
13. The tunes were largely transcribed from memory, but see Poston 1961; Moorat, 1912 and Whyton, 1964.
14. The terminology is Neisser's: ". . . a schema is like a format in a computer-programming language." (Neisser, 1976, p. 55).
15. Object-oriented languages are ideally suited to develop this aspect of frame-like structures, since they automatically support the creation of procedures (called "methods") which are local to frame-like data-structures ("objects"), and have built-in mechanisms for inheritance of values throughout a hierarchy of objects (in the case of Common lisp, "flavors").
16. We do not have space here to fully describe the implications of this way of structuring the frame system here (see Charniak, Reisbeck & McDermott, 1980; Alpay, 1987; Elsom-Cook, 1988).
17. Charniak gives the example of the sentence "As the boy walked down the aisle he took a can of tuna fish from the shelf and put it in his basket", where we have no trouble deciding that the context relates to knowledge of supermarkets.

References

Aitkenhead, A.M. & Slack, J.M. (1985) *Issues in Cognitive Modelling*. Lawrence Erlbaum
Alpay, L. (1987) *A Re-implementation, Extension and Evaluation of the medical expert system PIP*. MSc thesis September 1987, Cognitive Studies Department, University of Sussex
Anderson, John R. (1980) *Cognitive Psychology and its Implications*, W.H. Freeman & Co.
Anderson, John R. (1983) *The Architecture of Cognition*. Harvard University Press
Baddeley, A. (1980) Domains of recollection. *Psychological Review*, **89**, 708–729, 1980
Baker, M.J. (1989, in press) A cognitive model for perception of musical grouping structures (forthcoming) *Contemporary Music Review*, Spring 1989, special issue on Music and the Cognitive Sciences
Bartlett, F.C. (1982) *Remembering: A Study in Experimental and Social Psychology*. Cambridge University Press
de Beaugrande, R. (1982) General constraints on process models of language comprehension. In *Language and Comprehension* (1982) edited by Le Ny, J.F. & Kintsch, W., Lawrence Erlbaum
Bharucha, J.J. (1987) *MUSACT: A Connectionist Model of Musical Harmony*. Unpublished research paper, Dartmouth College, USA
Bischof, W.F. (1976) Psychology of language and memory. In Charniak, E. & Wilks, Y. (editors), *Computational Semantics*, North-Holland
Bobrow, D.G., Kaplan, R.M., Kay, M., Norman, D.A., Thompson, H. & Winograd, T. (1977) GUS, A frame-driven dialog system. *Artificial Intelligence*, 8, (1977), 155–173
Boltz, M. & Reiss Jones, M. (1986) Does rule recursion make melodies easier to reproduce? If not, what does? *Cognitive Psychology* **18**, 389–431
Broadbent, D.A. (1985) A Question of Levels: Comment on McClelland and Rumelhart. *Journal of Experimental Psychology: General* 1985, **114**,(2) 189–192
Charniak, E. (1978) On the use of framed knowledge in language comprehension. *Artificial Intelligence* **11**, (1978), 225–226

Charniak, E., Reisbeck, C. & McDermott, D.V. (1980) *Artificial Intelligence Programming*, Lawrence Erlbaum
Charniak, E. (1982) Context recognition in language comprehension. In Lehnert, W.G. & Ringle, M.H. (editors) *Strategies for Natural Language Processing*, Lawrence Erlbaum
Clarke, E. (1986) Theory, analysis and the psychology of music: A critical evaluation of Lerdahl, F. & Jackendoff, R. A generative theory of tonal music. *Psychology of Music*, 1986, **14**, 3–16
Cohen, G., Eysenck, M.W. & Le Voi, M. (1986) *Memory: a cognitive approach*. Open University Press, Milton Keynes, England
Cohen, G. (1983) *The Psychology of Cognition*, second edition, Academic Press
Cohen, P.R. (1985) *Heuristic Reasoning about Uncertainty: An Artificial Intelligence Approach*, Pitman, London
Deliege, I. (1987) Grouping conditions in listening to music: An approach to Lerdahl & Jackendoff's grouping preference rules. *Music Perception*, Summer 1987, **4**, 325–360
Deutsch, D. & Feroe, J. (1981) The internal representation of pitch sequences in tonal music. *Psychological Review*, 1981, **88**, 503–522
Elsom-Cook, M., & du Boulay, B. (1986) A Pascal program checker. *Proceedings of the European Conference on Artificial Intelligence 1986*, II pp. 90–95
Erman, L.D., Hayes-Roth, F., Lesser, V.R. & Reddy, D.R. (1980) The hearsay-II speech understanding system: Integrating knowledge to resolve uncertainty. *ACM Surveys* **12**,(2)
Feigenbaum, E. (1963) The simulation of verbal learning behaviour. In Feigenbaum, E. & Feldman, J. (editors) *Computers and Thought*, McGraw-Hill
Greene, J. (1986) *Language Understanding: a cognitive approach*, Open University Press, Milton Keynes, England
Grosz, B.J. (1979) *The Representation and Use of Focus in Dialogue Understanding*. Ph.D. dissertation
Heefer, A. & Leman, M. (1986) Chunking as a method of concept acquisition. In *Proceedings of the European Conference on Artificial Intelligence 1986*, II, pp. 79–83
Hinton, G.E. & Anderson, J.A. (1981) *Parallel Models of Associative Memory*, Lawrence Erlbaum.
Holtzman, S.R. (1981) Using generative grammars for music composition. *Computer Music Journal*, **5**,(1)
Jackendoff, R. (1987) *Consciousness and the Computational Mind*, MIT Press
Johnson-Laird, P. (1983) *Mental Models*, Cambridge University Press
Johnson-Laird, P. (1988) *The Computer and the Mind*, Fontana Press, London
Kay, M. (1980) Algorithm schemata and data structures in syntactic processing. In *Proceedings of the Nobel Symposium on Text Processing*, Nobel Academy
Laird, J.E., Newell, A. & Rosenbloom, P.R. (1987) SOAR: An architecture for general intelligence. *Artificial Intelligence* **33**, 1–64
Lerdahl, F. & Jackendoff, R. (1983) *A Generative Theory of Tonal Music*, MIT Press
Lischka, C. (1987) Connectionist models of musical thinking. In *Proceedings of the 1987 International Computer Music Conference*, University of Illinois at Urbana-Champaign, pp. 190–196
Longuet-Higgins & Steedman (1970) On Interpreting Bach. *Machine Intelligence* **6**, pp. 221–239
Longuet-Higgins (1976) Perception of Melodies. *Nature* **263**, pp. 646–653
Longuet-Higgins & Lee (1983) The rhythmic interpretation of monophonic music. In Sundberg, J. (editor) *Studies of Musical Performance*, Publications of the Royal Swedish Academy of Music
McAdams, S. (1987) Music: a science of the mind? *Contemporary Music Review*, 1987, Vol. 2 pp. 1–61
Miller, G.A. (1981) Trends and Debates in Cognitive Psychology. *Cognition*, **10**, 215–225, 1981
Minsky, M. (1977) Frame-system theory. In *Thinking: Readings in Cognitive Science*, edited by Johnson-Laird, P.N. & Wason, P.C., Cambridge University Press
Moorat, J. (1912) (arranger) *Thirty Old-Time Nursery Songs*, illustrated by Woodroffe, P. Thames & Hudson

Neisser, U. (1976) *Cognition and Reality*, W.H. Freeman & Co.
Pauker, S.G., Gorry, A., Kassirer, J.P. & Schwartz, W.B. (1984) Towards the simulation of clinical cognition: Taking a present illness by computer. In *Readings in Medical Artificial Intelligence*, eds. Clancey, W.J. & Shortcliffe, E.H., Addison-Wesley
Poston, E. (1961) *The Children's Song Book*, The Bodley Head, London
Peel, J. & Slawson, W. (1984) Review of a generative theory of tonal music, by F. Lerdahl & R. Jackendoff. *Journal of Music Theory*, 1984 **28**(2) pp. 271–294
Reisbeck, C. (1982) Realistic language comprehension. In Lehnert, V.G. & Ringle, M.H. (editors) *Strategies for Natural Language Processing*, Lawrence Erlbaum
Rosch, E. (1975) Cognitive representations of semantic categories. *Journal of Experimental Psychology: General* **104**(3) pp. 192–233
Rumelhart, D.E. & Ortony, A. (1977) The representation of knowledge in memory. In Anderson, R.C., Spiro, R.J. & Montague, W.E. (editors) *Schooling and the Acquisition of Knowledge*, Lawrence Erlbaum
Rumelhart, D.E. & McClelland, J.L. (1985) Levels Indeed! A Response to Broadbent. *Journal of Experimental Psychology: General* 1985, vol. 114, no. 2, 193–197
Rumelhart, D..E. & Norman, D.A. (1985) Representation of Knowledge. In *Issues in Cognitive Modeling*, (editors) Aitkenhead, A.M. & Slack, J.M., Lawrence Erlbaum
Schank, R. & Abelson, R.P. (1977) *Scripts, Plans, Goals and Understanding*, Lawrence Erlbaum, N.J.
Shortcliffe, E.H. (1976) *Computer-based medical consultations: MYCIN*. New York, North-Holland
Simon, H. & Sumner, R. (1968) Pattern in Music. In *Formal Representation of Human Judgement* edited by Kleinmuntz, B., Wiley & Sons
Simon, H. (1982) *The Sciences of the Artificial*, second edition, MIT Press
Sloboda, J. (1982) Music Performance. In Deutsch, D. (editor) *The Psychology of Music*, Academic Press
Sloboda, J. (1985) *The Musical Mind: The Cognitive Psychology of Music*, Oxford Psychology Series, Clarendon Press, Oxford
Steedman, M. (1972) *The Formal Description of Musical Perception*. PhD thesis, University of Edinburgh
Steedman, M. (1984) A Generative Grammar for Jazz Chord Sequences. *Music Perception* **2**, (1)
Steels, L. (1987) The Deepening of Expert Systems. *Artificial Intelligence Communications*, **0**, (1)
Stoffer, T.H. (1985) Representation of phrase structure in the perception of music. *Music Perception* **3**, (2) 191–220
Taft-Thomas, M. (1985) VIVACE: A rule-based AI system for composition. *Proceedings of the International Computer Music Conference*
Tenney, J. with Polanski, L. (1980) Temporal gestalt perception in music. *Journal of Music Theory*, **24**, (2) pp. 205–241
West, R., Howell, P. & Cross, I. (1985) Modelling perceived musical structure. In *Musical Structure and Cognition*, edited by Howell, P., Cross, I. & West, R., Academic Press
West, R., Cross, I. & Howell, P. (1987) Modelling music perception as input-output and as process. *Psychology of Music* **15**, (1)
Whyton, W. (1964) *100 Children's Songs*, Essex Music, London
Winograd, T. (1968) Linguistics and the computer analysis of tonal harmony. *Journal of Music Theory*, **12** 2–49
Winograd, T. (1983) *Language as a Cognitive Process. Volume 1: Syntax*, Addison-Wesley.
Winograd, T. (1980) What does it mean to understand a language? *Cognitive Science* **4**, 209–241
Winograd, T. & Flores, F. (1986) *Understanding Computers and Cognition: A New Foundation for Design*, Ablex Publishing Corporation, Norwood N.J.
Winston, P.H. (1975) Learning structural descriptions from examples. In *The Psychology of Computer Vision*, edited by Winston, P.H., McGraw-Hill

A computational model of rubato

Neil Todd

Department of Psychology, University of Exeter, Exeter, UK

Presented is a model of rubato, implemented in Lisp, in which expression is viewed as the mapping of musical structure into the variables of expression. The basic idea is that the performer uses "phrase final lengthening" as a device to reflect some internal representation of the phrase structure. The representation is based on Lardahl and Jackendoff's time-span reduction. The basic heuristic in the model is recursive involving look-ahead and planning at a number of levels. The planned phrasings are superposed beat by beat and the output from the program is a list of durations which could easily be adapted to be sent to a synthesiser given a suitable system.

KEYWORDS computational modelling, music cognition, musical performance, rubato, mental representation, mental process.

Introduction

One of the most ubiquitous expressive devices in musical performance is rubato. Most notably it is used in music of the romantic era, but is also evident in a variety of other styles. Research on music performance (Seashore, 1938; Shaffer, 1981; Clarke, 1984; Todd, 1985; Bengtsson & Gabrielsson, 1980; Sundberg & Verillo, 1980) involving the precise measurement of duration has shown that there are a number of basic observations which can be made. The first is that skilled performers can show a remarkable degree of reproducibility from one performance to the next (Shaffer, 1984; Gabrielsson, 1987). This precision in timing shows that the performance must involve the use of generative procedures and a precise internal representation of underlying expressive form. A second observation is the use of slowing to mark a phrase boundary (Todd, 1985), which has been shown to apply recursively at a number of levels (Shaffer & Todd, 1987).

In Todd (1985) a model of rubato was established which generated a duration structure from a structural description of a piece of music. The idea of the model was that the performer uses "phrase final lengthening" to signal a boundary — the degree of slowing determined by the

69

importance of the boundary. The input to the model was the time-span reduction of Lerdahl and Jackendoff's theory (1983). Whilst the model gave a reasonable description of the data from actual performances of some pieces there were, however, a number of objections to the model as it stood. This has led to the formulation of a new model. In this paper I will describe the new model and the reasoning which led to its formulation.

The reduction hypothesis and knowledge representation

The first problem with the Todd (1985) model stems from the fact that it inherits the "reduction hypothesis" of Lerdahl & Jackendoff's theory. That is, the listener, and therefore the performer, sees each event in a *single, coherent structure*. This hypothesis places too high a demand on working memory to be psychologically plausible. In terms of the model it means that when computing a boundary strength, every event in time-span reduction is taken into account, irrespective of how close, or how far apart, the events are in time. This leads to the prediction of more degrees of boundary strength, and therefore degrees of relative slowing, than can be discerned from the data. On the other hand, it is both psychologically plausible and musically necessary that the performer should have some kind of global overview of the piece as well as being able to "look ahead" to some degree in order to plan a phrase.

A solution to this problem, which is the first premise of the updated model, is to suppose that the internal representation — rather than being a single, simply connected tree — is composed of a set (or forest) of trees organised on a number of hierarchic levels with each subset of trees at one level being "bound" by a tree at a higher level. This accords with Anderson's ACT* theory of cognition (1983). In the theory knowledge comes in chunks or "cognitive units" which can be such things as propositions, spatial images or temporal relations. A cognitive unit encodes a set of no more than about five elements. Larger structures are created by the hierarchical embedding of cognitive units. Of particular interest to us here are cognitive units encoding temporal information which Anderson refers to as "temporal strings". The notion of temporal strings accords well with the idea of musical groups.

A model of performance constructed on this basis predicts a duration structure determined by the superposition of a number of hierarchic timing components, from a global component, spanning the whole piece, to a local component spanning a few beats with each component corresponding to structural level. This overcomes the objections discussed above because for any event at one level the number of other events directly connected is limited. At the same time it allows for "look ahead" and gives the performer global overview.

The process of performance

A second objection to the Todd (1985) model is that it is "off line". In other words it does not describe the process of performance. Whilst it is reasonable to suppose that the performer can hold the whole structure in long-term memory, indeed a musicians's ability to memorise is quite remarkable, it seems implausible that the performer could access the whole structure at any one time. In the early model the computations were done for each component and then added together. In an actual performance the computations are done as each phrase is accessed in turn and the components superposed note by note.

The obvious answer, and this is the second premise of the new model, is that in order to describe the process of performance the model needs to be formulated in computational terms and implemented in a suitable high-level language such as Lisp. In particular, what is important here is the idea that a process should be cast in terms of an "effective procedure" (Longuet-Higgins, 1978, 1981; Johnson-Laird, 1983), thus enabling the theory to be precise and testable.

The indeterminism of individual performances

Whilst such a theory does make predictions, given a certain input, the goal of the theory is not the prediction of individual performances as such, but the *principled explanation of performance data*. This is so in psychology in general, and music psychology in particular, because if the theory were completely deterministic it would negate the creative aspect of performance. Johnson-Laird (1983) has expressed this indeterminism of individual performances in the language of computer science:

> *If human beings are at least as complicated as Turing machines and their individual processes of thought differ as a result of their genes and experience, then their behaviour is most unlikely to become wholly predictable, because there is no effective procedure that can predict the behaviour of an arbitrary Turing machine. There is thus little danger of creating a psychology capable of modelling an individual's thoughts — an eventuality likely to destroy the spontaneity and significance of life. But there are no a priori reasons for supposing that it is impossible to develop scientific theories of general psychological abilities."*
>
> [Johnson-Laird, 1983; p. 12]

The computational theory of an expression system

These two issues discussed above, of representation and process, are central to any information-processing type approach to cognition and cognitive modelling. Our main task, therefore, in the construction of such a model is to make explicit, in the form of an algorithm, the process of performance and its input. However, as David Marr (1982) has said such a system can be viewed from three levels of explanation:

> At one extreme, the top level, is the abstract computational theory of the device, in which the performance of the device is characterized as a mapping from one kind of information to another, . . . In the centre is the choice of representation for the input and output and the algorithm to be used to transform one into the other. And at the other extreme are the details of how the algorithm and the representation are realized physically.
>
> [Marr, 1982; p. 24]

At the level of computational theory then, is useful to express the various processes of music performance in symbolic terms. Let N stand for the music notation or score, P for performance, and Ψ for the internal representation. Thus we can think of the process of performance as a mapping:

$$\pi: \Psi \to P \qquad (1.a)$$

where the mapping is carried out by a *performance procedure* or *function* π. In the same way the process of sight-reading can be thought of as a double mapping:

$$N \to \Psi \to P \qquad (1.b)$$

Conversely, we can think of the process of perception as the mapping:

$$\Lambda : P \to \Psi \qquad (2.a)$$

where the mapping is carried out by a *listening procedure* or *function* Λ. Again in the same manner the process of notation can be thought of as:

$$P \to \Psi \to N \qquad (2.b)$$

So, at the algorithmic level then, our task is twofold: a) to find a suitable representation for Ψ; and b) to make explicit an algorithm for performing the mapping $\Psi \to P$.

Methodology

The methodology adopted in order to implement the twofold task outlined above is threefold:

(a) *analysis* — which involves finding a value for Ψ, either from the score or the data;
(b) *synthesis* — which involves taking the value for Ψ and using it as an input to a performance algorithm which generates an output in the form of a graph or list of numbers; and
(c) *evaluation* — which involves the comparison of data with algorithm output.

This method is, of course, similar to the analysis-by-synthesis method of Sundberg and his co-workers (Fryden & Sundberg, 1984) but perhaps more closely related to the method of Risset and Wessel in their work on timbre (Risset & Wessel, 1982). The differences with the Sundberg method are that the starting point here is actual performances, rather than performer intuitions, and the evaluation process involves the direct comparison of data and model, rather than the subjective rating of generated output.

Analysis: score → representation vs. data → representation

We need to find a value for the internal representation Ψ. A distinction is made here between three possible representations. First, the *analyst's representation* Ψ_A, which is determined directly from the score; second, the *performer's representation* Ψ_P, which is also determined from the score but which is unobservable; and third, the *data determined representation* Ψ_D. So, we can represent the computational theory at this stage thus:

$$N \to \begin{cases} \Psi_P \to P_P \xrightarrow{\lambda} \Psi_D \\ \Psi_A \end{cases} \qquad (3)$$

To find a value for Ψ_A involves taking the score of the piece of music under investigation and production an anlysis of the grouping or phrase structure. At the moment the most useful analytic method is that developed by Lerdahl and Jackendoff (1983) despite its deficiencies (Slawson & Peel, 1985; Clarke, 1986; Baker, in press). After the analysis is complete the grouping is converted to a Lisp representation which becomes the input to an algorithm for generating a duration structure. (see figure 1).

```
(setq tsr '((A) (B) (A)))
(setq A '((a) (a)))
(setq B '((b) (b)))
(setq a '(3 1 2 1))
(setq b '(3 1 2 1))
```

Figure 1 A Lisp representation of Lerdahl and Jackendoff's bracket notation for grouping. At the top level there are two groups A and B arranged symmetrically in the order ABA. Group A contains the sub-group *a* repeated and group B contains the sub-group *b* repeated. The integers represent the metrical strength of a beat.

A value for Ψ_D determined by analysing the data from actual performances. The basic idea is that a slowing indicates a group boundary. This can be done systematically using an algorithm **listen** which takes that data as input and returns a Lisp representation of the grouping *tsr* (Todd, in press).

Synthesis: representation → performance

Having obtained *tsr* we need to make explicit the procedure π for mapping representation into the performance. We can represent the computational theory at this stage thus:

$$N \rightarrow \begin{cases} \Psi_P \xrightarrow{\lambda} P_P \xrightarrow{\pi} \Psi_D \xrightarrow{\pi} P_D \\ \Psi_A \xrightarrow{\pi} P_A \end{cases} \quad (4)$$

such that each representation Ψ_i has its corresponding performance P_i. The performance is modelled using an algorithm *play* (See Appendix 1). The basic heuristic of the algorithm is to look-ahead and plan the phrasing of a group at a given level then move down to the next sub-group, look-ahead and plan, and so on recursively. The planned phrasings are superposed onto an output plan (see *output*, Appendix 1) which continuously evolves as the performance unfolds. When a surface-group is reached the first element of the output plan is printed and discarded, and so on. When the surface-group is completed the program backtracks to the next level and so on until all the surface groups are played. The output from the program is a list of durations, which could easily be adapted to be sent to a synthesiser given a suitable system (see figure 2).

The precise durations within a phrase are determined by a parabolic function ρ_B embedded within the performance procedure. This function has the following form:

$$\rho_B(t, a_i) = a_1 + \frac{a_2}{(1-a_6)^2} \left\{ \frac{t}{a_3} - \frac{(a_4-1)}{a_5} - a_6 \right\}^2, \quad t = 1, 2, \ldots, T \quad (5)$$

where t is metrical time and a_i is a vector of parameters such that:

a_1 = *tempo,*
a_2 = *amplitude,*
a_3 = *length of phrase,*
a_4 = *boundary strength,*
a_5 = *upper limit of boundary strength,*
a_6 = *offset of parabola minimum.*

$(1-a_6)^{-2}$ is a normalisation factor such that if the boundary strength $a_4 = 1$ and $t = a_3$ (i.e. at the end of the phrase) then a_2 represents the true amplitude (Todd, 1985). As for the values of the parameters, a_1 and a_2 are input at the start of the algorithm *play* (see functions *start* and *set_up_vars*, Appendix 1); a_3 and a_4 are computed for each group as the program runs (see functions *plan* and *rubato*, Appendix 1); and a_5 and a_6 are set within the program with $a_6 = 0.52$. In Todd (1985) $a_5 = 11$ but in the new model $a_5 = 3$ because the number of possible boundary strengths is reduced (see function *set_up_vars*, Appendix 1).

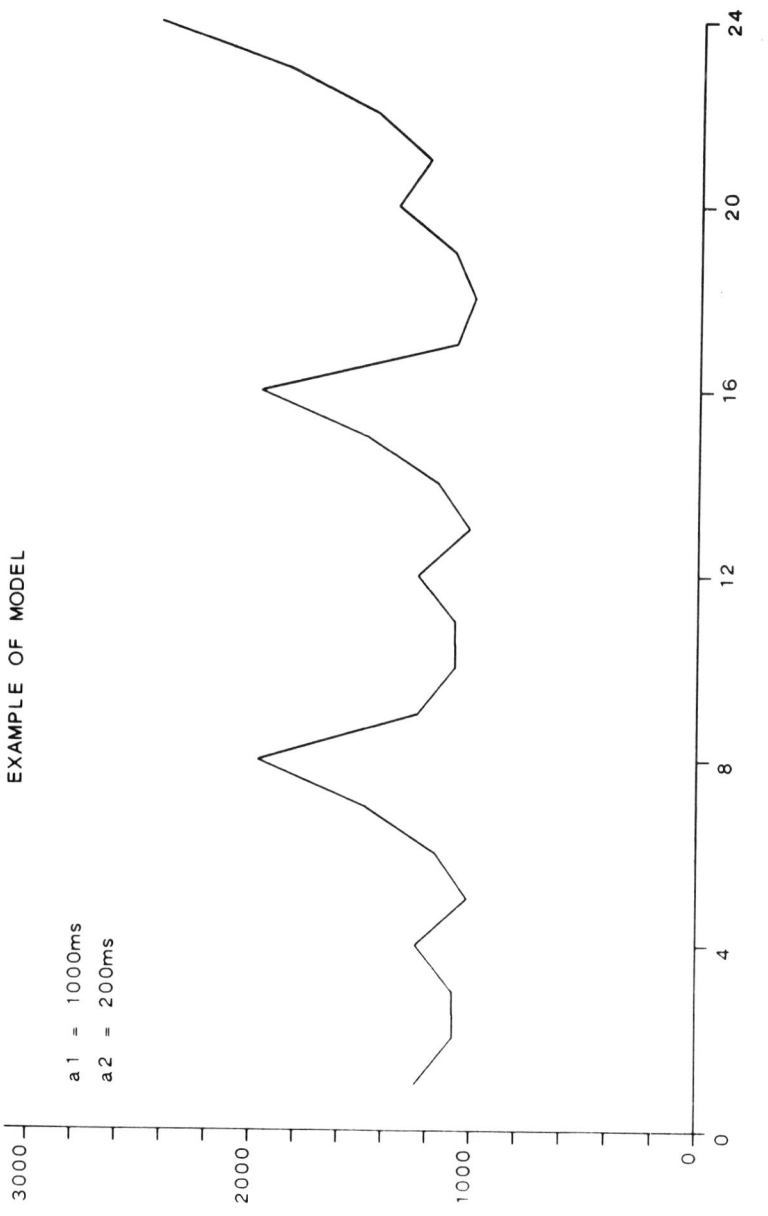

Figure 2 The output of the algorithm *play* taking as an input the grouping structure as in Figure 1.

Evaluation: $P_A \stackrel{\triangle}{=} P_P \stackrel{\triangle}{=} P_D$?

Having generated P_A or P_D we need to compare them with an actual performance P_P. In Todd (1985) the data and model (ie P_P and P_A) were compared visually using the criteria; a) the position of peaks or points of slowing; b) the relative heights of the peaks. Whilst this method is useful it is unsatisfactory for a number of reasons. First, the comparison of relative heights is only qualitative. So, obviously a more systematic and quantitative test is required. Hierarchical clustering (Johnson, 1967) is such a method which has been successfully applied in analysing speech (Grosjean and Gee, 1983) and I am currently working on ways of applying this to music performance.

A second problem lies in the indeterminism of individual performances as discussed above. Whilst it is often possible to observe considerable across-performer agreement (Shaffer & Todd, 1987) there are also many differences. Also, there is no reason why the analyst's interpretation Ψ_A should be the same as the performer's Ψ_P since there is no such thing as a single "correct" grouping. It is for these reasons that the input used is the representation derived from the data Ψ_D which is obtained via the algorithm *listen*. This procedure is certainly not intended to give licence to adjust the theory *post hoc* to fit each set of data — on the contrary the same performance mapping *play* is used in each case. Remember the goal of a theory of performance is the principled explanation of performance data. So, whilst we cannot predict a performance with any certainty what we can say for each performance is that if the following three assumptions produce a good match between P_P and P_D then the assumptions constitute a reasonable explanation:

(a) the performer has used slowing to indicate a grouping boundary;
(b) the performer's grouping analysis corresponds to *tsr*;
(c) the performer's mapping procedure corresponds to *play*.

The model then is really an analytical theory of performance rather than a prescriptive theory of performance. However, there are no reasons, if enought data is amassed, why probability weightings could not be assigned to various performances as a function of style and instrument.

Examples

Presented in Figures 3 and 4 are two examples of data from actual performances compared against the model. The first example is taken from a performance of the Adagio from the Haydn Sonata in B-Flat which was also used in Todd (1985) so that comparison with the old model is possible. The second example is taken from two performances of the Chopin prelude in F# Minor (Shaffer and Todd, 1987). The data were obtained using the method of Shaffer (1981).

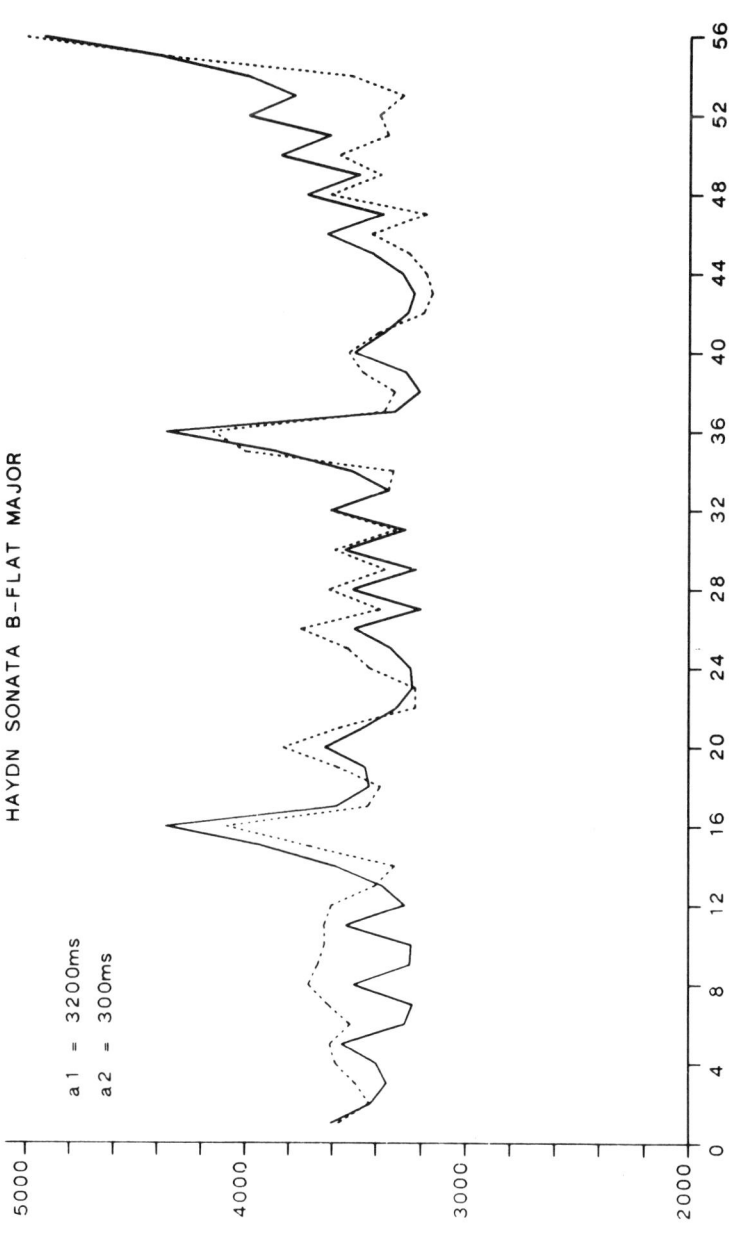

Figure 3 Comparison of model and data for Haydn Sonata. The figure shows the model (solid line) derived from the grouping analysis as in Appendix 3 compared against the data from a performance (dotted line).

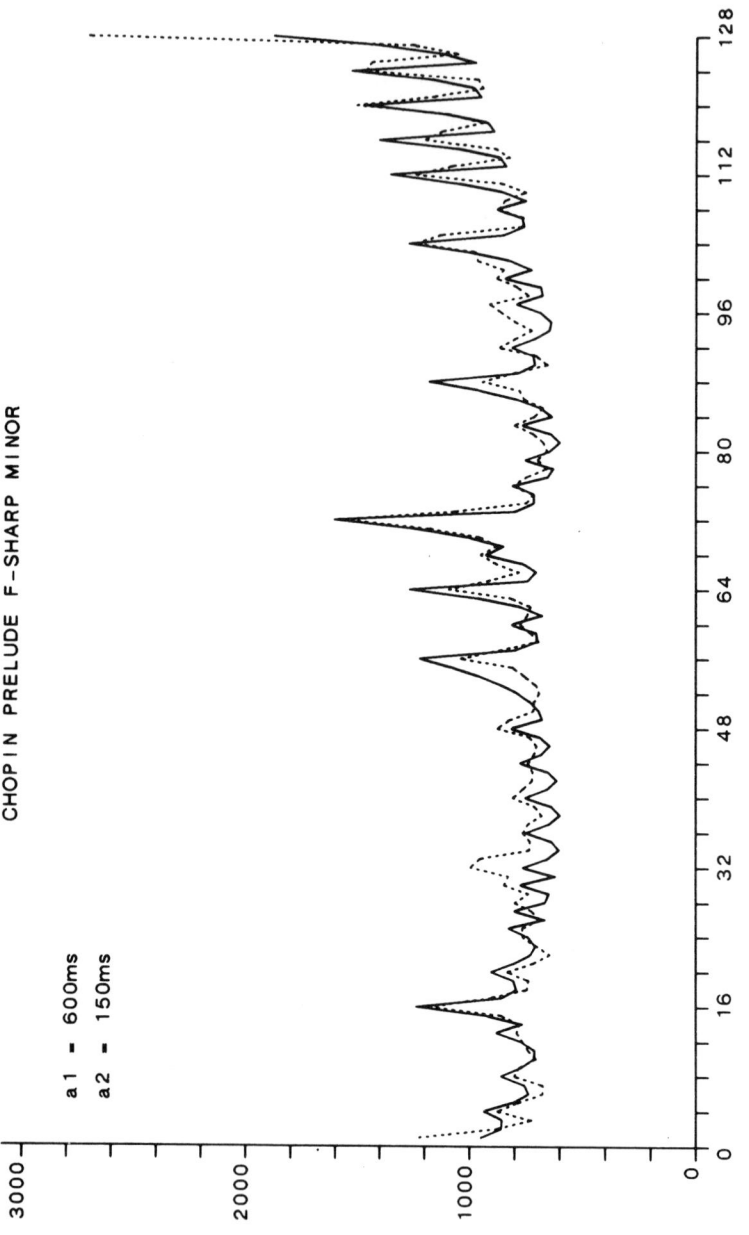

Figure 4 Comparison of model and data for Chopin Prelude. The figure shows the model (solid line) derived from the grouping analysis as in Appendix 4 compared against an average of data from two performances (dotted line).

Discussion

The paper started out by raising two objections to the Todd (1985) model. The first objection was concerned with the nature of the internal representation of grouping which forms the input to the model. The second objection was to do with the nature of the procedure for mapping the internal representation into duration. These objections led to the formulation of a new model.

An important conclusion to be drawn from this is that any theories of musical perception and cognition must take into account the psychological constraints of memory. As we have seen the unmodified adoption of the "reduction hypothesis" (Lerdahl and Jackendoff, 1983) leads to predictions which cannot be sustained.

The model, as it currently stands, still has many problems as far as psychological plausibility is concerned. Whilst an attempt has been made to take into account short and long-term memory limitations and the real-time nature of performance, the performance procedure *play* contains a number of sub-procedures for which it is hard to envisage realistic psychological mechanisms. As a next step along the road of psychological plausibility the model should be recast once more — perhaps in the form of a production system along the lines of Anderson's theory (1983) with its explicit memory modelling.

A further serious limitation of the model is that it does not attempt to account for note timing. This obviously requires an extension of the representation and performance procedure downwards which will also require the introduction of new timing principles, such as stress lengthening, in addition to the rubato function described above.

Finally, for the model to be tested completely it must be interfaced with a synthesiser. Whilst the method of direct performance data/model comparison is very powerful, at the end of the day the ultimate test of any performance theory must be "Well, what does it sound like?".

Acknowledgements

Thanks to Exeter University Computer Science department for the use of the Pyramid Unix machine. Thanks also to Fran Jenkin for checking over my first draft.

References

Anderson, J.R. (1983) *The Architecture of Cognition*. Harvard University Press
Baker, M.J. (in press) A Cognitive Model for Perception of Musical Grouping Structures. *Contemporary Music Review*
Bengtsson, I. & Gabrielssion, A. (1980) Methods for Analysing Performance of Musical Rhythm. *Scandanavian Journal of Psychology*, **21**, 257–268
Clarke, E. (1984) *Structure and Expression in the rhythm of piano performance*. Ph.D. Thesis. University of Exeter.

Clarke, E. (1986) Theory, Analysis and the Psychology of Music: A Critical Evaluation of A Generative Theory of Tonal Music. *Psychology of Music* **14**, 3–16

Fryden, L. & Sundberg, J. (1984) Performance Rules for melodies: Origins, Functions, Purposes. *International Computer Music Conference Proceedings*

Gabrielsson, A. (1987): Once Again: The Theme from Mozart's Piano Sonata in A Major (K.331). In A. Gabrielsson (Ed.): *Action and Perception in Rhythm and Meter*. Royal Swedish Academy of Music No. 55

Grosjean, I. & Gee, J. (1983) Performance structures: A psycholinguistic and linguistic appraisal. *Cognitive Psychology* **15**, 411–458

Johnson, S.C. (1967) Hierarchical clustering schemes. *Psychometrica* **32**, 241–254

Johnson-Laird, P.N. (1983) *Mental Models: Towards a Cognitive Science of Language, Inference and Consciousness.* Cambridge University Press

Lerdahl, F. & Jackendoff, R. (1983) *A Generative Theory of Tonal Music.* Cambridge, Mass.: MIT Press

Longuet-Higgins, H.C. (1978) The grammar of music. *Interdisciplinary Science Reviews* **3**(2) 148–156

Longuet-Higgins, H.C. (1981) Artificial intelligence — a new theoretical psychology? *Cognition* **10**, 197–200

Marr, D. (1982) *Vision: A Computational Investigation into the Human Representation and Processing of Visual Information.* San Francisco: W.H. Freeman and Company

Risset, J. & Wessel, D.L. (1982) Exploration of Timbre by Analysis and Synthesis. In D. Deutsch (Ed.), *The Psychology of Music.* New York: Academic Press

Seashore, C.E. (1938): *Psychology of Music.* New York: McGraw-Hill

Slawson, J. & Peel, W. (1984) Review of A Generative Theory of Tonal Music. *Journal of Music Theory* **28**,(2) 271–294

Shaffer, L.H. (1981) Performances of Chopin, Bach and Bartok: studies in motor programming. *Cognitive Psychology* **13**, 326–376

Shaffer, L.H. (1984) Timing in Solo and Duet Piano Performances. *Quarterly Journal of Experimental Psychology* **36**, 577–595

Shaffer, L.H., Clarke, E. & Todd, N.P. (1985) Meter and Rhythm in Piano Playing. *Cognition* **20**, 61–77

Shaffer, L.H. & Todd, N.P. (1987) The interpretive component in musical performance. In A. Gabrielsson (Ed.): *Action and Perception in Rhythm and Meter.* Royal Swedish Academy of Music No. 55

Sundberg, J. & Verillo, V. (1980) On the anatomy of the retard: A study of timing in music. *Journal of Acoustical Society of America* **68**, 772–779

Todd, N.P. (1985) A model of expressive timing in tonal music. *Music Perception* **3**, 33–58

Todd, N.P. (in press) Towards a Cognitive Theory Of Expression: The Performance and Perception of Rubato. *Contemporary Music Review*

Appendix 1: The algorithm "play".

The following algorithm was written in Franz Lisp Opus 38.91.

```
(defun start ( )
  (prog ( )
    loop
    (patom "Play which piece?" (setq piece_to_play (read))
    (patom "Name of data file?" (setq datafile (read))
    (setq port (fileopen datafile ' "w"))
    (patom "What tempo?") (setq tempo (read))
    (patom "What amplitude?") (setq amplitude (read))
    (load piece_to_play)
    (set_up_vars)
    (play 'tsr)
    (close port)
    (patom "Play more?") (setq answer (read))
    (cond ((eq answer 'no) (return 'finished)))
    (go loop)))

(defun play(Group)
  (cond
    ((null Group) ( ))
    ((beat Group) (play_beat))
    ((group Group)
      (cond
        ((surface_group Group)
          (prog ( )
            (plan_phrase Group)
            (play eval Group))))
        ((intermediate_group Group)
          (prog ( )
            (look_ahead Group)
            (plan_phrase Group)
            (play (eval Group))))
        ((piece Group)
          (prog ( )
            (look_ahead Group)
            (play (eval Group))))))
    (t (prog ( )
         (play (car Group))
         (play (cdr Group))))))
```

```
(defun set_up_vars ( )
   (prog ( )
      (setq a1 tempo)
      (setq a2 amplitude)
      (setq a3 0)
      (setq a4 0)
      (setq a5 3)
      (setq a6 0.52)
      (setq output ( ))))

(defun beat(Group)
   (cond
      ((numberp Group) t)
      (t ( ))))

(defun group(Group)
   (cond
      ((and (atom Group)
            (not (null (eval Group)))) t)
      ((t ( ))))

(defun surface_group(Group)
   (cond
      (beat (car (eval Group))) t)
      (t ( ))))

(defun intermediate_group(Group)
   (cond
      ((and (not (piece Group))
            (not (surface_group Group))) t)
      (t ( ))))

(defun piece(Group)
   (cond
      ((null (get Group 'phrase)) t)
      (t ( ))))
```

```
(defun look_ahead(Group)
  (look (eval (Group))))

(defun look(Group)
  (cond
    ((null Group)
      (prog ( )
        (putprop current_group
          (increment_depth current_group)
          'depth)))
    ((atom Group)
      (prog ( )
        (setq current_group Group)
        (initialise_depth current_group)
        (putprop current_group
          (set_up current_group)
          'phrase)))
    (t (prog ( )
        (look (car Group))
        (look (cdr Group))))))

(defun initialise_depth(Group)
  (cond
    ((null (plist Group)) (putprop Group '(0) 'depth))
    (t (putprop Group
        (append (get Group 'depth) '(0))
        'depth))))

(defun increment_depth(Group)
  (reverse
    (cons (add1 (car (reverse (get Group 'depth))))
      (cdr (reverse (get Group 'depth))))))
```

```
(defun plan_phrase(Group)
  (prog ( )
    (printc Group)
    (setq output (superpose
                  (plan (get Group 'phrase)
                        1
                        (length (get Group 'phrase))
                        (get_depth Group))
                  output))))

(defun get_depth(Group)
  (prog(Depth)
    (setq Depth (car (get Group 'depth)))
    (putprop Group (cdr (get Group 'depth)) 'depth)
    (return Depth)))

(defun plan(Phrase Time Length Depth)
  (cond
    ((null Phrase) ( ))
    ((atom Phrase) (rubato Time Length Depth))
    (t (cons (plan (car Phrase) Time Length Depth)
             (plan (cdr Phrase) (add1 Time) Length Depth)))))

(defun rubato (T A3 A4)
  (times (square (quotient 1.0 (difference 1.0 a6)))
         (square (difference (plus (quotient (float T)
                                             (float A3))
                                   (quotient (sub1 (float A4))
                                             a5))
                             a6))))

(defun play_beat( )
  (prog ( )
    (setq beatout (plus a1
                        (times a2
                               (car output))))
    (printc (fix beatout))
    (printc (fix beatout) port)
    (setq output (cdr output))))
```

```
(defun set_up(Group)
  (cond
    ((or (null Group)
         (and (atom Group)
              (null (eval Group)))) ( ))
    ((surface_group Group) (eval Group))
    ((atom Group) (set_up (eval Group)))
    (t (append (set_up (car Group))
               (set_up (cdr Group))))

(defun superpose(Phrase Output)
  (cond
    ((null Output) Phrase)
    ((null Phrase) Output)
    ((atom Phrase) (plus Phrase Output))
    (t (cons (superpose (car Phrase) (car Output))
             (superpose (cdr Phrase) (cdr Output))))))

(defun square(N)
  (times N N))

(defun print fexpr(L)
  (cond
    ((null (cdr L)) (prog( ) (print (eval (car L)))
                             (terpr)))
    (t (prog( ) (print (eval (car L))) (eval (cadr L)))
                (terpr (eval (cadr L)))))))
```

Appendix 2: Commentary on program

The executive function *start*;
a) inputs *piece_to_play*, which is a Lisp representation of grouping;
b) opens *port* for output to *datafile*;
c) calls the function *set_up_vars*;
d) calls the main function *play*;
e) closes *port*.

The function *set_up_vars* initialises
a) the six parameters of the encoding function as in Eqn. 5;
b) the output plan *output* which is a list of durations.

The main function *play* recursively operates on *tsr* and returns a list of durations. On each call the function will do one of four things:
a) if it is a piece, which is the top level of the structure, then the function *look_ahead* is called; *look_ahead* assigns the values *depth* and *phrase* to a property-list for each sub-group at that level;

b) if it is an intermediate-group then the function *plan_phrase* is called as well as *look_ahead*; *plan_phrase* applies the encoding function *rubato* to a group using as input the properties assigned at the level above by *look_ahead*; on each call of *plan_phrase* the result is superposed onto the output plan *output*;
c) if it is a surface-group then the function *plan_phrase* is called;
d) if it is beat, which in this implementation is just an integer, that the function *play_beat* is called; *play_beat* prints the first element of *output* to *datafile* and resets *output* less the first element.

The algorithm ends when all the groups have been played.

Appendix 3: Grouping analysis for Haydn Sonata 59

The grouping analysis was derived from the data of a performance of the Adagio from Haydn's Sonata 59 using the algorithm *listen* ($r_1 = 1$, $r_2 = 1.5$) (see Todd, in press). In the analysis *sgn* signifies *n*th surface-group and *ign* *n*th intermediate-group. This piece has two levels and therefore two timing components. At the top level there are three groups *ig1*, *ig2* and *ig3*.

```
(setq sg1 '(1 1 1 1 1))
(setq sg2 '(1 1 1))
(setq sg3 '(1 1 1))
(setq sg4 '(1 1 1 1 1))
(setq ig1 '((sg1) (sg2) (sg3) (sg4)))
(setq sg5 '(1 1 1 1))
(setq sg6 '(1 1 1 1 1 1))
(setq sg7 '(1 1))
(setq sg8 '(1 1))
(setq sg10 '(1 1 1 1))
(setq ig2 '((sg5) (sg6) (sg7) (sg8) (sg9) (sg10)))
(setq sg11 '(1 1 1 1))
(setq sg12 '(1 1 1 1 1 1))
(setq sg13 '(1 1))
(setq sg14 '(1 1))
(setq sg15 '(1 1))
(setq sg16 '(1 1 1 1))
(setq ig3 '((sg11) (sg12) (sg13) (sg14) (sg15) (sg16)))
(setq tsr '((ig1) (ig2) (ig3)))
```

Appendix 4: Grouping analysis for Chopin prelude

This grouping analysis was derived from an average of two performances of Chopin's Prelude in F# Minor using the algorithm *listen* ($r_1 = 1$, $r_2 = 1.18$, $r_3 = 1.4$) (see Todd, in press). In the analysis *tgn* signifies the nth top-level group. This piece has three structural levels and therefore three components. At the top level it is divided into two sections *tg1* and *tg2*.

```
(setq sg1 '(1 1 1 1))
(setq sg2 '(1 1 1 1))
(setq sg3 '(1 1 1 1 1))
(setq sg4 '(1 1 1))
(setq ig1 '((sg1) (sg2) (sg3) (sg4)))
(setq sg5 '(1 1 1 1))
(setq sg6 '(1 1 1 1 1))
(setq sg7 '(1 1))
(setq sg8 '(1 1 1))
(setq sg9 '(1 1))
(setq sg10 '(1 1 1 1))
(setq sg11 '(1 1 1 1))
(setq sg12 '(1 1 1 1))
(setq sg13 '(1 1 1 1))
(setq sg14 '(1 1 1 1 1 1 1 1))
(setq ig2 '((sg5) (sg6) (sg7) (sg8) (sg9) (sg10) (sg11) (sg12) (sg13) (sg14))
(setq sg15 '(1 1 1 1))
(setq sg16 '(1 1 1 1))
(setq ig3 '((sg15) (sg16)))
(setq sg17 '(1 1 1 1))
(setq sg18 '(1 1 1 1))
(setq ig4 '((sg17) (sg18)))
(setq tg1 '((ig1) (ig2) (ig3) (ig4)))
(setq sg19 '(1 1 1 1))
(setq sg20 '(1 1 1))
(setq sg21 '(1 1 1 1))
(setq sg22 '(1 1 1 1 1))
(setq ig5 '((sg19) (sg20) (sg21) (sg22)))
(setq sg23 '(1 1 1 1))
(setq sg24 '(1 1 1 1 1))
(setq sg25 '(1 1 1))
(setq sg26 '(1 1 1 1))
(setq ig6 '((sg23) (sg24) (sg25) (sg26)))
(setq sg27 '(1 1 1 1))
(setq sg28 '(1 1 1 1))
```

```
(setq ig7 '((sg27) (sg28)))
(setq sg29 '(1 1 1 1))
(setq ig8 '((sg29)))
(setq sg30 '(1 1 1 1))
(setq ig9 '((sg30)))
(setq sg31 '(1 1 1 1))
(setq ig10 '((sg31)))
(setq sg32 '(1 1 1 1))
(setq ig11 '((sg32)))
(setq tg2 '((ig5) (ig6) (ig7) (ig8) (ig9) (ig10) (ig11)))
(setq tsr '((tg1) (tg2)))
```

Rules for automated performance of ensemble music

Johan Sundberg, Anders Friberg and Lars Frydén
Department of Speech Communication and Music Acoustics, KTH (Royal Institute of Technology), Stockholm, Sweden

Recently developed parts of a computer program are presented that contain a rule system which automatically converts music scores to musical performance, and which, in a sense, can be regarded as a model of a musically gifted player. The development of the rule system has followed the analysis-by-synthesis strategy; various rules have been formulated according to the suggestions of a professional string quartet violinist and teacher of ensemble playing. The effects of various rules concerning synchronization and timing and also tuning, in performance of ensemble music are evaluated by a listening panel of professional musicians. Further support for the notion of *melodic charge*, previously introduced and playing a prominent rule in the performance rules, is found in a correlation with fine tuning of intervals.

KEYWORDS   music performance, timing, synchronization, tuning

Introduction

It is a well-known fact that musicians do not replicate in detail the music score. The score merely serves as a nominal description of the music requiring an interpretation, and this interpretation is signalled to the listener in terms of significant deviations from the nominal score which consequently seem musically important and meaningful.

Here we will present some recent results from a project where an analysis-by-synthesis strategy is applied to music performance. Numerous reports have already been published on this project (e.g., Friberg & Sundberg, 1986; Friberg, Frydén, Bodin & Sundberg, 1988; Sundberg & Frydén, 1985; Sundberg, Askenfelt, & Frydén, 1983a; Sundberg, Frydén, & Askenfelt, 1983b; Thompson, Friberg, Frydén, & Sundberg, 1986). The scenario is a highly skilled music teacher teaching the computer how to perform in a musically acceptable manner. Thus, a basic idea in this project is to make use of a musician's intuition and musical ideas as revealed by introspection and as developed over a long period of time through his experience of teaching.

The analysis-by-synthesis strategy for analyzing music performance complements the method of collecting measurements from actual performances, which has been applied in most investigations (see e.g., Bengtsson & Gabrielsson, 1977; Clarke, 1985; Edlund, 1985; Gabrielsson, 1987; Shaffer, 1981; Sloboda, 1983; Todd, 1985). The limitations and advantages of these two methods have been discussed extensively elsewhere (Thompson & al., 1986). Analysis-by-synthesis has been much less used (Clynes, 1983). There are certainly advantages and limitations associated with both these methods (Gabrielsson, 1985). An important advantage is that even those elements of music performance that are used only occasionally (and are hence difficult to find by means of a statistical processing of measurement data) can be revealed and analyzed. Moreover, if there are many reasons to shorten a note, it is a sizeable task to identify the various reasons by measuring performances. It is interesting that in performance research based on measurements, much more attention has been paid to regularly recurring events, such as the duration pattern of a bar, while expressive effects not affiliated with the bar unit have been largely neglected. In any event, there seem to be certain important advantages associated with the analysis-by-synthesis strategy as applied to music performance, and we have found it worthwhile to exploit these advantages.

In previous experiments, we have dealt with the performance of one part melodies and excerpts. Several rules have been formulated and tested, and when one or more rules have been applied, musically experienced judges report that the musical quality of the performance increases (Thompson *et al.*, 1986).

It seems certain that these rules must also apply in ensemble music in one way or another. In the following, we will first mention some rules that seemed to be of particular relevance in an attempt to synthesize performances of ensemble music. Then, two basic aspects of ensemble playing will be considered.

(1) How is temporal coordination achieved?
(2) What principles are used for tuning chords?

Most of the background of the first question has been descibed above already, the deviations from the nominal durations of the notes seem essential in music performance but will differ between different voices in a piece of music. We may thus ask whose timetable is accepted by the others, and at which places in the piece all the musicians synchronize their note onsets perfectly.

The background to the second question deserves more detailed comments. Tuning has been a classical concern in music theory. Reviews of measurements of tuning in performance have been offered by Ward (1970) and by Sundberg (1982), and, more recently, experimental work has been reported on perceptual aspects of tuning (Hall & Hess, 1984; Rasch, 1985; Vos, 1986). Theoretically, several tuning recipes compete.

One candidate is *just tuning*. It implies that all chords are played beat-free, which is often considered to be an advantage. This means that the fundamental frequencies in all simultaneously sounding major triads tuned to the frequency ratio 4:5:6, if instruments generating tones with harmonic spectra are used. An alternative is *equally tempered tuning*. In it, the octave is split into twelve equally wide intervals all having the frequency ratio $1:2^{1/12}$.

Just tuning is sometimes referred to as pure. However, in the present article, the term pure will be used for "sounding appropriately tuned" or "perfectly in tune". As will be shown, this is sometimes quite different from being in accordance with just tuning.

Figure 1 summarizes measurements made on various types of musical performance. The interval sizes have been normalised, such that the data show the deviations in cents from what the interval is in the equally tempered scale. It can be seen that just tuning is far from universally applied in music performance. Rather, the intervals are generally played wider than just, except for the minor second which is played considerably narrower than just.

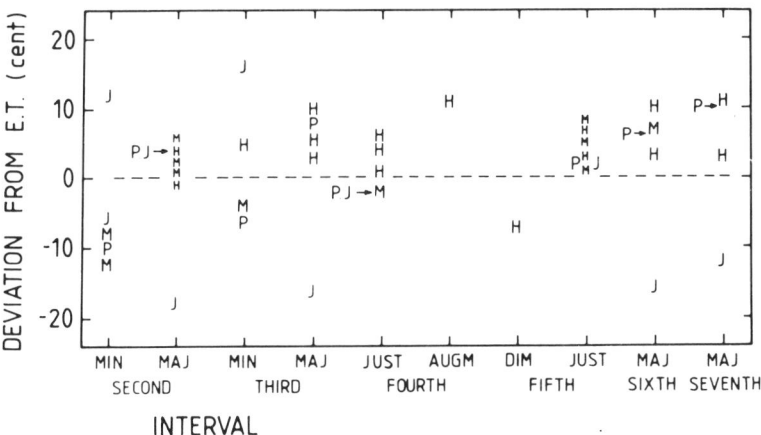

Figure 1 Mean interval sizes observed in solo (M) and ensemble (H) performances. J and P show the corresponding values in just and Pythagorean tuning. Data adapted after Ward (1970).

In ensemble music performances, most musicians are free to decide themselves the exact fundamental frequency of the notes they are playing. This allows context-dependent intonation. Thus, they can adjust the frequency of each note such that each chord receives optimal tuning or such that each melodic interval is optimally sized. According to general opinion among musicians, this context-dependent tuning of each note is essential in ensemble performances. For instance, all professional players of bowed instruments would agree that they have to move their finger position if a note is changed from F sharp to G flat, and Shackford (1961; 1962a; 1962b) found these two pitches to be clearly differentiated in string music performance.

In his survey of data on tuning in performance, Ward (1970) found that most intervals except the minor second are played *wider* than in the equally tempered scale. However, in an investigation of chord intonation in barbershop singing, several intervals were found that were *narrower* than in the equally tempered scale (Hagerman & Sundberg, 1982). Furthermore, within a single note, the fundamental frequency is sometimes observed to change, apparently from one value to another (Sundberg, 1982). This suggests that the fundamental frequency averaged over an entire note may be misleading.

Ideal melodic tuning is sometimes incompatible with the demand to play beat-free chords. Thus, the melodically desirable narrow minor second often conflicts with the demands of just tuning. Let us take the progression dominant to tonic as an example. Melodically, it normally contains a minor second from the third of the dominant to the root of the tonic. Using instruments with harmonic spectra, a beat free third requires the fundamental frequency ratio of 4:5. This third is 16 cents flatter than the corresponding value in the equally tempered scale. Consequently, if the third of the dominant chord is tuned beat-free, the semitone step up to the root of the tonic will be 16 cents wider than in the equally tempered tuning. Thus, there is a conflict between what is perceived as optimal harmonically and melodically. Therefore, a third tuning scheme must be postulated. Henceforth, though as yet poorly defined, the tuning that yields intervals sounding melodically pure will be referred to as *melodic tuning*.

In any event, it can be assumed that the equally tempered scale, though used in some keyboard instruments, cannot *a priori* be regarded as the only possible solution to the tuning problem in ensemble performance. The details of the musicians' tuning strategies are largely unknown, and a primary task was therefore to look for better tuning and intonation alternatives.

Procedure

Figure 2 gives an overview of the strategy. The input is the musical score, which, voice by voice, is written into a Macintosh microcomputer. This input can be complemented by various details of interpretation, such as phrase and subphrase boundaries, harmonies, ties, etc. The input is then processed by a program (called RULLE), which automatically computes the performance and converts it into control signals for a synthesizer, using the MIDI standard. The synthesizer used is mostly a specially constructed machine, SISYPHOS, a sampler-type machine that reads previously stored wave forms at a speed determined by the fundamental frequency. One advantage with this device is that fundamental frequency can be controlled with an accuracy of +/− 0.85 cent.

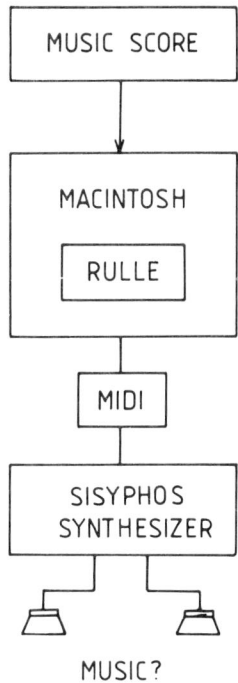

Figure 2 Block scheme showing the analysis-by-synthesis strategy used in the present project. The score is written into a Macintosh microcomputer, in which the RULLE program converts it into control signals in a MIDI format, which are sent to a synthesizer.

Context-dependent performance rules (Friberg & Sundberg, 1986) are introduced into the RULLE program, which is written in the Le_Lisp computer language. These rules shorten and lengthen the durations of single notes, increase or decrease their sound level, perform fine tuning of pitch, generate crescendos and decrescendos, and distribute markers at phrase and subphrase endings as defined in the input notation. The program allows the testing of the musical effects of each rule on the performance. In this way, the effect on performance of every single rule can be tested, demonstrated, and assessed.

In most cases, the effects of the rules are quite clearly demonstrated by this experimental setup, and only exceptionally there has been any disagreement between the authors as to whether or not a rule improved a performance. Nevertheless, in order to evaluate the various rules formally, we have had a panel of 2 professional violin players and 8 advanced music conservatory students to assess the effects. In this experiment, the subjects listened to different computer generated renderings. Their task was to rate the musical quality of the performance with a number between 0 and 7, 0 being poorest and 7 being the best.

Results

A. Rules for monophonic music performance

Melodic charge

Musical notes do not form a society of equality. On the contrary, some notes are remarkable or unexpected, while others are more predictable. It seems necessary to take this into account during playing. Assume, for example, that the note of C sharp occurs in a C major tonality, which is a remarkable event in traditional harmony. If the player does not stress this remarkable note when playing, the performance sounds musically insensitive at this point. We have arrived at the following method for marking a note's remarkableness.

Each note is assigned a value reflecting its *melodic charge*. The basis of this concept is borrowed from the circle of fifths, as illustrated in Figure 3: a note's melodic charge reflects its distance along the circle of fifths from the root of the prevailing chord. Note, however, that the distribution of melodic charge is assymmetrical around the circle; the numbers on the subdominant (left) side of the circle are negative and greater as compared to the numbers on the opposite side, which are positive. For example, three fifth steps down from the root correspond to a melodic charge of −4.5, while three fifths steps up correspond to the charge value of 3.0. In previous reports on this project, the absolute value, only, of the melodic charge has been used. Unless otherwise stated, the term melodic charge will henceforth be used for the absolute value of the melodic charge, as before.

While the concept of melodic charge may seem farfetched, the usefulness of the circle of fifths to describe in a compact form musically relevant aspects of pitches in traditional tonal music is well-known. As shown in Figure 4, melodic charge shows a significant correlation with the mean probe tone ratings for the notes in the major scale, that Krumhansl & Kessler (1982) reported from an experiment whose listeners rated how well different notes served as a continuation of a reference

Rules for music performance 95

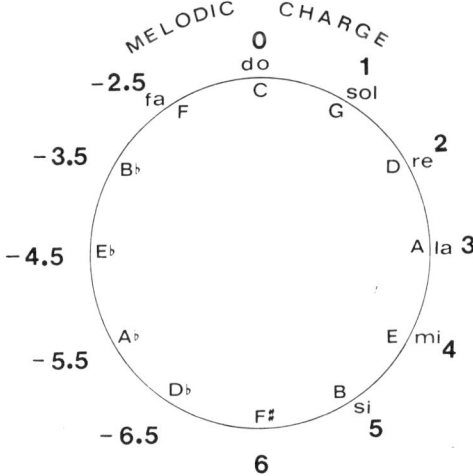

Figure 3 Definition of *melodic charge* of the scale tones in tonal music by means of the circle of fifths. Note that the values are asymmetrically distributed around the reference which is the root of the prevailing chord, and that the charge is negative in the left (subdominant) half of the circle.

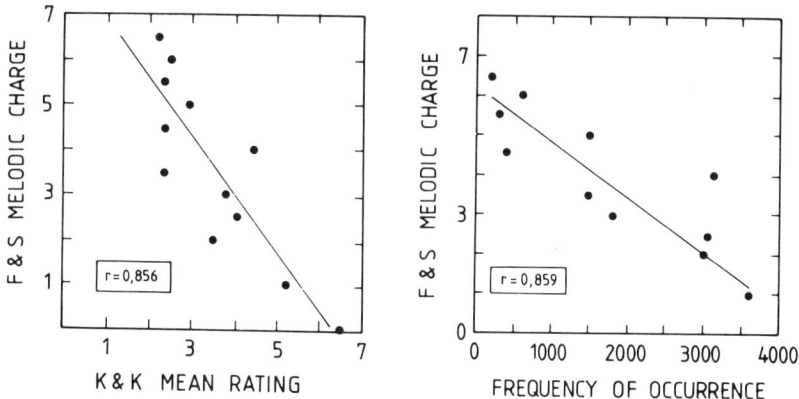

Figure 4 Correlation of melodic charge with (left) the probe tone ratings for the tones in the major scale according to Krumhansl & Kessler (1982) and (right) the frequency of occurrence of the various scale tones in Schubert themes, as reported by Knopoff & Hutchinson (1983).

scale (Sundberg & Frydén, 1987). Also, as shown in the same figure, melodic charge clearly correlates with the frequency of occurrence of the various scale tones in Schubert themes, as reported by Knopoff & Hutchinson (1983). This suggests an interpretation of melodic charge: assuming that rarely occurring notes are remarkable, a note's melodic charge may reflect how remarkable it is.

According to our rules, melodic charge is signalled in three different ways in a performance: (1) by a lengthening of the note's duration by an amount equal to 2/3 of the melodic charge, in msec; (2) by an increase of the note's sound level by an amount of dB equal to 0.2 times the melodic charge, and then the sound level differences between adjacent notes is smoothed; and (3) by an increase of the note's vibrato extent by 0.03 times the melodic charge, in percent. The effect is illustrated in Figure 5.

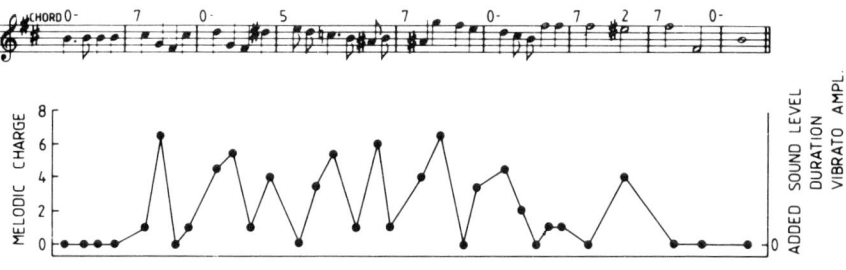

Figure 5 The effect of melodic charge on performance according to the rule system: (1) a lengthening of the note's duration; (2) an increase of the note's sound level; and (3) an increase of the note's vibrato extent.

Harmonic charge

The principle of inequality seems to apply also to chords. For instance, a G major chord appearing in a C major tonality is not very remarkable, while an A major chord occurring in the same tonality is much more remarkable. Again, it sounds musically insensitive if a player overlooks this when playing.

We have derived a quantitative measure of the remarkableness of chords from the chord notes' melodic charges, and we have called the resulting entity *harmonic charge*. The harmonic charge of a chord is a weighted sum of the chord notes' melodic charges as determined with the root of the tonic as the reference: for a triad it equals the melodic charge of the root plus 2/3 of the melodic charge of the third plus 1/3 of the melodic charge of the fifth. The values thus obtained are then normalized such that the harmonic charge of the tonic becomes zero. Figure 6 shows the harmonic charge values for some chords.

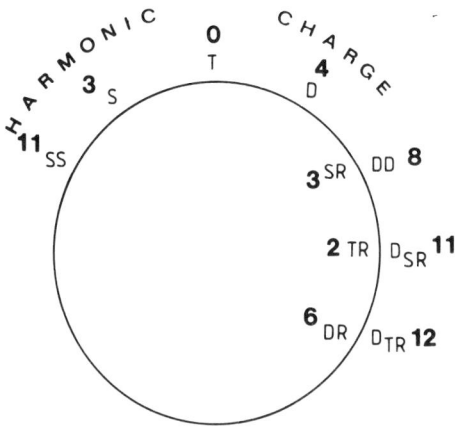

Figure 6 Harmonic charge values for some chords symbolized by their harmonic function in tonal music: T=Tonic, S=Subdominant, D=Dominant, R=Relative. In a C-major context the chords are the following: SS=B flat major, S=F major, T=C major, D=G major, DD=D major, SR=D minor, D_{SR}=A major, TR=A minor, D_{TR}=E major, DR=E minor.

Harmonic charge may seem as farfetched as melodic charge. However, once again listeners experiences can serve as a support. Krumhansl & Kessler (1983) presented different probe chords to listeners following a reference cadence that defined the tonality and asked the subjects to rate how well the probe chords fitted as a continuation of the reference cadence. The probe chord ratings show a significant correlation with harmonic charge, as shown in Figure 7.

According to our rules, the harmonic charge is reflected in the performance in terms of crescendos and decrescendos, as well as in minute accelerandos and rallentandos and tenutos, as illustrated in Figure 8. The sound level increases toward increases in harmonic charge and vice versa; the amplitude of the first note after each chord change is increased by a number of dB equal to a constant times the harmonic charge value of the new chord, and the intermediate notes are given intermediate amplitudes. In this way, crescendos and decrescendoes are created. Crescendos that are too slow are hard to detect and are avoided by delaying crescendo starts until 1.9 seconds before the chord change, whenever needed. Unlike crescendos, decrescendos start immediately after the chord change.

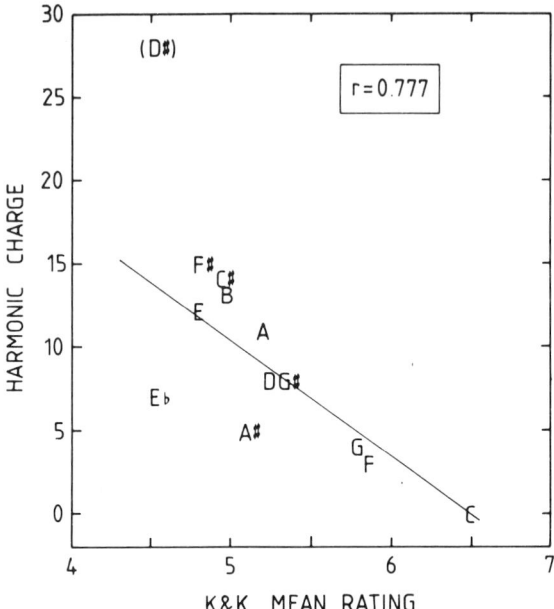

Figure 7 Harmonic charge versus the probe chord ratings reported by Krumhansl & Kessler (1983).

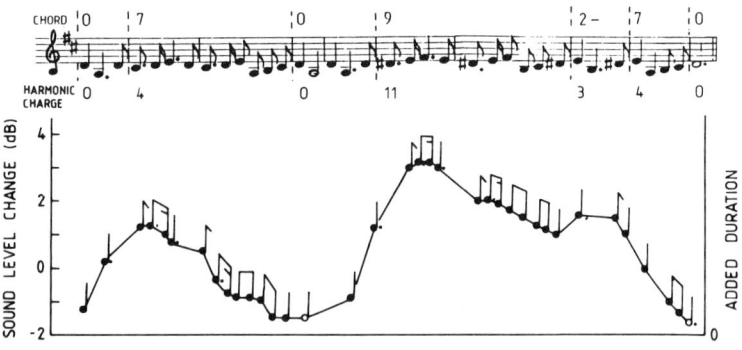

Figure 8 The effect of harmonic charge on performance according to the rule system: (1) crescendos and diminuendos; (2) concomitant tempo changes; and (3) small tenutos.

Apart from these long-term sound level variations, the harmonic charge also generates expressive variation of the notes' durations. In a crescendo, the durations of the notes are lengthened by a factor proportional to the increase in sound level, as illustrated in Figure 8. In addition, a small tenuto is added to the first note appearing together with a new, harmonically charged chord.

B. Rules for ensemble music performance

Synchronization

Two performance rules out of a total of about 20 have been presented above. As mentioned, the musical effects of these rules on performances have been approved by panels of musically experienced listeners. It seems reasonable to assume that these rules might also be valid in ensemble playing. If so, each member of an ensemble will arrive at a time pattern that is suited for his own voice or instrument. As a result a number of competing timetables will emerge in an ensemble, and some decision must be taken as to which one is going to take precedence.

One way of maintaining synchronization is that each musician should simply stick to the nominal durations. There are strong indications that this is not the normal solution in ensemble performance. We may merely point to well-known phenomena such as final ritard, tenuto and other means of expression which are clearly used in ensemble performance. We have tried out two alternative ways of achieving synchronization between voices.

One possibility is that all musicians in an ensemble introduce all the perturbations of the nominal durations that are required, but scale them such that the entire ensemble is synchronized once per bar, e.g., on the main beat. This once-per-bar principle would maintain a coordination and yet offer some leeway for individualization of the various parts. This was selected as one of the two alternatives for the listening test.

Another possibility is that everything that is vertically aligned in the score is also perfectly aligned in time and that the player, who is playing the shortest or melodically most charged note, dictates the timetable for the remainder of the ensemble. Note that this principle does not require everything to be played as nominally written in the score. This principle of synchronization on the shortest notes was selected as the second alternative for the listening experiment.

We used the following strategy in order to automatically derive a performance from the score. First, all voices were processed by all rules affecting amplitude or vibrato. Secondly, a new voice was derived from the score. This voice was built from the shortest note that appeared in the score at each moment. In those cases where there were several notes with the shortest note value, that note was selected which had the highest melodic charge. The "synchronization voice" thus obtained jumps boldly from one part to the other, as is illustrated in Figure 9. Once this synchronization voice has been constructed, it is processed by all performance rules that affect the duration of the notes, and all ensemble members play in synchrony with this voice.

Figure 9 The excerpt from String quartet No 5, C major, second movement by Franz Berwald used in the synchronization test. The circled notes show the synchronization voice, obtained by selecting, at each moment, that voice which plays the shortest and melodically most charged notes.

Our panel of musicians rated the quality of three synthetic performances "with regard to ensemble playing, i.e., how simultaneously the musicians played". The excerpts are listed in Table 1. Each was presented three times in random order on a test tape avoiding repetitions of the same excerpt in sequence. In the examples, the synchronization was organised according to either of the two principles mentioned. The examples were presented over loudspeakers to all subjects at a comfortable listening level. The subjects gave their answers on terms of ratings between 0 and 7 on standard sheets.

Table 1 Results from the listening experiment in which professional musicians rated the quality of "togetherness" in synthesized performances of three excerpts, where the synchronization was organised according to either the "once per bar" principle or the "shortest note" principle (see text).

Excerpt Synchronization strategy:	"Once per bar" Mean rating	SD	"Shortest note" Mean	SD
H.L. Hassler: Bars 1 to 10 from Madrigal "Nun fanget an" for 5 voices	5.18	1.05	5.02	1.43
F. Berwald: Bars 58 to 69 from String Quartet No 5, C major	2.20	1.19	4.13	1.33
J.S. Bach: Bars 17 to 33 from the Ricercar a 6 voci from Musikalisches Opfer	4.85	1.56	5.37	1.40

The results, also shown in Table 1, showed no preference in the case of the Hassler example, where both principles yield very similar results. However, there was a clear preference for the principle of synchronisation on the shortest notes particularly for the rhythmically vivid Berwald excerpt, and less so for the Bach excerpt. According to an analysis of variance, the subjects differed significantly in their answers, and the excerpts significantly influenced the results. However, averaging over all excerpts, the principle of synchronization on the shortest notes gave significantly better ratings than the synchronization on the bar.

These results indicate a preference for the principle that all notes aligned in the score should be synchronized in the performance and that a possible timing strategy is that the player who plays the shortest and melodically most charged notes decides the timetable for the other players. This suggests that at any moment, every member of an ensemble has to listen carefully to what the other players are playing and synchronise with the timing of the most vivid musical motion, unless there is a conductor to take the responsibility for the synchronization.

Tuning

In the same listening session, different tunings were also evaluated by the panel of ten professional musicians. The two tunings tried were just tuning and equally tempered tuning. In addition, we also wanted to try melodic tuning, but as available data on melodic tuning were incomplete, we first had to carry out a preliminary tuning experiment.

In an experiment, we asked a very proficient violinist to tune a set of rising melodic intervals. The tones were produced by a synthesizer controlled from the Macintosh computer by the experimenter who changed the tuning of the interval according to the desires of the musician. Each interval was tuned at least two times. Repeated attempts to tune the same interval mostly showed a variation of a couple of cents only. His interval settings are presented in Figure 10 together with those shown previously in Figure 1.

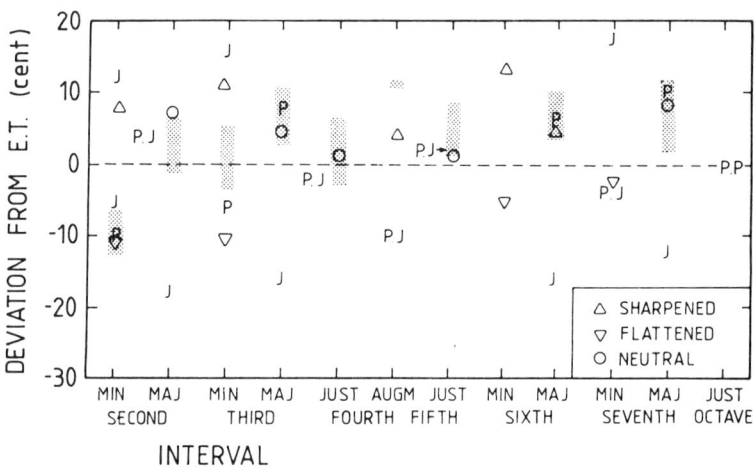

Figure 10 Deviation from equally tempered tuning of melodic interval as adjusted by a professional violin player. P and J show how Pythagorean and just tuning deviate from equally tempered. The hatched areas show the values plotted in Figure 1 representing tuning data derived from measurement on musical performance.

There is a clear tendency to increase the contrast between flattened and sharpened notes, so that flattened notes are tuned flat and sharpened notes are tuned sharp, as compared with the equally tempered tuning. In traditional harmony, a flattened note is typically followed by a falling minor second (e.g., as in the sequence A flat → G) while a sharpened note is typically followed by a rising minor second (e.g., as in the sequence G sharp → A). Therefore, the tendency to increase the contrast between flattened and sharpened notes can also be seen as a tendency to decrease the size of the melodic minor second.

These interval tunings appear to be related to the signed melodic charge of the upper (target) note of the interval. Figure 11 shows the

Rules for music performance 103

settings, expressed as deviations from just tuning (left) and from equally tempered tuning (right). In both graphs, the settings are given as a function of the signed melodic charge of the target note of the interval, assuming the lower note of the interval as the reference. The pitch symbols refer to the names of the target note of the interval, using C as the lower reference note. Intervals "aiming" upward, i.e., potentially followed by a rising semitone, e.g., a D sharp, are symbolized by sharps, and intervals "aiming" downward in the same sense, e.g. and E flat, by flats.

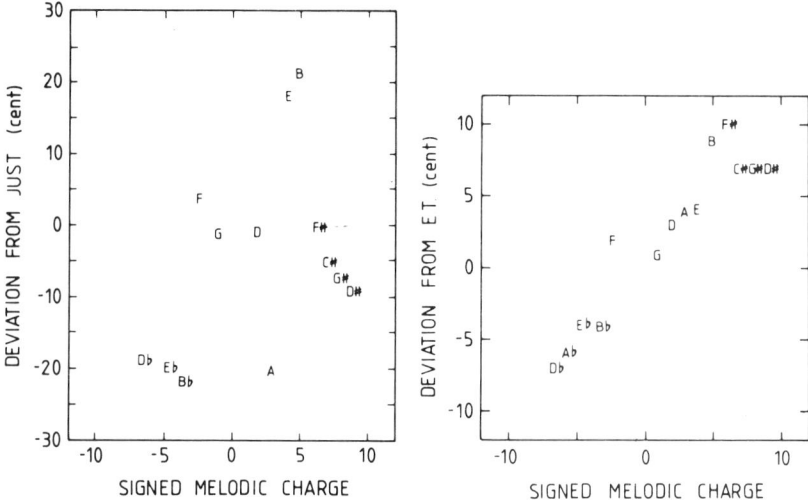

Figure 11 Deviation from just tuning (left) and from equally tempered tuning (right) of the melodic interval tunings shown in Figure 10 plotted as function of the notes' difference in signed melodic charge.

When expressed as deviations from just tuning, an overall tendency can be observed for the intervals to be expanded with increasing signed melodic charge. However, the scatter is considerable, and the data points are clustered in groups.

If, however, the data are expressed as deviations from the equally tempered scale, as in the right graph, an almost linear function is obtained. This result is interesting, as it suggests the possibility that the equally tempered scale may serve as a frame of reference for interval tuning in music performance practice. Thus, the equally tempered scale may not necessarily be only a mathematical construct, but may also represent a psychological reality.

The straight line approximation derived by linear regression analysis ($r=0.924$) yields almost just fifths, 701.4 cent wide on the dominant side of the circle of fifths, and slightly more on the subdominant side. These settings yielded a series of interval settings that we accepted as a fair approximation to melodic tuning.

Thus, in the listening test, subjects listened to three excerpts played in three different tunings: (1) just tuning, (2) equal temperament, and (3) melodic tuning. In addition, we also tried (4) a combination of just and melodic tuning. The reason was that neither melodic, nor just tuning sounded acceptable throughout. Rather, both sometimes sounded badly out of tune, though in different places in the pieces. For the fourth alternative, all successive notes were tuned in melodic tuning at the onset of the note, and after 10 msec, the tuning changed to just over a 70 msec period according to a cosine curve.

The excerpts are listed in Table 2. They represent different styles of harmony. One consisted of the first 8 bars from Gesualdo's madrigal "Belt, poi che t'assenti" which contains frequent examples of chromatic changes of notes. The second example was a 15 bar extract by Purcell ("Fancy" in F major) which contains many instances of melodic minor seconds. The third example was a choral written in four voices by the contemporary Swedish composer Sven Erik Bäck ("Du som gick före oss". "Thou, who went ahead of us").

Table 2 Average rating and change in rating of just, melodic, and just-to-melodic tunings, as compared with equally tempered tuning.

Tuning	Excerpt	Mean Rating	SD	Change re Eq. Temp.
EQ. TEMP	Gesualdo	3.5	1.53	
	Purcell	3.9	1.69	
	Bäck	4.75	1.14	
	All examples	4.05		
JUST	Gesualdo	3.77	1.99	+0.27
	Purcell	1.37	1.46	−2.53
	Bäck	4.35	1.56	−0.40
	All examples	3.16		−0.89
MELODIC	Gesualdo	1.63	1.50	−1.87
	Purcell	3.6	1.94	−0.3
	Bäck	3.55	1.56	−1.2
	All examples	2.93		−1.12
MEL-JUST	Gesualdo	3.27	1.51	−0.23
	Purcell	2.28	1.22	−1.62
	Bäck	4.35	1.52	−0.40
	All examples	3.30		−0.75

Each excerpt was presented in each of the four tunings, and, as before, each example occurred three times in random order on a test tape that the subjects listened to over loudspeakers at a comfortable loudness level. The subjects' task was to rate the quality of the tuning, taking both harmony and melody into consideration, and they gave on a protocol sheet their ratings along a scale from 0 to 7, 7 being the best. The mean ratings are shown in the same Table 2.

According to an analysis of variance, all factors produced significant differences: subjects, excerpts, and tuning ($p<0.01$, in all these cases). A major reason for this significance was the fact that the subjects answered very consistently when rating the three copies of each example.

Much to our surprise, the panel seemed to prefer the equally tempered tuning to just melodic, and just-to-melodic tuning. However, this preference was dependent on the music, as mentioned.

For the Purcell example, containing several minor second intervals, melodic tuning was almost as highly rated as equally tempered tuning, while for the Gesualdo and Bäck examples, composed in a homophonic, chordal style, just tuning was almost as highly rated as equally tempered tuning. The melodic-to-just tuning was slightly better than the just for the Purcell example and slightly better than melodic for the Gesualdo and Bäck examples.

These results offer good reasons for rejecting the hypothesis that just intonation can be regarded as an optimal general solution in ensemble performance. Also, it can be concluded that in tuning, the musical context must be taken into account; chords apparently sound better in just tuning while minor second sound better in melodic. Our melodic-to-just did not represent an alternative superior to the equally tempered tuning but still improved results slightly in cases where just and melodic sounded badly out of tune.

Discussion

The present investigation considered two aspects of ensemble performance: synchronization and tuning. As regards synchronization, the results suggest that musicians have to follow, at each moment, the timing of a *crucial voice* which consists of elements of various voices. This seems convincing in the sense that most musicians would agree on the necessity of invariably listening to the other players. During rehearsals, an important goal may be to learn the other voices and their possible time tables.

This rule for the synchronization of ensemble playing may need to be complemented by other, style-dependent rules. For instance, in certain contexts one instrument may lead over the others, e.g. in order to avoid masking effects (Rasch, 1978; 1979; 1981). In jazz music, certain dialects seem to exist where one voice may lead or lag as compared with a stable reference beat. In general, the existence of a rule seems to add one more possibility for musical expression, through violating this law.

In regard to tuning, the results show that equally tempered tuning is better than both just and melodic tuning, if applied throughout a piece. The reason may be simple exposure to the tuning of pianos, organs, and synthesizers. It may even be that our use of a synthesizer, increased the jury's prejudices in this respect. An interesting future experiment would be to repeat our listening test using a violin sound.

The melodic-to-just tuning was not rated as highly as we had hoped. There may be several reasons for this. One is that the timbre used in our experiment was strongly periodic and had prominent high partials that exposed tuning deficiencies in terms of salient beats. Also, it seemed that the pitch transitions were too apparent. It is possible that musicians use vibrato to conceal tuning adjustments during playing. Furthermore, if melodic-to-just tuning is applied in music performance, it would constitute a source of error in fundamental frequency measurements; it is not completely evident how an average over time should be computed.

However, since a string player is free to make a context-dependent choice of fundamental frequency, it is not correct to infer that equally tempered tuning is better than the other tunings when the other players are also free to vary intonation. On the contrary, it seems likely that tuning is context-dependent, such that both the harmonic and the melodic functions of each note are taken into consideration. For instance, the musician playing the melody part in a homophonic piece might play according to melodic intonation, while the accompanying instruments, providing the underlying harmony, play in just tuning. In a predominantly polyphonic piece, on the other hand, melodic tuning may be more frequently used, e.g. for salient melodic intervals. The assumption that interval sizes are context dependent is also supported by the fact that some subjects found it difficult to give an overall rating, as they found both merits and deficiencies in most examples. In a future analysis of the context dependency of tuning, analysis-by-synthesis would offer an efficient tool.

It could be argued that the preliminary tuning experiment, on which the melodic tuning was based, used a stereotyped context, namely the interval between a note and the note preceding it. It is not clear whether these tuning data can be expected to be representative of music performance, where other contextual factors are also relevant, such as the note's position in the scale. In the tuning experiment, the major and minor intervals were tuned with an imagined context, viz., that they were followed by a rising or falling minor second. Nonetheless, a more detailed analysis of the relevance of the context to tuning would be needed.

Nevertheless, the settings for the melodic tuning seem convincing. First, there was a fair agreement between these data and averages found in actual performances. Second, the subject was mostly able to replicate his settings with a high level of accuracy. Third, his settings fitted nicely into the framework of the signed melodic charge.

The last mentioned fact is quite interesting. What does this correlation between tuning and the signed melodic charge suggest? According to our previous research, a performance gains in musical quality if melodic charge is marked. One may speculate that sharpening and flattening intervals is used as an *expressive means* in order to mark the melodic charge of the notes. This speculation is supported by an investigation by Makeig & Balzano (1982) showing that differently sized octave intervals had different expressive meanings.

The fact that the musicians' tunings of the intervals clearly correlated with the melodic charge of the target note is interesting also from another point of view. Melodic charge is derived from the circle of fifths, and the same correlation coefficient was obtained if the position on the circle of fifths was used rather than the melodic charge in Figure 11. This means that melodic tuning is very similar to a theoretical construct called Pythagorean tuning. In this tuning all fifths are tuned just, or to 702 cent. In our musician subject's tuning, the mean fifth was slightly more narrow, or 701.4 cent. This minute difference may seem small but gains in importance, the greater the number of fifths there is in an interval.

Finally, the use of rules to describe musical performance should be commented on. Before discussing this problem it is necessary to distinguish between two aspects of a rule. One is the class of notes that are modified by the rules, i.e., the *target notes* of the rule. The other is the amount of modification that the rule generates in the target note's sound variables. This aspect will be referred to as the *rule quantity*.

Music is a form of communication by means of acoustic signals. This implies that there are some conventions shared by the player and the listeners. The rules offer efficient tools for describing such conventions. On the other hand, a given piece of music can be performed in a number of different ways, while the use of rules seemingly implies that there is one single performance possible.

One way of having the same rule system produce different performances is to allow *variation of rule quantity*. Many experiences support the assumption that this occurs in reality. We have noted on a number of occasions that introducing a new rule into the system necessitated a reduction of quantities of one or more of the existing rules. We have also noted that comparatively acceptable performances could be generated with only a small number of rules, suggesting that some rules are not compulsory; the quantity of these *optional rules* may then be regarded as reduced to zero.

There may also be *alternative rules*. For instance, emphasis is expressed in several different ways in our system: sound level, duration, and vibrato amplitude. A rule may merely be a line in the musician's and the listener's internal dictionary which translates items of musical expression, such as emphasis, phrase ending etc., into sound events, such as change in sound level, lengthening etc. This dictionary probably contains synonyms, and in selecting which synonym to use, the musician would take into account the style of the piece, among other things. On the other hand, some rules may not be style-dependent: in a recent experiment, it was found that rules developed for traditional tonal music clearly improved the performance also of contemporary music (Friberg et al., 1988).

Acknowledgement

This research is supported by the Bank of Sweden Tercentenary Foundation.

References

Bengtsson, I. & Gabrielsson, A., (1977) Rhythm research in Uppsala, in *Music Room Acoustics*, J. Sundberg (ed.), Publications issued by the Royal Swedish Academy of Music Nr. 17, Stockholm, pp. 76–181
Clynes, M. (1983) Expressive microstructure in music, linked to living qualities, in *Studies of Music Performance*, J. Sundberg, (ed.) Publications issued by the Royal Swedish Academy of Music Nr. 39, Stockholm, pp. 76–181
Clarke, E. (1985) Structure and expression in rhythmic performance, Chapter 9, in *Musical Structure and Cognition*, P. Howell, I. Cross, & R. West, (eds.) Academic Press, London, pp. 209–236
Corso, J.F. (1954) Unison tuning of musical instruments *J. Acoust. Soc. Am.* **26**, pp. 746–750
Edlund, B. (1985) *Performance and Perception of Notational Variants*. Acta Univ. Upsaliensis, Studia musicol. Upsaliensia N. S. 9
Friberg, A. & Sundberg, J. (1986) A Lisp environment for creating and applying rules for musical performance, in *Proc. Int. Computer Music Conference*, P. Berg, (ed.) The Hague, pp. 1–3
Friberg, A., Frydén, L., Bodin, L–G., & Sundberg, J. (1987) Rules for computer controlled performance of contemporary keyboard music. *Speech Transmission Laboratory Quarterly Progress and Status Report*, 4/1987, pp. 79–85
Gabrielsson, A. (1985) Interplay between analysis and synthesis in studies of music performance and music experience. *Music Perception* 3:1, pp. 59–86
Gabrielsson, A. (1987) Once again: The theme from Mozart's piano sonata in A major (K. 331), in *Action and Perception in Rhythm and Music*, A. Gabrielsson, (ed.) Publications issued by the Royal Swedish Academy of Music Nr. 55, Stockholm, pp. 81–104
Hagerman, B. & Sundberg, J. (1980) Fundamental frequency adjustment in barbershop singing. *J. of Research in Singing* **4**, pp. 3–17
Hall, D. & Hess, J.T. (1984) Perception of musical interval tuning. *Music Perception* **2**, pp. 166–195
Krumhansl, C.L. & Kessler, E.J. (1982) Tracing the dynamic changes in perceived tonal organization in spatial representation of musical keys. *Psychological Review* **89**, pp. 334–368
Knopoff, L. & Hutchinson, W. (1983) Entropy as a measure of style: The influence of sample length. *J. of Music Theory* **27**, pp. 75–97
Makeig, S. & Balzano, G. (1982) Octave tuning — two modes of perception. Paper presented at *Symposium on Psychology and Acoustics of Music*. Lawrence, Kansas.
Rasch, R.A. (1978) The perception of simultaneous notes such as in polyphonic music. *Acustica* **40**, pp. 21–33
Rasch, R.A. (1979) Synchronization in unperformed ensemble music. *Acustica* **43**, pp. 121–131
Rasch, R.A. (1981) *Aspects of the Perception and Performance of Polyphonic Music*. Dissertation, published by R. Rasch, Utrecht
Rasch, R.A. (1985) Perception of melodic and harmonic intonation of two-part musical fragments. *Music Perception* **2**, pp. 441–458

Shaffer, L.H. (1981) Performances of Chopin, Bach, and Bartok: Studies in motor programming. *Cognitive Psychology* **13**, pp. 326–376

Shackford, C. (1961, 1962a and 1962b): Some aspects of perception I, II, and III. *J. of Music Theory* **5**, pp. 162–202; **6**, pp. 66–90; and **6**, pp. 295–303)

Sloboda, J.A. (1983) The communication of musical metre in piano performance. *Quart. J. of Exper. Psychology* **35A**, pp. 377–396

Sundberg, J. (1982) In tune or not? A study of fundamental frequency in music practise, in *Tiefenstruktur der Musik*, Festschrift for Fritz Winckel, C. Dahlhaus & M. Krause, (eds.) Technische Universität Berlin pp. 69–97

Sundberg, J. & Frydén, L. (1987) Melodic charge and music performance, in *Harmony and Tonality*, J. Sundberg, (ed.), Publications issued by the Royal Swedish Academy of Music Nr. 54, Stockholm, pp. 53–58

Sundberg, J., Askenfelt, A., & Frydén, L. (1983a) Musical performance: A synthesis by rule approach. *Computer Music J.* **7**, pp. 37–43

Sundberg, J., Frydén, L., & Askenfelt, A. (1983b) What tells you the player is musical? An analysis-by-synthesis study of music performance, in *Studies of Music Performance*, J. Sundberg, (ed.) Publications issued by the Royal Swedish Academy of Music Nr. 39, Stockholm, pp. 61–75

Sundberg, J. & Frydén, L. (1985) Teaching a computer to play melodies musically, in *Analytica*, Festschrift for Ingmar Bengtsson, Publications issued by the Royal Swedish Academy of Music Nr. 47 pp. 67–76

Thompson, W.F., Friberg, A., Frydén, L., & Sundberg, J. (1986) Evaluating rules for the synthetic performance of melodies. *Speech Transmission Laboratory Quarterly Progress and Status Report* **2-3**, pp. 27–44; to appear, in revised form, in *Psychology of Music*

Todd, N. (1985) A model of expressive timing in tonal music. *Music Perception* **3**, pp. 33–57

Vos, J. (1986) Purity ratings of tempered fifths and major thirds. *Music Perception* **3**, pp. 221–258

Ward, W.D. (1970) Musical perception, in *Foundations of Modern Auditory Theory*, J.B. Tobias, (ed.) Academic Press, New York, pp. 407–447

Structural, cognitive and semiotic aspects of the musical present

David Clarke

Department of Music, Dartington College of Arts, Totnes, Devon, UK

Music's relation to time is viewed primarily as a phenomenological issue. The psychological concept of the perceived, or specious present is accordingly adopted and investigated, since it is through the medium of this conscious state of attention that musical structures are perceived. Special consideration is given to the kinds of structures and the quality of presence associated with the teleological mode of temporality described as linear time. The specifically hierarchic nature of these structures raises the question of the level at which the perceived present obtains and how hierarchies function within it. In turn this leads to a reappraisal of the way in which the present is determined in linear-time music.
  These issues are grounded in a discussion of specific musical structures, and Schenkerian analytical techniques are shown to be useful in providing models for certain important aspects of temporal perception. Finally, a description of the signification of the musical present is attempted applying concepts taken from the semiology of Saussure.

KEYWORDS perceived present, linear time, hierarchic structures, present as process, prolongation, signification, paradigmatic and syntagmatic relations.

Introduction

Our contemporary culture's increasing responsiveness to musics from a multiplicity of historical, sociological and geographic sources makes more hazardous than ever before the activity of propounding musical universals. Nevertheless, it does remain possible to posit a small number of extremely general attributes common to all the phenomena we understand as music. Three such characteristics form the premises from which this paper proceeds: first, that music is presented in time; second, that music is a system of signs; third, that music is realized only in perception.
  This is neither a complete list, nor do the properties enumerated — individually or collectively — pertain exclusively to music. However, the temporal, semiotic and cognitive dimensions of all musical existence do map out a particularly interesting field of theoretical inquiry which this paper will be concerned to broach; the unrealized general, or grand,

theory of music to which such universals point forms the background against which it proceeds. As my title suggests, the main perspective from which this inquiry will be conducted is that of temporality, focusing specifically on the experience of the Present in music. But also implicit is the fact that this experience is conditioned by the cognitive processing of musical structures, and that the temporal nature of these perceived structures has a particular bearing on a musical work's significance (or "meaning" in its broadest sense).

I should stress at the outset that this study is undertaken from the standpoint of a music theorist rather than a music psychologist — but a theorist who nevertheless recognizes the need to evaluate the role of perception in determining musical structures and signification. While this inquiry is unlikely to present substantial new insights into the separate disciplines of analysis, cognitive psychology or semiotics, I hope that the light which these activities throw upon one another in an investigation of time perception may be of interest to practitioners in all three fields.

A few preliminaries of a philosophical nature will help us to define the area in which a study of the relationship between music and time can most effectively be undertaken. First let us note that time would seem separable — theoretically at least — into an objective and a subjective mode of being. Evidence for the former is supplied by, for example, an unattended piece of rotting cheese whose decay continues despite the absence of a perceiving subject. Time, manifested here in a process of entropy, shows itself to be just as much part of the physical world "out there" as any of the other, material objects that one may or may not perceive through one's senses. Conversely, we might ask to what extent time may exist purely subjectively, as part of our inner, mental world. In other words, if I had no sensory access to the outside world would I still have any experience of time? I think the answer to this is Yes, provided I were able to engage in some form of mental symbolic activity, such as language, whose signification derived at least in part from the placing of elements in a sequence: where meaning depended on a recognition of the difference between "before" and "after".

For most of my waking life, however, time is a fusion of these two realities. As an intentional being I am constantly involved in forming internal representations of the external world from my sense data. As with other phenomena "out there", I can have no experience of time in the outside world except through my perceptions. Yet I cannot perceive time as if it were an object: I cannot see, hear, touch, taste or smell it. Rather, my experience of time is mediated through the processes involved in the mental representation of phenomena that I *can* see, hear etc.

Music is one such phenomenon. Frequently it is highly structured, and the correspondingly complex symbolic activity involved in its cognition will be decisive for my apprehension of time. Conversely, the way in which those structures are perceived is dependent on the cognitive abilities of the mind. Hence an investigation of musical temporality will be far from an abstract discussion of time and sounds, but will rather need to consider quite explicitly the relation between structure and perception. Hence the approach will be phenomenological rather than ontological.

The present as a psychological concept

An essential aspect of the relationship between perception and time is that the former, strictly defined, can take place *only in the present*. "To perceive", says Paul Fraisse "implies essentially a reaction to the present situation" (1964, 67–8). The present is the domain where intentionality meets reality. Hence it is more than just a passively experienced slot of time, a neutral now: it is the focal point of my conscious activity. It is from this domain that my experience of time takes its perspective. Hence as perceptions recede into the past they enter the domain of memory and take on a different mode of being; and the future is experienced as a complex of implications formulated from what is taking place in the present and the relation of those events in turn to memories of the past.

In psychology the nature of the present has been a subject of discussion since at least the end of the last century. William James' appraisal of the so-called "specious", "perceived" or "psychological" present, made in the 1890s, still has currency in modern thinking. Under this account the present is not a durationless point in time, like a mathematical point in space with theoretically no area, but a ". . . saddle-back of time, with a certain length of its own, on which we sit perched, and from which we look in two directions into time" (1892, 280; quoted in Fraisse, 1964, 85). Hence time is not perceived as a seamless flow, but as a series of discrete presents of brief, but nevertheless measurable duration. This, then, is directly connected to the commonly recognized tendency of the mind to divide up perceived phenomena into segments or "chunks". The precise duration and nature of the present is accordingly determined by the length of a segment and the events in it. However, psychologists seem to agree that the present in any case can only ever last a few seconds. The upper limit of its duration has been variously placed at around five seconds by Fraisse, for example (1964, 92), and seven seconds by Michon (1978, 92). Michon's article reviews numerous aspects of research into the cognitive mechanisms which seem to underlie the perception of the present. Among other things he characterizes the psychological present, after James, as "the time interval . . . in which we experience the flow of events as being simultaneously available to perceptual or cognitive analysis" (1978, 90). This once again reinforces the notion of the present as an aspect of consciousness, and its differentiation from the functions of memory.

The perceived present in music

In view of the above observations, it seems entirely appropriate that a study of musical temporality should take the notion of the present as its starting point. Unsurprisingly, the perception of different types of musical structure fosters different apprehensions of the present. Indeed, as Jonathan Kramer (1981) has pointed out, one of the hallmarks of our contemporary, pluralistic musical culture is a wider range of possibilities in this respect than ever before. However, limitations of space here will compel extreme selectivity in the range of our inquiry; hence we shall focus exclusively on a single, well established mode of temporality: that which Kramer defines as "linear time".

Linear time is determined by the goal-orientated, teleological types of structure, often, but not always associated with tonality, and especially germane to symphonic movements. What is so remarkable about such music is the way in which the present is very powerfully experienced as being determined by preceding events and in turn influencing the direction of future ones. A further reason for selecting this temporality lies in the relatively greater discernibility of its structures, and their closer relation to cognitive processing than might be found in, say, a piece of post-war total serial music. Nevertheless it is hoped that the results of such an investigation will provide the basis for future comparison with other temporalities — moment form, for example, in which the present is experienced less as part of a dynamic process of becoming and more as a non-evolving state of being.

Although we shall be concerned ultimately to formulate general theoretical statements about cognitive and semiotic aspects of linear time, the usefulness and accuracy of such assertions is greatly enhanced if based on detailed examination of specific musical structures. Hence the most appropriate strategy is to be more selective still and focus on a single, short musical extract. To this end we shall consider the beginning of the main, allegro part of the first movement of Haydn's 104th Symphony. This is as good a representative as any of the sonata-allegro form which was so central to the high classical style, and which so epitomizes the teleological drive that is characteristic of linear time in music. Furthermore, the articulated phrase structure essential to this style offers the mind strong clues, though not always unambiguous ones, as to segmentation — a point of obvious relevance in view of the relationship, described above, between the perceived present and the tendency of the mind to "chunk" material.

Figure 1 quotes the opening eight-bar period of the Haydn allegro. Possible schemata for segmentation are indicated in two ways. First, below the stave is a grouping analysis based on various time spans, loosely modelled after Lerdahl & Jackendoff (1983) — though I should stress that this is in the interests of concise presentation rather than as a formal adoption of their theory. It will be observed that the arrangement of groups is predicated primarily on harmonic factors and that this

The musical present 115

Figure 1 Haydn, Symphony no. 104, I, bars 17–24. Analysis of constituent motives and grouping structure.

corresponds to the second scheme of segmentation, namely the motivic analysis presented above the stave.

For the purposes of this discussion the most pertinent question to ask initially of figure 1 is, Which level of grouping most closely models the time span perceived by the mind as the present? Let us first consider in a little more detail Michon's description of the perceived present. Of the various properties of the present which he summarizes two are especially apposite to the case in question:

> The contents of a present are simultaneously available and are as such continuously open for restructuring; that is, the information contained in it is open to revision under different cognitive (or at least higher order) interpretive hypotheses.
>
> [The present] has a width that is highly variable and that seems to have an upper limit of 7 or 8 sec, although its average seems to be in the order of 2 or 3 sec. Its perceived width depends on the number and the sequential structure of the events in it.

(1978, 92)

Looking first at the foreground of figure 1, it is clear that motive *a* and its associated level of the grouping structure exemplifies both these conditions. The duration of the motive comes close to the average cited by Michon, and its contents are "simultaneously available". I take this latter attribute to be a corollary of the fact that in my cognition of motive *a* the details of my mental representation are not formed concurrently with the minutiae of the musical presentation. Thus, when the initial F# of the melody moves to G I do not seem to create a representation for this fragment and then add to it a further one when G moves to E, and so on. Rather, all this information (and indeed also that pertaining to the lower voices) is held in an open state in my consciousness until a boundary is reached — in this case the D major triad of b.2 — at which point I generate a representation of the complete motive and the relationships between all its constituent elements. That this action cannot take place at any earlier point in the motive suggests the time span of motive *a* (corresponding to level 1 of the grouping analysis) as the shortest possible "Now". I would hold that this is also true for motives *b*, *c* and *d*, though their components do suggest the latent possibility of still lower level subgroups (indicated in figure 1 using roman numerals); a possibility which in the case of motive *b* is made manifest in the subsequent development of the musical discourse.

Moving now to the opposite extreme of the hierarchic structure of figure 1, we encounter an interesting conundrum. For the entire eight-bar phrase encompassed by level 3 would also seem to meet the criteria for the perceived present. The duration of the phrase corresponds to the upper limit cited by Michon (this, perhaps, a significant general characteristic of the classical style). And the fact that our perception of the end of the phrase is coloured in an immediate way by all the preceding contents suggests that these are in some way "simultaneously available" — though in just what kind of way is a question we shall shortly have cause to address. Thus the perceived present can be shown potentially to obtain at or between two durational extremes; that is, at any of the levels shown in figure 1.

How is such an ambiguity to be resolved? Specific points made in a recent approach to this issue by Eric Clarke (1987) will help provide an initial focus. Clarke seems to favour an interpretation which takes the upper limit of the perceived present as a single governing level:

> ... *the perceptual present arises at a single level* ... *Hierarchical relations between low-level structures can be identified with the perceptual present, but these smaller sub-units are not themselves perceptual presents.*
>
> *(1987, 230)*

Positing this broader time span as a kind of "default" level, Clarke then elaborates on the function of lower-level groups within it:

> *Just as there is a privileged level of meter (the "tactus") which corresponds to the rate at which one might tap one's foot* ... *so also might there be a particularly salient level of grouping structure in music which corresponds to the level at which the perceptual present is formed. Within groups at this level, relationships between events have dynamic properties (i.e. are musical processes), while relationships between such groups are more static and constructive (i.e. are formal in nature). (Ibid.)*

This last point relates closely to the way in which musical elements are simultaneously available, and ultimately raises questions about how we understand the perceived present. Clarke's description of the dynamic, processive relationship between events within groups has already been exemplified in the previous discussion of motive *a* and its associated group at level 1 of figure 1. Such qualities obtain precisely because, experienced within the perceived present, all the elements of this group "are simultaneously available and as such are continuously open for restructuring" (Michon, 1978). This simultaneous availability becomes qualitatively different, however, once the group attains closure at its own hierarchic level, i.e. at the onset of the next motive. For one of the consequences — or even defining qualities — of closure is that relationships within the group concerned become far less mutable. Hence this material is subsequently "available to perceptual and cognitive analysis" *only as a complete group* (as a static and constructive aspect of form, to paraphrase Clarke). That availability obtains at the next hierarchic level where cognitive analysis is concerned with determining the relationship between entire groups from the previous level. (As Clarke points out, this interpretation relates directly to Meyer's observation that what is processive at one level is formal at the next, and vice versa (Meyer, 1973, 80).)

Stressing the temporal context of the above account leads to a particularly important realization. A low-level group of such a hierarchic structure is experienced *initially* as a dynamic, open process, and *subsequently* as a static, closed element of form. In other words, an individual group is experienced differently at two different points in time: a phenomenological difference which in terms of time consciousness can only be described as an opposition between past and present. That lower-level groups such as those at level 1 of figure 1 are capable of being experienced as a present at all, leads one to query Clarke's assertion that "smaller sub-units are not themselves perceptual presents" (assuming of course that the sub-units to which he refers correspond in duration to those in our own discussion). However, the intention here is not simply to argue a competing case for a lower "default" level of the perceived present, since I would accept in addition the existence of a higher-level present (corresponding to level 3 of figure 1). It seems to me, then, that we should rule out the notion of a single, fixed level at which presence obtains, and contemplate instead a model for the present which accommodates this dichotomy. I would therefore advance the hypothesis that in the cognition of music in a linear temporality the present should be understood not as a mental "bucket" of more or less fixed capacity, waiting to be filled with structural information, but rather *as a process* from a lower to an upper threshold of duration. The upper threshold is determined by the power of the mind to hold events within its conscious grasp and by the existence of a corresponding higher-level phrase or group length in a musical structure. The lower threshold is determined by the shortest possible coherent segment, or "chunk" into which the musical foreground can be articulated.

Two questions now arise. First, what factors determine the chunking process at the immediate foreground level, and second, what is the cognitive nature of the process which leads from this lower threshold to the upper threshold of the perceived present? The former question points to a vast field of inquiry, and highlights the significant number of unstated criteria involved in segmenting even so short and seemingly uncomplicated an example as figure 1. An adequate exploration of those criteria, however, would require a separate and lengthy study; and because the latter question concerns this inquiry more directly I shall respond to the first by merely outlining the broad nature of the principles involved.

Key forces in the demarcation of segments are related factors such as closure, boundary recognition and Gestalt principles. The function of closure — especially its implications for musical continuity when it is not attained simultaneously in all parameters — is discussed with varying degrees of formality by Meyer (1973), Narmour (1977) and Sloboda (1985). Michon (1978) reviews many of the contingencies surrounding boundary and pattern recognition; while Lerdahl and Jackendoff (1983), and Tenney and Polansky (1980) present in rather different ways, though with equally impressive thoroughness, formal descriptions of Gestalt principles as they affect the perception of hierarchic musical structures. In addition, grouping may be influenced by idiosyncrasies of structure and content peculiar to individual musical texts, whose recognition would seem to depend on repetition and increasing familiarity with the work concerned. Finally, segmentation also depends on the action of codes: structures (such as those acquired from an understanding of tonality) which form part of a listener's cognitive "software", acquired from exposure to a wider repertory of related music. This last comment underlines the role played by cultural factors.

In practice the shortest possible coherent segments (at least as regards tonal-metric music) form groups often identified motivically — as in figure 1, level 1. This is emphatically not to say that motivic features are necessarily the most important structural elements of such music; rather that because thematic segmentation is rarely divorced from other parametric processes, and because thematic elements create a particular focus for attention and memory, motives take on a kind of emblematic role for an entire group. Since we have used the term "perceived present" to refer to both a cumulative temporal process and groups at either extreme of its duration, it would seem desirable in the interests of clarity to introduce some additional nomenclature. I therefore nominate the term "immediate now" to signify a group at this minimal durational threshold of the perceived present.

Considering our second question, we may surmise that in the course of the temporal expansion of the perceived present to its upper threshold each immediate now subsequently enters some form of immediate memory storage, in which state it remains available as a determinant in the cognition of succeeding Nows. For example, motives *a* and *b* of figure 1 influence one's perception of *c*, but because they are not sounding Now, in the same sense as *c*, that influence must be in the form of a structure, or complex of information, encoded from these motives as they left the domain of the immediate now. (Although in this form *a* and *b* are experienced less immediately than the contents of the Now, it should be stressed that the loss of immediacy is only relative. Within the perceived present these encoded forms retain a significant degree of immediate availability which still permits one end of the phrase to encroach upon the other without the need for active retrieval from memory.) In the following section we shall consider the extent to which these functions can be represented analytically and what this might suggest about the corresponding mental representation. Of primary concern will be the tonal aspect of the process, since tonal information, unlike data pertaining to metre and grouping, is highly context specific.

The perceived present and tonal structure

Curiously, depite the fact that Lerdahl and Jackendoff's generative theory of tonal music (1983) is ostensibly far more overtly and axiomatically predicated on cognition than Schenkerian theory, the latter is nevertheless able to demonstrate some quite salient points about time perception, and for this reason will be adopted here. Figure 2 furnishes a Schenkerian analytical representation of the Haydn passage quoted in Figure 1. As is usual in such notation note values, the presence or absence of stems etc. are used to indicate the degree of subordination or superordination of each element relative to the others. In level 1 of figure 2, motive *a* and all other pitch material within its associated time span (hereafter, segment *a*) is shown to function tonally as a prolongation of the tonic triad of D major. The first-inversion dominant chord in segment *b* is likewise shown as part of a tonic prolongation.

At this point there emerges the suggestion of a relationship between the perceived present and the Schenkerian notion of prolongation. To paraphrase Forte and Gilbert (1982), the prolongation of a note or chord means that it remains in effect even when it is not literally sounding.[1] At a foreground level this principle correlates directly with the reality of the psychological present whose contents are "simultaneously available to perceptual or cognitive analysis".[2] Thus the F♯ of motive *a* — see figure 2, level 1 — while not physically present for the entire duration of the idea, remains available to consciousness along with all the other subsequent notes. Through such simultaneous availability the final D of the motive can be related to the initial F♯ as constituents of a single triadic sonority. The Schenkerian notion of unfolding, represented by the diagonal beam in level 1, aptly models the cognition of these two pitches as the earlier and later phases of a single structure perceived as continuously present. Level 2 represents this effective simultaneity according to Schenkerian

120 David Clarke

Figure 2   Tonal/prolongational structure of Haydn extract (cf. figure 1).

practice, by folding up the two pitches into the chord which they prolong.
The difference in the analytical notation of levels 1 and 2 suggests a corresponding difference in cognition. Level 1, as we have noted, models elements as they are held in consciousness during the immediate now; but what of level 2? While the contents of this level are clearly only just in the process of receding from consciousness, we might surmise that they are already on their way into some domain of memory or storage. In a study such as this it would be over-ambitious to attempt anything like a detailed account of this psychological process, particularly since there are so many open questions surrounding memory among psychologists.

However, one particularly important general attribute of memory can be singled out as relevant here, and is described as follows by Dowling & Harwood:

> The role of memory in hearing a piece of music is somewhat like the role of memory in listening to a conversation. To understand present utterances or events, one needs to have a notion of the gist of what went before but need not be able to recall literally all that was said. Usually, one comes away from a conversation with a knowledge of its overall meaning but with little exact recollection of details. (1986, 163.)

In this connection Dowling & Harwood make reference to the distinction between semantic and episodic memory, as researched by Tulving (1972) and Tulving & Thomson (1973). Certainly the former concept is germane to level 2 of figure 2, since it does seem to portray the gist, or semantic essence of the contents of the foreground level (especially clear in the case of segments *a* and *b*). A dash suffix is used here and subsequently to refer to segments transformed into this abstracted state, while their actual mental counterparts will be informally termed "semantic representations".

Figure 2, then, modelling the conversion of material as consciously perceived into semantic representations, provides a workable structural analogue for the processes which generate the perceived present. Because, however, Schenkerian graphic analyses describe material synchronically, figure 2 does not quite accurately model the sequence of events as it unfolds in real time. For example, the semantic representation of segment *a*, labelled *a'* in level 2, is only extrapolated once *a* itself has attained closure — i.e. once segment *b* is under way. In an attempt to represent the temporal process more accurately, Figure 3 shows the build-up of the overall present as a series of "frames", each frame corresponding to the minimum unit of coherence described above as the immediate now. (Note that for convenience, only the treble register is used in this diagram.)

Admittedly this form of graphing is in some ways a little clumsy. None the less, in other ways it gives quite a clear picture of certain significant mechanisms in the evolution of the perceived present. For instance it shows how the representation of the immediate now is determined not only by currently sounding events, but also by the semantic representation of elapsed Nows. The diagram also alludes to an easy osmosis between these two levels, made possible in reality, one assumes, because similar types of tonal encoding can be recursively applied to each level. Furthermore, we can see clearly demonstrated in Figure 3 the cumulative nature of the perceived present. Significantly this takes place at the level of semantic representation.

The present may be said to end when all the material is represented in semantic memory — though the knowledge that this indeed is all the material belonging to this particular present is dependent on the recognition of near-simultaneous closure in various parameters in the

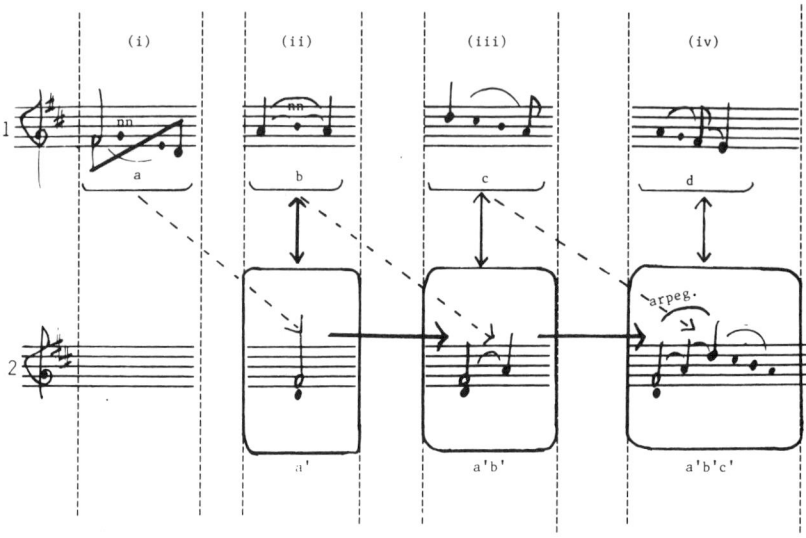

Figure 3 Interaction of hierarchic levels in real time (cf. figure 2). Diagonal, broken arrows indicate abstraction of contents of "immediate now"; horizontal, solid arrows indicate accumulation of abstract representation in semantic memory between successive frames; vertical arrows indicate interaction between each Now and semantic representation accumulating from previous Nows.

eighth bar of the passage. The effect of this closural congruence on the tonal structure is to cause all the elements of level 2 of Figure 3 to be encoded as a prolongational motion from the tonic to the dominant, as represented in level 3 of Figure 2. Cognitively speaking, this level would seem to correspond to the deeper reaches of semantic memory, functioning in a more strongly differentiated way from the processing of the immediate now than is the case with level 2. Characteristically, since the information content of this time-span is fixed only at the phrase boundary, its effect is only really felt in the next perceived present where it influences the mental representation at both the other lower levels. Here, then, is a clear illustration of how in linear time, events of the past impinge on our cognition of events in the present.

The signification of the present in linear time

Owing to its close bonds with the past (from which relationship can be predicated implications for the future) the musical present in linear time takes on a particularly idiosyncratic quality. It becomes a critical focal point for our attention since its contents are always changing, and as a corollary our appraisal of past and future also undergoes constant modification. The present therefore is more than just a repository of structural information or a stimulus to our cognitive faculties; it is an experience of transformation, through which time is made meaningful. That meaning is not of course susceptible to translation into words, but since it is an aspect of the present conceptually separable from the structural and cognitive processes which bring it into being, it is appropriate to describe some of its peculiarities in a language formulated specifically to deal with signifying behaviour. Hence the last part of this inquiry considers the present from the standpoint of semiotics.

The approach taken here essentially derives from Ferdinand de Saussure, whose *Course in General Linguistics* (1974) has been a seminal source in the development of semiology and structuralism during the twentieth century. Two Saussurean concepts in particular will prove valuable. The first of these is the linguistic sign. Under Saussure's definition this is a unity compounded from two elements: a signifier and signified. He described the signifier as a "sound-image": not sound itself, but a kind of psychological imprint of sound (such as the sound "tree"). This distinction makes it possible for a signfier to exist in a written as well as spoken form. Yet although the signifier is not literally a material phenomenon, Saussure does attribute to it a relative material quality when compared with the signified (1974, 67, 117–120). The signified is a concept, for example the concept of tree (as opposed to any particular physical manifestation). The linguistic sign is considered a unity because signifier and signified, while theoretically separable, are in practice mutually associated. For an English speaker, then, any presentation of the sound-image "tree" also brings with it the concept, and, conversely, any conceptualization of a tree has a powerful tendency to summon up the associated acoustic pattern (1974, 66–67).

However, signs are not simply defined by a one-to-one relationship between sound-image and idea. What Saussure terms the *value* of a sign is determined by its relationship to all the other signs within the language system. It is not the place here to go into a detailed discussion of this principle, save to consider that it obtains on two contrasting axes defined by what Saussure described as syntagmatic and associative relations. Figure 4, adapted from the *Course* illustrates the double aspect of this relational principle for the word "tenable". Here is a word whose linguistic value derives from relationships generated from and between its two components "ten-" and "able". On the one hand the two elements are related syntagmatically; that is, through being placed in a contiguous linear sequence. (This relationship also obtains on a larger scale through

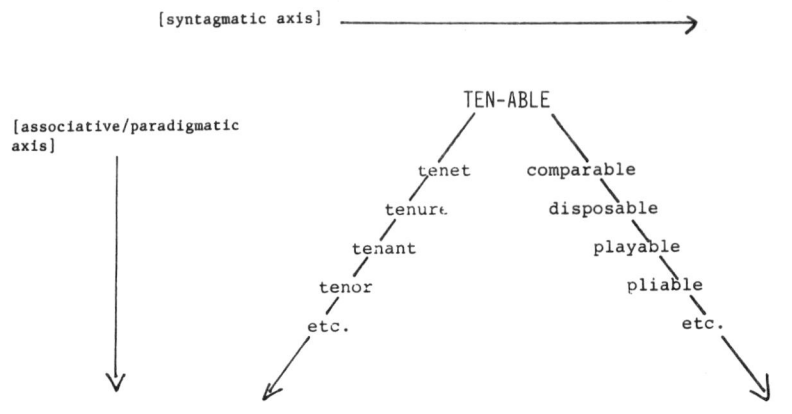

Figure 4 After Saussure: syntagmatic and associative (paradigmatic) relations in language.

the sequential ordering of whole words in a sentence, and it is not difficult to imagine how a changed syntagmatic relation — i.e. a re-ordering of words — produces a different signification.) On the other hand each element of the word "tenable" also acquires its value from its unique position in a larger complex of terms which are not actually present in the utterance but which are related by association. Hence "tenable" takes its value from related terms such as "tenet", "tenure", "comparable", "disposable", etc. It virtually goes without saying that Figure 4 represents a mere handful of exemplars from a potentially vast network; but the point is that the unique value of the uttered term derives from its difference from all the related, absent ones. In the ensuing discussion the practice of later generations of theorists will be followed, substituting the term "paradigmatic relations" for "associative relations".

Let us now begin to explore how these theoretical notions from Saussure might be relevant to the temporally experienced musical structures described above. I should initially point out that our concern will be entirely with signification generated within a musical text. This is not to deny the possibility of extra-musical signification, through such means as Leitmotive, or the particular personal associations of time and place a piece may have for each of us; nor is it to resist the idea of a work signifying through its relationships with all other works in a given cultural context (so-called intertextuality). However, it will be more manageable and more consistent with the scope of this study so far to concentrate on the internal signifying structures of a musical work.

At the beginning of this section the present in linear time was described as an experience of transformation through which time is made meaningful. We might therefore surmise that the present is some kind of sign. If so, to which elements can we assign the roles of signifier and signified? The signifier is least problematic in this respect. I would have little hesitation in identifying this feature with the currently sounding contents of the immediate now, as represented in level 1 of Figure 3. Available to me quite literally here (as part of the cognitive processing going on in my own brain) and now, there is no more immediate standpoint from which these contents could be *signified*.

If level 1 of Figure 3, depicting the mental imprint of material sound-images, corresponds to the domain of the signifier, could it be that level 2 corresponds to the domain of the signified? One may cautiously assent to this notion, though only after weighing up the similarities to, and differences from the linguistic signified under Saussure's formulation.

First let us consider the similarities. To begin with, the contents of semantic memory, like the linguistic signified, are of an inherently conceptual nature. Moreover, the signification of each Now of Figure 3 is determined, like the linguistic sign, by the fusion of material and conceptual domains. In other words, the signifiers of level 1 invoke the conceptual elements of level 2 to produce the sign we call Now.

The differences between the musical sign and the linguistic sign all essentially have to do with the relatively far greater mutability of the former compared with the latter. Whereas in language a signifier such as "tree" always takes the concept of tree as its signified, a musical signifier such as motive *b* of the Haydn extract, will most probably have a different signified each time it reappears. (Consider, for example the motive's many recurrences in the development section of the first movement of the "London" Symphony, each time fused with a different semantic network owing to the increasing accumulation of antecedent events.) Granted, the linguistic sign is also mutable, owing to the arbitrary nature of the signifier-signified relationship (Saussure, 1974, 74–78); however, in language the process takes place over decades and centuries rather than the seconds and minutes of expanding musical structures.

Linguistic and musical sign systems are also contrasted by a difference in the very nature of their signified, as further consideration of Figure 3 reveals. We should recall that the set of frames shown here represents the series of different stages through which the perceived present expands from its smallest to its largest durational threshold. While the signifier which defines each of these stages (or Nows) is a closed form, the signified remains open and available to structural reappraisal. Thus in each frame the signified is modified — an observation which pinpoints the fact that level 2 represents not several different signifieds, but a single signified in a process of evolution. All of this contrasts rather strongly with the linguistic signified, which has a higher degree of fixity, or stability. It is true that linguistic signifieds, as parts in a relational system, are prone to change; however, what is essential to the signified is not change itself but the stable state in which it exists before and after change. My concept of a tree could be altered if, for example, its relationship to (or difference from) my concept of an animal were altered — if, say, trees began to take walks. But my concept of a tree would still be either one thing or the other; it would be experienced as a state of being, not becoming.

Part of the discrepancy between musical and linguistic signification noted in the last observation has to do with the fact that musical relationships viewed from a syntagmatic (and hence diachronic) perspective have been contrasted with linguistic relationships of a synchronic and implicitly paradigmatic nature. To consider the added signifying dimension of the sign "tree" when it functions in a larger syntagm, as in the sentence "the tree was toppled in a storm", would be to come closer to the musical condition represented in Figure 3. To pursue this point in any depth would require a foray into linguistics extending beyond the scope of this paper, and indeed beyond Saussure's own coverage. Instead, we may undertake the complementary activity and consider the extent to which paradigmatic relations in music resemble the linguistic features described above.

Figure 5 quotes the melody of the consequent to the eight-bar antecedent phrase cited in Figure 1. On one level a paradigmatic

Figure 5 Haydn, Symphony no. 104, I, bars 25–31; melody only (answering phrase to figure 1).

relationship exists between these two phrases as a whole, but for our present purposes we shall be concerned with the paradigms manifested between constituent motives of the respective phrases. A specific example would be the relationship between motives c of the first phrase and c' of the second. The basis of the relationship between these two elements is similarity: they become mutually associated through a cluster of common features such as their conjunct, unidirectional motion in minims, and their occurrence at the equivalent point in the larger phrase structure.

A semiotic interpretation of this situation might incline towards considering the nucleus of shared properties as a conceptual network

The musical present 127

which is the common signified of two (potentially more) signifiers — as diagrammed in Figure 6. However, this disregards the temporal aspect of musical signification. In real time (i.e. diachronically speaking) the two signifiers of Figure 6 are perceived not simultaneously but consecutively.[3]

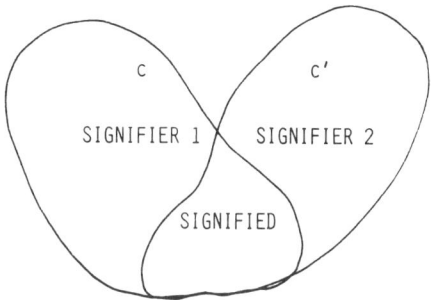

Figure 6   Model for signification on paradigmatic axis in music, considered synchronically.

Thus when the second signifier is presented, the first has already entered semantic memory and therefore no longer exists as a signifier but in the abstract, conceptual form characteristic of a signified. Figure 7 is an attempt to demonstrate the process along analogous lines to Figure 3, with signifiers and signifieds occupying planes comparable to levels 1 and 2 of the latter. The second frame of the diagram shows that as signifier 2 is presented as a sound-image the conceptual network, signified 1 (abstracted from signifier 1), maps on to it, producing an interaction between levels reminiscent of Figure 3.

In Figure 7, however, there is an important qualitative difference in

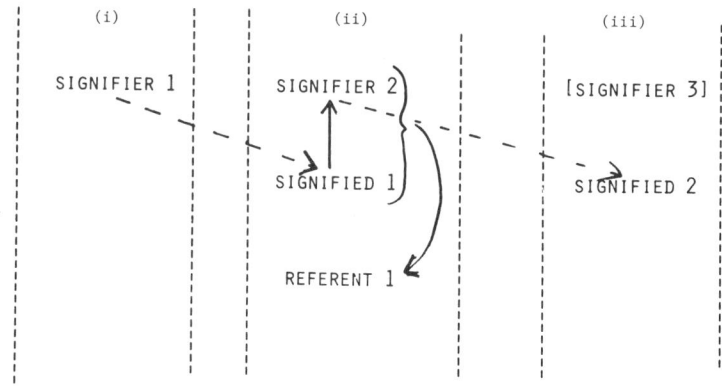

Figure 7   Model for signification on paradigmatic axis as manifested in real time.

signification owing to the fact that the interaction between levels is based on a relationship not of contiguity, as was previously the case, but of similarity. As signified 1 maps on to signifier 2 the formal parallels between them mean that the latter engages in a process similar to rehearsal. I would suggest that this acts as a kind of retrieval process which wants to recall signifier 1 — or, more precisely, wants to re-convert signified 1 into a mental representation corresponding to its original sound image. I use the term "wants to" because this is a tendency rather than a fully-fledged or literal process of recall. For example, when I perceive motive c' of figure 5, motive c of figure 1 does not attain comparably material status: c' alludes to c but c does not actually become present again. Nevertheless this does constitute a kind of reference to c which is of a different, relatively more material order than the conceptual network which we have posited as the signified of c. Although the allusion to c, considered informally, is also part of what is signified by c' (one might even think of it as a kind of second order signified), a separate term is required to define it, and to this end I have used the label "referent" in Figure 7.

The involvement of a referent is an important factor in the qualitative distinction between paradigmatic and syntagmatic relationships (it is worth recalling Saussure's own observation that paradigmatic and syntagmatic relationships "each [give] rise to a separate order of values" (1983, 121)). An essential property of the referent is that it is more akin to a form than a process, being closed and therefore stable. In this sense it is closer in nature to the linguistic signified than is the evolving musical signified which emerges on the syntagmatic axis. Another distinguishing feature emerges as a corollary. Syntagmatic relations, as represented in Figure 3, draw on the past as they imbue the present with meaning, but in view of the open, evolving nature of their signified there is no stable feature from the past to which they can look back or make reference. By contrast, paradigmatic relations generate just such a feature, the referent, which supplies a temporal, retrospectively oriented depth of field.

The ambiguous nature of the referent, as something less abstract than the conceptual signified and yet also less tangible than the material signifier, makes the relationship between present and past a subtle and mutable one. Because the signifier always sounds here and now, it always has the greatest immediacy and makes the strongest impact on our consciousness. While elements of the past can be referred to, they do not have the same sensory impression of presence as the signifier. Hence the referent takes on the quality of something displaced or at a distance; indeed it might be described as a subliminal awareness of a now absent signifier. The depth of our awareness of the past depends on the preponderance of paradigmatic relationships. In a sonata-form movement, for example, there is a general tendency for expositions to present a fairly steady influx of new ideas, and for development sections to modify pre-existing ones. In the latter therefore, signification through paradigmatic relations intensifies, and so accordingly does our impression of the absence of signifiers in the guise in which they were heard in the exposition. A recapitulation might be understood as providing a balance in this respect by stating signifiers in a form identical or relatively similar to those of the exposition.[4]

Finally, we might ask whether the interaction between signifier and signified in a syntagmatic relationship might not also produce a third term, equivalent to the referent. In fact, I believe this to be the case. It will be recalled that the signified on the syntagmatic axis is part of an evolving process and is therefore open and active. Thus, while derived from the past, its orientation is towards the future. In other words, musical implication is predicated upon the relationship which the current sound-image has with the abstracted semantic contents of the past. This strongly suggests that a study of musical temporality must also include an account of the role of implication. But here one can only register the importance of the issue; the investigation of structural, cognitive and semiotic aspects of the musical future is a subject for a further paper.

Future directions

The most appropriate way to conclude this paper will be to continue in the vein in which the previous section ended and to consider other avenues of further exploration suggested by our wider discussion. First, one thinks of the need to ground in empirical testing the modified formulation of the perceived present advanced earlier (this a task for experimental psychologists rather than music theorists). Second, many of the ideas raised here require further exploration in terms of larger stretches of music such as entire movements or works. Extended to such dimensions it would seem that the adaptation of Schenkerian analytical notation for diachronic modelling (as in Figure 3) would become unwieldly, and this would necessitate some more elegant means of describing "frames".

It would be misguided, however, to leave unexplored the potential for Schenkerian concepts to throw light on cognitive processes. Particularly important here is the relation between middleground structure and the faculty of semantic memory. If the latter is an authentic, definable aspect of mental activity then there are significant consequences for our understanding of musical meaning, not least because of the suggestion of faculties shared with language cognition. Moreover, it could be that in the act of composition the process is reversed, so that events of the musical surface are generated from this semantic domain. This would suggest support for Schenker's claims for composition as a process whereby the musical foreground is generated from middle- and background levels (though whether semantic memory extends to an organizing level corresponding to the Schenkerian *Ursatz* is likely to remain an open question). Again music theorists must depend on experimental psychologists for a more precise understanding of how semantic memory functions in practice. However, theorists have the possibility to reciprocate by detecting the operation of such faculties in musical structures, and by offering formal descriptions of such structures as a basis from which psychologists might generate hypotheses.

As regards semiotics, aspects of Saussure's linguistic model have been shown to be adaptable to temporal signification in music. However, if one is to tackle issues of musical signification manifested by larger-scale and more complex structures, a fuller critique of Saussure's concepts and an investigation of ways of developing them will become crucial.

Clearly, much of the present study has been of a conjectural and partial nature, but I hope that at the very least it may add fuel to discussion and help to further the fascinating and potentially highly fruitful exchange of ideas between the domains of music theory, cognitive psychology and semiotics.

Notes

1. "Prolongation refers to the ways in which a musical component . . . remains in effect without being literally represented at every moment". (Forte & Gilbert, 1982, 142.)
2. The important caveat should be added here that prolongations at higher levels of Schenkerian analytical structure cannot have the same psychological counterpart since they frequently extend substantially beyond the realm of the perceived present. The perceptual basis of higher-level structures in Schenkerian analysis has frequently been queried (most heatedly regarding the fundamental structure, or *Ursatz*). I do not propose to enter the debate here, save to conjecture that the interaction between hierarchic levels most probably corresponds to a psychological interaction between faculties such as the perceived present and various domains of memory.
3. In other words, paradigmatic relations are presented syntagmatically. Though this may seem curious and even contradictory, it in fact ties in very closely with the behaviour of poetic language. To paraphrase a famous statement by the structuralist critic Roman Jakobson, "the poetic function projects the paradigmatic axis into the syntagmatic axis" (Jackobson, 1960). A fuller discussion of the significance of this phenomenon will be included in a forthcoming paper by the present author.
4. For a fuller account of the signification of the present in a wider sonata-form context, and how this contrasts with moment form see D. Clarke (1986).

References

Clarke, D.I. (1986) *Language, form and structure in the music of Michael Tippett*. PhD dissertation (2 vols.). University of Exeter
Clarke, E.F. (1987) Levels of structure in the organization of musical time. *Contemporary Music Review*, **2**, pp. 211–238
Dowling, W.J. & Harwood, D.L. (1986) *Music Cognition*. New York: Academic Press
Forte, A. & Gilbert, S.E. (1982) *Introduction to Schenkerian Analysis*. New York and London: W.W. Norton & Co.
Fraisse, P. (1964) *The Psychology of Time*. Translated by Jennifer Leith. London: Eyre and Spottiswode
Jakobson, R. (1960) Closing statement: linguistics and poetics. In *Style and Language*, T.A. Sebeok (ed.) pp. 350–377. Cambridge, Mass,: MIT press
James, W. (1892) *Psychology: Briefer Course*. New York: Holt
Kramer, J.D. (1981) New temporalities in music. *Critical Inquiry*, **7(3)**, pp. 539–556
Lerdahl, F. & Jackendoff, R. (1983) *A Generative Theory of Tonal Music*. Cambridge, Mass.: MIT press
Meyer, L.B. (1973) *Explaining Music*. Chicago and London: University of Chicago press

Michon, J. (1978) The making of the present: a tutorial review. In *Attention and Performance VII*, J. Requin (ed.) pp. 89–111. Hillsale, New Jersey: Erlbaum

Narmour, E. (1977) *Beyond Schenkerism: The Need for Alternatives in Music Analysis*. Chicago and London: University of Chicago press

Saussure, F. de (1974) *Course in General Linguistics*. Charles Bally & Albert Secheye (eds.) with Albert Reidlinger. Translated by Wade Baskin. London: Fonatana/Collins

Saussure, F. de (1983) *Course in General Linguistics*. Charles Bally & Albert Secheye (eds.) with Albert Reidlinger. Translated and annotated by Roy Harris. London: Duckworth

Sloboda, J.A. (1985) *The Musical Mind: The Cognitive Psychology of Music*. Oxford: Clarendon press

Tenney, J. with Polansky L. (1980) Temporal gestalt perception in music. *Journal of Music Theory*, **24(2)**, pp. 205–241

Tulving, E. (1972) Episodic and semantic memory. In *Organization of Memory*, E. Tulving and W. Donaldson (eds.) pp. 381–403. New York: Academic press

Tulving, E. & Thomson, D.M. (1973) Encoding specificity and retrieval processes in episodic memory. *Psychological Review*, **80**, pp. 352–373

New approaches to the composition and analysis of electroacoustic music

Composing strategies and pedagogy

Simon Emmerson

Music Department, City University, Northampton Square, London, UK

Musical material suggests itself to composers in a variety of ways, many unexpected. But is the way in which a composer comes to particular decisions of importance to the teaching process? This paper examines the ideas of *experimentation* and *testing* with respect to research into composition. A model of the learning process is elaborated which seeks to disentangle the self-supporting justifications which grew up in the wake of post-war serial composition and analysis. An approach based on aural testing and 'experimental analysis' is advocated. The contribution of electroacoustic music is examined. It is argued that criteria of judgement in the learning process should be broadened to include those of a wider 'community of interest' and that compositional tools should be developed for the community as a whole, especially in the area of research into large scale forms. Finally, some observations on the consequences of this model to the broader world of music promotion are made.

KEYWORDS music research, pedagogy (teaching), analysis, composition, electroacoustic music.

Some imaginary strategies

In the first instance I will confine my examples to familiar pitch-based music which may be notated, although similar examples may be found from the realm of non-pitched (and unnotatable) music such as electroacoustic music.

Let us take four imaginary composers in isolation from one another and improvise a simple scenario. Each is a little frustrated at the lack of progress on a work in hand and has entered a state of mind open to outside influence — although none is entirely conscious of this.

Composer no. 1 awoke at 5am with the simple solution to a composing problem he had considered the previous evening : a symmetrical hexachord for a piece he was working on called 'Mirrors'. After all, he mused, the relation of the micro- to macrostructure should be strong and based upon the same gestalt image. He scribbled the hexachord in the notebook by his bed (Figure 1). He fell asleep and had forgotten the reasons for his choices in the morning.

Composer no. 2 rose at 7am as usual and as part of his morning meditation consulted the *I Ching* concerning the pitch material for the work he was engaged on. Using a similar method to that used by Cage in *Music of Changes* (for a general discussion see Kostelanetz, 1971), he came up with a hexachord (Figure 1).

Figure 1 A typical hexachord

Composer no. 3 started work at 10am by reading some poetry. He was intending to set Pablo Neruda's *The Heights of Macchu Picchu*. A particular stanza had affected him : "Sube conmigo amor americano" (Neruda, 1966, p. 30). As a game, he followed the rules of such as Bach, Schumann, Brahms, Berg and several more recent composers, and copied out those letters corresponding to musical pitch names (with the German possibilities of 'B' for B flat, 'H' for B natural and 'S' for E flat). This resulted in the letters S,B,E,C,G,A which when transcribed gave a hexachord (Figure 1).

Composer no. 4 cannot now remember whether, on that particular day, it had been the sound of the electronic arpeggio at Charles de Gaulle airport, or the plucked metallophone inside one of those children's toys which are pushed along on wheels endlessly repeating their usually "out of tune" melody; in any case he strummed at the piano in an attempt to recreate what he had heard and came up with an arpeggiated hexachord (Figure 1).

These strategies may be summed up:

1. Gestalt morphological modelling : using broad ideas of symmetry, balance etc. mapped from a macro-structural idea to the microstructure.
2. Chance procedures (within constraints : in this case the well tempered pitch seive).
3. Code modelling : there are bound to be weaker and stronger versions of this game! 'ABEGG' (Schumann *Abegg Variations. Op. 1*) and AGAHE (Brahms *String Sextet No. 2, Op. 36*) are somewhat easier to crack than 'AD SCHEBEG', 'ABA BEG' and 'A EBE' (Berg *Chamber Concerto*)! In most cases the Neruda text would probably be unknown

to the audience and the connection would therefore remain entirely esoteric.
4. Real world modelling : this takes many forms of which the given one is a particularly banal example; another is that of the influence of the experience of flying (in propeller aircraft) on an American tour by Stockhausen at the time of composing *Carré* (Cott, 1974, pp. 30–31).

It must be stressed that I am referring to strategies that are not fully perceived by the composer, and indeed may appear to have emerged spontaneously.

But these contrasting strategies have produced the same result in each of our imaginary cases here. It is evident that prior knowledge of these strategies can influence both the listener and the teacher. In what ways do I, as a teacher, behave differently because I *know* the composer used the *I Ching* rather than his knowledge of symmetrical pitch groups?

I do not intend, within the relative confines of this paper, to address the complex relationship of poiesis to esthesis (terms used in the sense developed by Jean-Jacques Nattiez, for example in Nattiez, 1982). That there is a relation, I treat to be self-evident. And it is most important to stress that I am not assuming that the simple 1:1 mapping of composer's idea to audience perception will be the subject of 'assessment' in the sense of 'success' or 'failure'. We must never rule out the possibility that successful art may be based on misconception.

A simple model of composition

I want to suggest a simpler causal model. We need only assume that a parameter in the poietic model is significant if a change in that parameter results in some change — *any change* — in the esthesic (perception) model. It does not matter if the audience fails to unravel the composer's code in all its detail, only that the composer's code is a *necessary* condition for the esthesic perception.

This paper is based upon several simple generalisations concerning twentieth century Western art music:

— that from the relatively shared language of the eighteenth century, through the increasingly personal developments of the nineteenth, have emerged the almost private musical languages of the twentieth. This has reduced appreciation of contemporary music to generalities, the details requiring expert (often non-aural) knowledge to analyse.
— that communication between composer and audience rests to some extent on a common code or at least common expectations and assumptions. This is not to endorse a conservative position that any specific system (tonality, for example) embodies such generalities; it is but one of many possible instances of them.
— that the discovery (not the invention) of some of these general codes is an essential task for all composers. I will not argue at this stage for

universal forms, though these may exist at some very high levels of abstraction. Furthermore, these generalisations are capable of a wide variety of interpretations in practical art and are not style specific.
— that the primary judgement of music is *aural* : while we may subsequently demand rational explanations for our reactions, we give 'Primacy to the Ear!' (following Schaeffer, 1973).

The aim of composition pedagogy must be to give the composer a set of tools; we have said that the relation of what is done with these tools to what is perceived by an audience will be complex and be influenced by much beyond conscious control.

In the case of pitch-based musics — especially those with a strong traditional code — the learning process takes much for granted, the relation of the paper symbol to the resulting sound, for example. With the fragmentation of the language mentioned, the problem of pedagogy is that it has retained these assumptions about the relation of symbolic to perceived information.

This has been highlighted by the exception to the rule : electroacoustic music. The revolution that this might have brought about in the pedagogy of music has only partly been realised. Working with sounds on tape (or from computer systems) one is immediately confronted with an aural result and, if following broadly the aesthetic assumptions behind this paper, a judgement to be made and a decision to be acted upon. There may still be symbolic manipulation : composers keep mnemonic notebooks and use a variety of structuring and combinatorial strategies (of which more in a moment), but only for their own use, not for 'interpretation' by others.

Nonetheless, *we* are interested in the composer's secrets, his sketches, notebooks and anything that can help us build up a picture of his methods, to prize open his privacy, not for our voyeuristic gaze (encouraged, paradoxically, by the successful and famous) but for the much more practical task of building the bank of commonly held tools to which I referred.

While my model draws on experience of the composition of electroacoustic music, it is intended to draw inferences for all genres of contemporary music.

It follows from the assumptions above that the composer is faced with the first judgement : "It doesn't matter why I combined these sounds : *Do they sound right together?*". This leads us to the simplest of heuristic models (Figure 2).

Whereas before, such systems were considered somewhat in isolation, I wish to embed this one firmly in the composer/listener chain. The 'ACTION' remains (for the moment, at least) firmly in the area of the composer's poiesis; it is when we come to 'TEST', however, that we hit that precise point at which our 'research' begins.

The notion of test has both local and more general aspects. The composer brings to bear previous experiences of his/her own and other

Composing strategies and pedagogy 137

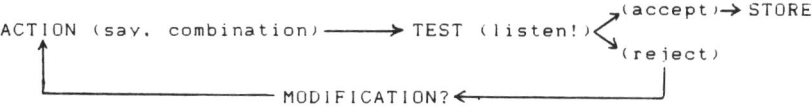

Figure 2 A simple model of composition

performances. But is this enough if we are aiming for discoveries of more universal application? It is my contention that the notion of testing works during the process of composition must be extended in the first instance to groups of like minded people — and that does not mean stylistically uniform — and conceivably to audience participation also!

The second point about our first model is that — we may take our cue from child psychology here — the model is also about learning *what actions produce what types of result*. This is the origin of experience. Actions are rarely arbitrary (though we shall examine when they may legitimately be so) and are drawn from an 'ACTION REPERTOIRE'. A successful action is reinforced.

Elaborating the model of composition

So far the model, elaborated though it is becoming, has an inherently conservative streak. As it stands, a successful group of actions would be reinforced and a stable repertoire established for endless use (as tends to happen in commercial music). But the TEST procedure is neither absolute nor stable. The model is embedded within the social psychology of its real time. The term 'judgement' has a paradoxical component: we must establish sufficient agreement to allow communication, but build in the ability to evolve to suit changing situations. The parallel with spoken language is unavoidable. To survive in an evolving world the variability of TEST demands an input to ACTION REPERTOIRE called 'NEW ACTIONS'.

This leads to an elaborated model for our learning procedure, embodying ACTION REPERTOIRE, NEW ACTIONS and the notion of REINFORCEMENT (to generate the ACTION REPERTOIRE *ab initio* and to differentiate its elements) (Figure 3).

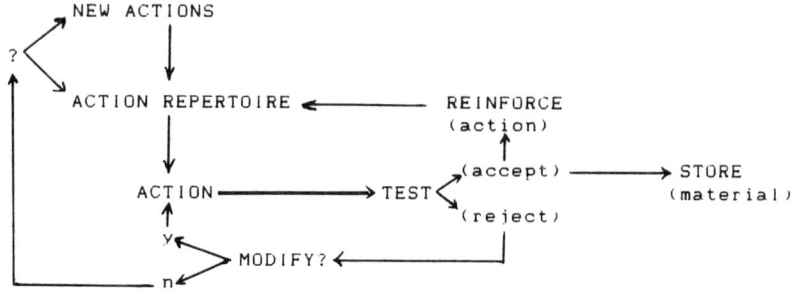

Figure 3 An elaborated model of composition

But where can these NEW ACTIONS come from? *It doesn't matter!* We can free ourselves from justifying this input until at least one rotation of our model, then perhaps it may join a corpus of the repertoire open for further corroboration or rejection. The parallel with the Darwinian view of evolution is unavoidable; random mutations are quite acceptable, even to be encouraged, *providing they are subsequently tested!*

It is the business of the psychologist of music to examine the TEST procedures and to establish a hypothesis concerning the preference rules embodied therein. The composer need not be conscious of these rules to use them or to participate in their development. And they are rules which change with time and context.

The structuralist fallacy was that the ACTION REPERTOIRE was to too great an extent defined by the preference rules within TEST in a tautological and self-justifying manner.

Conscious and unconscious strategies

Conscious strategies can easily be handled. They are codified and often explicit in the composer's writings. But the relation of conscious to unconscious strategies is of fundamental importance. A composer presents me with a short fragment of work consisting of two sound textures. I measure their durations as 5 and 8 seconds. Are these part of a *conscious* use of the Fibonacci sequence, or an intuitive combination of sounds? For our poietic analysis it *does* matter. Naturally, if the composer presents me with more material, I may be on firmer ground. If the following fragments consist of durations of 13 and 21 seconds, nature would bow out to artefact and I would come down on the side of structuralist preconception! If, however, 5 and 8 second durations cropped up consistently at climactic points in otherwise complex duration mixtures, I would begin to form hypotheses about the composer's unconscious mind, and conceivably about the behaviour of certain sound materials.

Measures of the composer's unconscious decisions may allow more penetrating generalities about the nature of composition compared to what we know may have been acquired consciously by the composer through learning (even fashion).

We must, once again, not confuse this assertion with pre-judging the aesthetic result. It is not that conscious methods may *never* succeed. The question is more subtle and must be asked in a more complex way. For example, Stockhausen's *Telemusik* is overtly constructed from the application of Fibonacci series numbers to various aspects of the work — durations of sections, number of occurrences etc. But we must go beyond those analyses which are merely descriptive of the composer's exhaustive and conscious techniques. The second order question is posed. *Why is the piece successful in spite of its overt pre-conception?* (I am allowed to put the question in such a loaded form because of the preponderance of similar Fibonacci applications in Stockhausen's other works of the period which have none of the same impact as *Telemusik*.) In other words, what *particular* relation of material to duration in *Telemusik*, not controlled specifically by the composer's conscious strategies, makes the piece sound *right?* This type of question is all too rarely asked.

Composition and analysis research

We will only know the answer through the development of *composition and analysis research*. For example, let us take Stockhausen's *Telemusik*, Parmegiani's *Dedans-Dehors*, Xenakis's *Pithoprakta*, Ligeti's *Atmosphères*. We can imagine an iconoclastic series of *études* which explore the possibilites suggested in such works in a more organised and tested manner. (May I stress once again the absence of any objective and time-independent conclusions. The suggested experiments are to develop experience and tools for future work, not an objective set of rules as in tonal harmony and counterpoint.)

It would be possible to change the time scale, double the density, transpose the textures, change the timbres — in other words to TEST the results. (See Erikson, 1975, pp. 181–184 for a criticism of the Xenakis work.) These experiments would only harm any *undeserved* reputations of the originals. The composers claimed an experimental aesthetic. But *experiment* means the establishment of a working hypothesis which is modified or overthrown through too many counterinstances (see Popper, 1959, and, from the standpoint of a more radical analysis of the history of science, Kuhn, 1962). I propose the establishment of an *experimental analysis* as a partner to *experimental composition*. Indeed in the longer term distinctions between the two would be minimal.

Testing hypotheses

We have not discussed preliminary ideas on the nature of testing musical esthesis, upon which the basis of a developing language resides.

In order to counterbalance the pitch-oriented analytical tradition, which has all too often missed the global (textural, timbral and gestalt) aspects of musical perception, I will take as my starting point articles by Denis Smalley (Smalley, 1966) and Trevor Wishart (Wishart, 1986) on the nature of electroacoustic music, though the principles may be applied to almost any genre of music.

Smalley follows Schaeffer (1966) in describing the perceptual qualities of sound events in terms of *typology* (outside time) and *morphology* (in time). The terminology is descriptive of sonic phenomena, ascribing all combinatorial strategies to 'aural judgement'. Overtly, Smalley rejects all conscious artifice based on pre-conceived (or, more correctly, *pre-perceived*) strategies. The composer may set trajectories only within possibilites suggested by the aural impact of the material. But behind Smalley's exposition of strategies of sound object combination, lies a *covert* strategy that we must examine. He hints that the strategy that the ear subconsciously, or at most half-consciously, follows is governed by *archetypes*. The model of 'attack-resonance-decay' is somehow built into our perceptual apparatus. Along with other writers of the French school, Smalley argues for *reduced listening* — the need to listen to sounds for their sonic structure alone, independent of their origins. This is sometimes known as *acousmatic* listening, after the disciples of Pythagoras who had to listen to the master from behind a curtain with no direct apprehension of the source of the sound. But Smalley is careful to see this acousmatic behaviour as provocative to the ear/brain system. The sound source may be removed from sight, but the ear searches actively. He suggests the term *surrogacy*. Where we recognise the source of the sound through listening alone, as in a simple instrumental or environmental recording, we apprehend a *first order surrogacy*. The electro-acoustic composer may go further, however, and create sounds, either electronically or by processing recordings which are models of such real world sounds and may evoke them even though having no such origins; this he terms *second order surrogacy*. He finally describes sounds even further removed from such perceptual deductions as possessing *remote surrogacy*.

Lying behind these strategies is the underlying assumption that there exist *archetypes* of sound structures which allow comprehensibility. This is a crucial point. In discussing how composers of electroacoustic music approach the creation of larger scale structures. Smalley makes an intuitive leap that needs further investigation. He argues that the models of morphological archetypes may be used *at a higher (ie. formal) level*, for example the acoustic model of 'Onset-Continuant-Termination'. Although the chain may be elaborated and deliberate ambiguities introduced, he strongly suggests that these archetypes (whether learnt or inherited) *circumscribe the possibilites of our musical discourse*. We are not free to invent combinations of sounds as we choose without risking a lack of comprehension; we must discover the relations — based on what we know of the archetypes — within which we may operate. *If we aim at comprehensibility, we are not free to invent freely without reference to these discovered relations.*

But there has been a leap between 'object combinations' and 'formal structures' which contains a hidden assumption. Firstly, the idea that simple sound gestures are surrogates for actions in the real world is not new, but is directly pertinent to electroacoustic music. The composer and audience will have relatively little problem with this lower level 'sound bank' — often the attacks and resonance of more or less familiar objects. The leap to use a similar group of models to build the *larger-scale* structures needs further justification.

At the same time, however, it also suggests a line of *research*. The problem is that even the immediacy of electroacoustic music is reduced at the level of *formal* work. That is, the immediate feedback of sounds is clear and concise when they are short. Repeated listenings may be within the shortest memory times. But listening to whole sections of a work and building up longer structures returns us to long term memory. This in turn tends to be determined by longer term experience.

This suggests strongly that a distinction may emerge in the TEST model outlined above between lower level gesture testing (and feedback) and higher level formal testing. At the lower (sound object) level, experience is seen as concrete, pertaining to the acuity of the ear (and its use in short term memory). At the higher (formal) levels, experience is seen as the accumulation of a repertoire of strategies, that is, possible larger scale combinations relying on long term memory.

Smalley's implication is that *both* may be based on morphological archetypes. The nature of ACTION REPERTOIRE and its concommittant TEST procedures change with longer time spans. This builds a new aspect into our model which cannot be expressed simply on paper: CYCLE TIME. This disturbs our model, not in form, but in practice. The radical break that electroacoustic music introduced was the possibility of immediate sound feedback in the studio. The time for one cycle of this model was reduced progressively to within a short-term memory time. At the level of form, or at least larger scale strategic thinking, however, the revolution is left incomplete. To work in terms of overall form still requires 'outside time' representations, of which transcription to paper is still the most commonly found. The slower cycle times of our model at this level are a potential trap.

Testing longer term strategies may be laborious and the composer fall back all too easily on non-musical models and other preconceived ideas. I will argue that test procedures in such instances must be carried out by a *community of interest* and not by the individual composer alone.

Indeed, we may make the radical proposal that *all* preconceived strategic rule systems should *not* initially be in ACTION REPERTOIRE, but in the first instance in NEW ACTIONS. There would be some strange bed fellows : Cage's *I Ching* procedures, serialism, number games, stochastics and other such procedures, letter games etc. The list is of course familiar from the new music of the 1950s and 1960s. The failure of both pedagogy and analysis was to equip these action strategies with their own built in preference rules, and thus to create self-supporting models.

I must pause to reiterate and emphasis a point. I am *not* arguing that all music created by such rule-based systems is as a consequence somehow invalid or irrelevant. Composers can transcend the limitations of the 'systems' they purport to use. The question concerns the *reestablishment* of relations between conscious poietical actions and their results in esthesis. Or more simply put between the composer and the audience.

The aim is to establish a repertoire of actions and strategies not a rigid preference rule system. This may sound simply like the older word 'technique', but it is intended to embrace the experimental ethos characteristic of this age which has lost its central cultural assumptions. Experiments may 'fail' and contribute positively to this knowledge and experience.

Pedagogy and beyond

The simple heuristic model proposed here has the built in assumptions subsequently elucidated. The most important of these is that experiments are judged. It may be seen to be dodging the thorny question of judgement *criteria* for the moment, but let us assume that we have established some kind of *community of interest* whose views we trust and value. I hazard the following observations as to the pedagogical consequences of the views embodied in the model outlined here:
1. TEST procedures may not be carried out by the composer alone. If we are to research the relation between poietical and esthesic spheres then the composer *cannot be the sole judge*. Reference to other members of the community (composers, performers and listeners) is essential.
2. ACTION REPERTOIRES do not therefore remain private property. Crudely a mere 'exchange of ideas' must be replaced by more sophisticated notions of 'experience management': this is a more tricky notion than 'knowledge management'. It is my contention that composition has moved to too great a degree towards 'objective' or 'knowledge-based' criteria and has forgotten the role of shared 'subjective' experience and exploration.
3. The consequences of NEW ACTIONS need research: indeed, the relation of poiesis to esthesis *demands* research. This may include a vast range of new inputs, influences, styles and techniques. The relation of

ACTION REPERTOIRE to result (in STORE) is already the domain of research in the psychology of music.
4. The role of ACTIONs in our model is circumscribed by the available technical and musical resources. In the electroacoustic world this is strongly influenced by the available studio technology. Future software development will define the MODIFY function more clearly.
5. Careful comment must be made on TEST. In the final analysis it is literally *unanalysable!* Whereas the automation and software control of the other aspects of the model is possible, I have indicated that it was a *fallacy* of previous 'systems' of composition that TEST was defined in a circular manner such that it could not fail to confirm the ACTION REPERTOIRE. This is a crucial point. It may be that psychologists of music wish to analyse just what it is that makes a particular strategy sound 'right'; this analysis may contribute to the community of experts which determines ACTION given certain premises. But it cannot replace TEST — the sole arbiters of taste remain human!

And finally, what lies beyond pedagogy? Our model suggests drastic consequences for the future of (Western) music. For we cannot claim that at the end of some arbitrary period of study a composer emerges fully equipped with a language. Here I step outside the normal confines of a conference paper to express opinions as to how the relationship of pedagogy to music at large in the community might develop in the late 20th and early 21st centuries.

The model elaborated above is essentially incompatible with the system which has been with us since the late classical era for the commissioning, promotion and publication of musical works. The 'masterwork syndrome' militates against true experimentation in several ways:
1. The composer may create only one version of the work. The flexibility, sometimes found in the music of other cultures, to accommodate different times of day, different locations etc. is usually proscribed.
2. The composer's work is usually tested 'once and for all' in its final form. Revisions and new versions are discouraged and often impossible. Hence further testing fails to take place.
3. Each work is promoted as a potential masterwork with associated vested interests militating against honest (that is *not* to say 'objective') assessment of its merits. A few chosen ones (the critics) hold absurdly disproportionate power over the fate not only of the work but of the composer and represent the smallest part of the community of interest to which I referred, and from whom a contribution is needed.

The consequences of this list would be the subject of another paper.

Postscript

The author was composer no. 3, sitting in the library at the Music School at Durham University on a visit to the studio around Easter 1975. I have used that hexachord in one form or another (which for some reason I felt to be intensely symbolic), in all my works until recently. But I was unconscious of an enormous poietic fallacy. Only while preparing this paper did I notice that, of course, as there are only nine 'musical letters' and my text omits three (F,H,D), statistically any number of short phrases might have produced an identical result! This precisely illustrates the point that we must not confine ourselves to overt results in the examination of poiesis, but to the *motivations* which create the ACTION REPERTOIRE!

Bibliography

Erikson, R. (1975) *Sound Structure in Music*, Berkeley: University of California Press
Cott, J. (1974) *Stockhausen : Conversations with the Composer*, London: Robson
Kostelanetz, R. (1971) *John Cage*, London: Allen Lane
Kuhn, T. (1962, rev.1970) *The Structure of Scientific Revolutions*. Chicago: University of Chicago Press
Nattiez, J-J. (1982) Varèse's "Density 21.5" A study in semiological analysis. *Music Analysis* 1,(3) pp. 243–340
Neruda, P. (1966) *The Heights of Macchu Picchu* (tr. Nathaniel Tarn), London: Jonathan Cape
Popper, K. (1959) *The Logic of Scientific Discovery*. London: Hutchinson
Schaeffer, P. (1966) *Traité des Objets Musicaux*, Paris: Editions du Seuil
Schaeffer, P. (1973) *La Musique Concrète*, Paris: Presses Universitaires de France
Smalley, D. (1986) Spectro-morphology and Structuring Processes. In *The Language of Electroacoustic Music*, S. Emmerson (Ed.) pp. 61–93. Basingstoke: The Macmillan Press
Wishart, T. (1986) Sound Symbols and Landscapes. In *The Language of Electroacoustic Music*, S. Emmerson (Ed.) pp. 41–60. Basingstoke: The Macmillan Press

An approach to the analysis of electro-acoustic music derived from empirical investigation and critical methodologies of other disciplines

Michael Bridger

Middlesex Polytechnic, Trent Park, Barnet, London, UK

Roland Barthes' S/Z (a virtuoso analysis of a short story by Balzac) yields a number of principles susceptible to modification for application to the analysis of electro-acoustic music, amongst which are his fundamental notion that a work of art carries within itself indicators of appropriate analytical method and his insistence on the primacy of experiential encounter between writing and reader (music and listener).

This paper is an account of a recent research project in which an analytical approach to a group of electro-acoustic works was developed from the reported experience of listeners, aided by diagrammatic scores that helped to focus attention and identify points for discussion. Barthes' system of codes of meaning was adapted, and further useful insights came from film criticism, the work of Roman Jakobson (particularly with respect to communication systems and the metaphor/metonymy dichotomy), and Arthur Koestler's notion of 'matrices of bisociation'.

KEYWORDS analysis of electro-acoustic music, listeners' response, diagrammatic scores, Roland Barthes, Berio, Cage, Ligeti, Stockhausen, Varèse

Roland Barthes' S/Z (1975) is one of the most celebrated critical works in any field to have appeared in recent years. Widely quoted and commented upon, it has been a liberating and enabling stimulus for criticism and analysis over a wide range of literature and other arts. There are many reasons for this, not least being the sheer exuberance and vitality of Barthes' virtuoso dissection of Balzac's story, *Sarrasine*. The sense of a provocative, iconoclastic originality that pervades Barthes' writing is an encouraging precedent for anyone attempting to comment on electro-acoustic music — a bold first step is needed in the absence of agreed, established orthodoxies of analytical apparatus, vocabulary or evaluative criteria.

So, one can at least adopt the pioneering spirit of Barthes in this task. At

the more detailed level of procedure, his fragmentation of Balzac's text into a series of "lexias", or reading units, offers a tempting precedent, and his deployment of a set of five "codes of signification" operating within those lexias seems promising too. These were the twin starting points I adopted some years ago in a project attempting to bring a group of electro-acoustic pieces within a common analytical and criticial environment. The works involved were:
Berio — *Visage*
Cage — *Fontana Mix*
Ligeti — *Artikulation*
Stockhausen — *Gesang der Jünglinge*
Stockhausen — *Telemusik*
Varèse — *Poème Electronique*
These works were selected according to several criteria:

— they are all by composers with established reputations in other musical genres, and were composed within a few years of each other;
— they are all works for tape alone, with no live performance element;
— they have been readily available on disc, and therefore can be regarded as relatively widely disseminated and accessible examples of this music.

As it eventually transpired, *S/Z* did indeed provide useful precedents in this investigation, but not quite in the ways originally expected. The first problem arose in trying to find a useful equivalent to Barthes' division of the text into lexias. Not that there is any difficulty in identifying sections and articulations within these works — in the case of *Telemusik*, for instance, the segmentation is especially apparent. Moreover, since Barthes' own methodology for division of test into lexias was remarkably arbitrary, a degree of idiosyncracy would be justified in the case of less clear-cut structural articulation. But it seemed hard to use this initial division as the springboard for the main analytical process, centred in Barthes' model around five codes of signification.

In the end, it was not so much the fine detail of Barthes' methodology, but rather its general principles and the way in which he arrived at it that were the most helpful factors — in particular his notion that a work of art carries within itself indicators of appropriate analytical method and his insistence on the primacy of experiential encounter between text and reader. A remarkable example of these features is the way in which Barthes "discovers", or contrives to discover, the five codes of signification in just the title and first sentence of the story.

His preoccupation with reading (a process of interaction and recreation which in his eyes acquired an almost mystical quality) took on the nature of a communal project in *S/Z* since it was written during a period of teaching, and Barthes suggests that this was an important factor in the book's evolution. Having been involved in teaching aspects of electro-acoustic music to undergraduate students for many years, I decided to take whatever opportunities I could to develop not only views on this music, but also a framework for eliciting those views, less from my one prejudices, judgments and speculation, than from discussion and empirical investigation.

It is, of course, difficult to push discussion and analysis of electro-acoustic music beyond loose generalities in the absence of scores for much electro-acoustic music. Of the works I had selected, only *Telemusik* has a published score by its composer, though there is a remarkable graphic score for *Artikulation* devised by Rainer Wehinger (Wehinger, 1970). In order to be able to deal with the pieces equally, and at a level of some detail, I evolved a simple graphic notation. Using a chart recording device, a trace of each work's dynamic level was produced on a paper roll. A speed was selected that would allow some fine detail to be captured whilst encompassing the entire piece within a manageable length of paper — one minute of music to a single sheet of A4 paper seemed a reasonable compromise. Both channels of the stereo recording were combined, in order to make the task of following the trace as easy as possible. In general it seemed that a facility for following the traces was easily acquired, once an initial tendency to interpret the peaks as related to pitch rather than to intensity could be overcome.

Even at this preliminary stage, it became apparent that valuable information about a work's dynamic structuring was revealed, and that the possibility for the listener to be visually reminded of the preceding few seconds of music as well as being primed for periods of high or low activity was an aid both to attentiveness and to a more analytical appreciation. It became possible, for instance, to discuss points of interest in the music by reference to 'page four' or to 'about three minutes twenty seconds', thus identifying specific sections in a way hitherto impossible. It was found surprisingly easy to judge the progress of the music on paper in this way, even at times when there may be a few distinctive features in the trace; unlike a conventional score, where a flurry of semiquavers is accommodated by an elongated bar, in this diagrammatic form the passage of time is represented at an even rate to which the listener becomes rapidly acclimatised.

Encouraged by this apparent success in producing vestigial scores which could be followed during listening, used as a basis for discussion and reference, and which revealed, quite objectively, important features of the music, the possibility of further development was considered. It was clearly important to find some way of indicating the spatial imaging of these pieces, which is so striking a feature of them in their stereophonic format, even though much reduced from the multi-channel originals of most of them. At the same time, the addition of verbal descriptions of the salient sounds of the music seemed necessary, though open to the possibility of misinterpretation and the inevitable subjective recourse to onomatopoeic analogy. A number of other ideas were explored, most of which would have involved the systematic classification of specific sound parameters throughout each piece, along the lines developed by Fennelly (1967), Schaeffer (1952) or Smalley (1981) but all such approaches had to be abandoned, overwhelmed by the sheer complexity and diversity of the material.

However, musical analysis can operate at many different levels of detail, and for the purposes of my project attention to salient features rather than minutiae was appropriate. Two interlinked features rather than minutiae was appropriate. Two interlinked sets of criteria had then to be defined: how to identify and classify salient features, and how to define ways in which they relate and interact in expressive and structural terms. Both these issues were explored in discussion arising out of teaching over a number of years and I found a remarkable degree of unanimity with respect to observation, classification and interpretation of the works' sonic profiles (contrasting strikingly with the disparity that was often evident between critical or evaluative views of the same pieces amongst the same groups of listeners).

Since the works under scrutiny are diversely hybrid in nature, in most cases bringing electronic sounds into varying relationships with sound from other sources, it is perhaps not surprising that appearances in the music of identifiable elements of conventional *music*, of the human *voice*, or of recognisable *concrète* sounds were three characteristics that seemed always to attract listeners' attention. Three further characteristics, this time not of sound types, but rather of ways of organising, differentiating, developing that material into expressive statements (again derived from discussion with listeners) were *location, dynamics* (interpreted broadly to include both volume and activity levels) and those recurrences, juxtapositions or transitions that were perceived as having *structural* significance. In total, then, six 'codes of signification' emerged, as against Barthes' five. Although the parallel with Barthes' scheme is not very close with respect to its detail, the fundamental approach is the same, namely to deduce from the group of works under scrutiny a taxonomy of their codes of signification and then to draw attention to the detailed operation of these codes.

Barthes' proposed hermeneutic code does have a pervasive relevance in this medium. Perhaps even more than in literature, the over-riding mechanism is hermeneutic, in the sense that the astute and attentive listener constantly searches for clues about a considerable number and variety of areas of enigma. Underlying the approach I adopted is the contention that the six codes identified above, along with a verbal description of salient sounds (which brings electronically generated sound into the net), account for a substantial part of the fabric of this music and also that, to an extent closely dependent on context, individual codes, or several simultaneously, can temporarily acquire, as the music proceeds, enhanced capacity for expressive significance in a hermeneutic field.

Parallel with these macroscopic and largely referential qualities, of course, minute characteristics of the electronic components of this music form another layer of structural and expressive potential; an aspect that may well be expected to have assumed a more far-reaching and innovative significance in this investigation, were it not for the repeated experience, as reported by listeners, that the primary impact of this music is accounted for by the elements (or 'codes') previously identified rather than by its purely electronic elements.

Visual indication of this conjectured periodic emergence of significant features was tackled by the use of fluorescent markers of the type commonly used for highlighting documents, thus enabling attention to be drawn to particular features of the music by indications superimposed on the trace of dynamic level. This had the advantage of preserving clarity and simplicity so that the valuable application of the traces as guides for listening and discussion, as mentioned earlier, would not be compromised. On the contrary, it was found that following the traces became easier.

As I have implied, listeners were involved in some way in all stages of this investigation. However, since the involvement of listeners took the form of discussion rather than objective testing, and since it continued alongside other evolving aspects of the investigation, statistical analysis was neither possible nor appropriate. The resulting attempt to achieve an element of objectivity was, therefore, undeniably informal, but should perhaps be viewed more favourably when compared with the customary exclusion of any consensus of reported *listening* experience from most musical analysis.

The main points that emerged in the course of this project follow, grouped together in line with the codes identified above.

Electronic sound

In these works, which combine electronically generated sound with other sounds, listeners tended always to notice the proportions in which these elements are combined, ranging from totally electronic in *Artikulation* to totally concrète in *Fontana Mix*. The differing ways in which these elements are related were also noted. In *Gesang der Jünglinge*, the establishment of qualities of *affinity* between the boy's voice and the electronic material is readily apparent, embracing all facets of sound generation — timbre, tessitura, envelope, duration. In *Visage* quite the reverse is found, with a stark *differentiation* between the female voice and its electronic 'oppressors' contributing powerfully to the work's evocation of a dramatic scenario.

Clearly, the greatest deficiency of available technology at this time was in the more subtle qualities of timbre, and listeners seldom seemed convinced that this characteristic of the medium showed real potential. Other aspects of electronic sound production were genuine extensions of resources available by acoustic means — the possibility of very rapid sequences of pitches, of extremes of pitch, of prolonged, uninterrupted textures with a quality of stasis never possible before in music, of sliding and microtonal pitches — these and many other characteristics were imaginatively exploited, and I found these qualities remarked on by listeners.

The technique of ring modulation differs from other electronic means in the way that it can not only be used to generate complex timbres out of simpler waveforms (as in *Artikulation*), but can also incorporate natural or musical sound as one of the combined elements. Apart from the intrinsically interesting timbres that can result from this process, there is a potential quality involved of metamorphosis, transformation or unification that can have a powerfully symbolic resonance. This is a key factor in *Telemusik*, in which deliberately heterogeneous musical material is subjected to intensive ring modulation that in acoustic terms blends elements into a homogeneous sound world, and that, in philosophical terms, symbolises the vision of global unity that so excited Stockhausen at the work's inception. It seemed to me that listeners seldom appreciated the intention of these transformations, to the extent that a common reaction was to wish for a more recognisable appearance of the various materials employed in the work.

Voice

Two points were apparent at once: firstly, that all these works make significant use of the human voice, secondly that these uses vary in a remarkable number of ways, and to remarkable extents. At the simplest level of observation, three titles in themselves (*Gesang der Jünglinge, Poème Electronique, Artikulation*) betray a linguistic or vocal preoccupation as a formative principle, so it is hardly surprising that in these works a strong involvement of the voice is found, but in the other three works also, appearances in the texture of voice recordings are moments that especially attract the listener's attention.

Considering first the types of voice employed, there are closely recorded solo voices (a boy in *Gesang der Jünglinge*, a woman in *Visage* and *Poème Electronique*), male voices from broadcasts in *Fontana Mix*, priests chanting in *Telemusik*, voices singing in chorus in *Fontana Mix* and *Poème Electronique*, and so on through what proves to be an extensive panorama. At the most superficial level, it is clear that simply as a source of variety of timbre, the voice provided a rich vein of possibility, and there are a few moments in the works when one feels that the interest in the voice is in fact primarily timbral, perhaps especially so in *Gesang der Jünglinge* and *Poème Electronique*. But such a de-personalised response to a voice is rare in a musical context, just as it inevitably is in real life, and a more powerful expressive element derives not from acoustic properties, but from the voice as a vehicle for delineation and interpretation of emotional states. Thus the woman in *Visage* is taken to be oppressed, turbulent, personally involved in a situation of imminent crisis; the boy in *Gesang der Jünglinge* seems aloof, clinical, detached, unresponsive to both the acoustic, and (by a process of metaphor) the emotional environment in which he is placed. Taking another pair of works in which polarities of this sort can be detected, the fragments of voice in *Fontana Mix* are assumed to be randomly overheard snippets, removed from the original contexts that could have created a sense of personal expression; in contrast, the electronically processed fragments incorporated in *Telemusik*, though similarly transplanted into the composition, somehow do preserve a quality of communication at a primary level. Within the single work of *Poème Electronique*, the distraught female voice and the fragments of chanting provide a further continuum of expressive potential.

Curiously, the most obvious and direct means by which a voice can communicate, that of language, is evident throughout these works only in ways that diminish its force. The torrent of pseudo-language in *Visage*, creating the sense of linguistic expression in one way, but no sense at all in another, aptly encapsulates a stance towards language evident in all these pieces which, even bearing in mind the relatively small size of the sample, is unlikely to be coincidental. In *Gesang der Jünglinge* (the only case here in which an actual text is featured with moments of clear, precise intelligibility), for example, the possible impact of semantic content is neutralised by the unresponsive, impersonal quality of the boy's delivery of that text. Looked at as a whole, the composers seem to have been intrigued by the possibilites inherent in a sophisticated and teasing game with the paradoxes of vocal and linguistic communication, in which both metaphorical and metonymic processes can function all the more powerfully because of the prevailing aura of ambiguity.

By another pleasing paradox, the piece amongst this group most directly concerned with language, as revealed both by its particular sound quality and by its title (*Artikulation*) makes no use whatsoever of actual voices or even of actual linguistic elements, being constructed instead entirely of particles of synthetic sound generated, treated and aggregated into longer structural units by processes derived from those of language, but once again without any recourse to, or even suggestion of, semantics.

Music quotation

A wide variety of types of reference to other music is evident, ranging from the direct incorporation of fragments of recordings of conventional music, conventionally played, to pitch processes which, even though non-tonal and realised in electronic sound, can be felt to operate in a manner akin to that of more familiar idioms. Inevitably, rather more subjective judgements were involved in this categorisation than in the area of voice discussed above, but even allowing for this, a complex network of association, reference, extension and deliberate exclusion is revealed closely parallelling the multi-layered and ambivalent attitude to language discussed in the previous section.

The most straightforward involvement of conventional music in this hybrid form is the direct inclusion of recorded material, and even within this one category a range of expressive effects, and presumably of expressive intentions, is revealed. In *Fontana Mix*, some of the most striking ingredients are the fragments of choral and orchestral sound that make fleeting appearances, but as with the voice elements mentioned above, the immediately apparent structural principle of random collage denies the possibility of a committed emotional response. The brief fragment of organ music, strategically placed towards the end of *Poème Electronique*, on the other hand, creates both by its placing and the clearly intentioned repetition a much more telling impact.

Partly because of their particular sound quality, but also because of the unfamiliarity of their idiom, the recordings of music of oriental cultures incorporated in *Telemusik* perform a different function. Central to their role is the sense of fusion and assimilation created by filtering and ring modulation; there is seldom sufficiently unaltered substance remaining to allow the sense of mere quotation which could otherwise occur. The single, peremptory strokes on Japanese percussion instruments which mark the beginning of each section of the work are another original and unique device, effective both as a means of structural articulation and as representative symbols for the awesome, autocratic power of the ancient culture from which they emanate, and which, by his own account, so impressed the composer as a formative influence on this work.

Apart from the actual incorporation of recordings of musical material, some of which have been discussed above, the points of contact between this group of works and traditional musical syntax are remarkably few and far between, creating the inescapable impression that, in these particular works at least, their composers felt some obligation to develop ways of forming an expressive language appropriate to their new medium without excessive recourse to procedures strongly associated by long tradition with other established musical forms. Adoption of any sort of metrical procedure, except on a very short time-scale, is particularly rare (though, of course, this is also true of much music written at this time for conventional media); where there is a repetition of short-term rhythmic patterning in a way suggestive of meter, more often than not an overt derivation from the device of the tape loop preserves the integrity and self-sufficiency of the medium.

The most direct involvement of melodic process in these works is in the context of the fragments of singing included from time to time, which have been alluded to in the preceding section dealing with use of the voice. There are other instances of melodic idioms and devices as well, however, ranging from the cryptic three-note motif that recurs to such telling effect in *Poème Electronique* to the relatively extended appearance in *Gesang der Jünglinge* of strings of pitches that evoke the quality of note-rows. Rapidly executed sequential clusters of clearly defined pitches, most noticeably in *Gesang der Jünglinge*, but in other pieces also, often occupy an aesthetic grey area that brings the exploratory nature of this music forcefully to mind. Passing too quickly for the ear to focus on individual pitch components and thereby to form clearly delineated structures in the musical areas of perception, as would happen in conventional music, these events nevertheless project a strong profile that is clearly melodic within the extending parameters of this exploratory musical idiom.

A parallel extension and transformation into this medium from conventional musical syntax can be discerned in the area of harmony. As in the case of melody, there are few appearances of sound events that could be classified as chords, as commonly understood, but there are a comparatively large number of complex resonances that have a chord-like quality, even though (like the melodic clusters mentioned above) lacking the clearly defined pitch relationships one would expect in other music. In *Poème Electronique* there are, of course, examples of relatively simple formations of clearly pitched electronic sounds which can be classed unequivocally as chords, but what is noticeably absent in these instances, as elsewhere, is any sequential procedure even approximating to the notion of harmonic progression. Unmistakeably, at those moments where a chord-like event occurs, it tends to be savoured as a unique sonority rather than as a contributory component of a syntactical succession.

Superficial timbral association between electronically generated sound and established instrumental colours is not a strong feature of these works; indeed it would be quite out of character with all that has been discussed so far if there were any sense of a deliberate synthetic recreation of familiar timbres. At those points where a sound is briefly reminiscent of an orchestral voice, as with one or two clarinet or flute-like sonorities in *Gesang der Jünglinge*, it is because these sounds are so easily produced electronically that they belong as much to the vernacular of electronic music as to that of instrumental music.

Concrète sound

Immediately recognisable natural or industrial sounds are relatively rare in this group of works. The barking dog at the end of *Fontana Mix*, and the similarly placed sound of a plane taking off in *Poème Electronique*, establish a sense of impending closure (presumably by design in one case, by accident in the other!), and are striking examples of how effective a recognisable sound can be in the context of a hybrid sound world. But there are, on the other hand, many more instances of sounds that *suggest* a possible *concrète* origin, but which cannot be distinguished by the listener from electronic sound with any degree of certainty. This is in no way an inadequacy of the medium, of course, but is rather an area of ambiguity, which has latent expressive possibilities just as potent as those that the introduction of a recognisable sound may have.

If the concept of *concrète* sound is widened in a way that some theorists think legitimate, the occurrences certainly of the human voice, but also perhaps of musical instruments, can be regarded as further examples of concrète material. In the sense that the listener to all this music is presented with a succession of problems of sound identification which form part of the hermeneutic complex discussed earlier, the simple, broad classification that one sound is electronic, another sound is not, and a third may or may not be, is a significant factor in the overall decoding and *Gestalt* formation process.

Dynamics

In the absence of almost all the syntactical devices of conventional music that together enable the construction of musical phrases from smaller germs of material, and progressively longer aggregations of those phrases until the level of a whole movement or complex of movements is achieved, it is at once apparent that reliance was all the more necessary on the rather more crude and less finely differentiated aspects of musical language grouped together here under the heading of dynamics.

Dealing first with the question of volume level, it would probably be true to say that even though the actual material of this music is so innovatory, the fundamental long term dynamic profiles are relatively similar to those of other music. Climactic moments, predictably, still tend to be loud, with, for that reason, a strategic caution evident in the placing of those moments; loud and soft sections alternate in familiar patterns; transitions from loud to soft are accomplished with degrees of emphasis ranging from sudden to imperceptible. When played back on large, purpose built amplification systems, performance of this music can legitimately employ an extended dynamic range beyond the capabilities of acoustic instruments, but in the context of the audience aimed at with the stereophonic record (the format dealt with in this project) this is an irrelevant distinction since even recordings of orchestral music can be amplified to suit personal taste, and it is not uncommon for high levels to be preferred.

On the other hand, the nature and rate of event-flow of these works is considerably further removed from the conventional practice of other music. In particular, the range from the stillest moments, perhaps to be found in *Telemusik*, to the most active is very extensive indeed, a characteristic of the genre that derives from the technical capabilities of the equipment involved. In tonal, or even non-tonal instrumental music, so many layers of musical syntax operate simultaneously that the sheer grain of the texture is seldom a predominant, primary feature, but in this music, with little possibility of reliance on most of the traditional procedures, it is not surprising to find that textural flow and density is elevated to the status of a major structural principle. A comprehensive taxonomy of the various ways in which this aspect of the idiom functions would have to include both states and processes, degrees of homogeneity and heterogeneity, alternation and transition between sections of different status, regularity and asymmetry, congruence and noncongruence with other parameters, overall formal patterns and strategies, each of which elements of classification, along with many more, could be further subdivided and more finely graded to account for the range of models provided by even this small group of works.

It must certainly be true that the high incidence in this music of cells of sound drawn from widely differentiated sources, and the equally wide fluctuation with respect to rhythmic and other aspects of patterning of this material, together form a most significant part of the listening experience at the level of abstract, non-referential attention and appreciation, over and above the hermeneutic quest for referential identification mentioned earlier.

Location

Along with the electronic generation of sound, the possibility of harnessing sound location and movement for artistic purposes was perhaps an innovation of equal potential in electro-acoustic music. Except for a very few instances, such as certain works of Venetian choral music, the fact that the ear is a minutely accurate detector of sound location had previously been, for simple logistical reasons, a quite unexplored region of aesthetic experimentation. Yet there is no axiomatic, fundamental reason why this parameter of sound should not be as susceptible to exploitation for expressive purposes as any other; especially when one bears in mind the life-preserving urgency of response to sound direction that was even more necessary at earlier stages of our evolution than it is today. Complex schemes of placing and movement in three dimensions, binaural rather than merely stereophonic, are possible in specially designed speaker arrays for concert projection of this music, but even within the more restricted terms of reference of the present study, dealing only with the stereo record format, a surprisingly varied catalogue of procedures can be enumerated.

One potential of the medium that is rather less exploited in these works than might be expected is the use of panning from one channel to the other, a device that can be startlingly effective for the listener since it evokes a response not only to position but to movement — an environmental clue which, to continue speculation about the role of hearing as a biological defence mechanism, is likely to stimulate a strong flow of adrenalin! There are examples of panning in all these works except *Fontana Mix*, but they are often indistinct and no more than a single transit in one direction, thus exploiting only one very limited ploy from what could be an extensive arsenal. On the other hand, it may be that this economy enhances the effectiveness of the device on those occasions when it is used, and this view is especially supported by consideration of the role of panning in the spatial deployment of *Gesang der Jünglinge* and *Visage*.

Strategies of static placing and relative distribution are much more highly organized, with the gamut of possible permutations fully exploited. Thus there are moments when both channels have similar but not identical material, when both channels are active with differentiated material, when a previously heard sound reappears in the same or opposite channel (both can be effective gambits), when one channel becomes silent, or re-enters after a silence. And so on — a full list, which would include many composite and intermediate categories, would be varied and extensive.

The most straightforward use of location is as a congruent reinforcement of some other characteristic; the start of a new section, the introduction of new material, a sudden loud sound, a contrast or an association between two sound types — all of these events and many more occur along with an accompanying underlining of placing in one or other of these works. Beyond these examples of linked usage, paralleling other features of the music, are quasi-dramatic spatial distributions, especially in *Visage* and *Gesang der Jünglinge*, where the solo voices are often deployed on a sophisticated stereophonic continuum that reinforces the narrative element of these works. In *Fontana Mix*, in keeping with its other elements, a much more random distribution is employed; in *Poème Electronique* a balanced marshalling of the diverse elements between the channels.

One factor that seemed to interest listeners in discussing these works was the nature of mental processes and conditioning at a sub-conscious level that may have influenced decisions about placing to right or left. The travel of our written language, as well as musical notation, from left to right; the predominant tendency towards right-handedness which no doubt accounts for that orientation — these and other aspects of life and consciousness are likely to predispose directional decisions even in an abstract medium such as electro-acoustic music. If this were to be investigated in detail, several fundamental, but necessarily speculative decisions would have to be made about possible aspects of transference into a composer's mind of physical gestures, stances, orientations and movements. Does the composer envisage his stance as facing his audience (the traditional confrontation of a performer), or as facing towards his sound material, in the same orientation as the audience? Is it possible that a panning of sound from left to right may tend to symbolise an expansive, open-palmed gesture of generous display, as a guide might indicate an impressive view? Conversely, could a panning from right to left suggest clenched-fist aggression? How would any such correspondence operate in the case of a left-handed composer? All interesting questions, but ones for which there are insufficient instances in this group of works to justify any theorising beyond this initial speculation.

Structure

The duration of these pieces varies from under four minutes (*Artikulation*) to over 21 (*Visage*) — by analogy with other musical genres, from the scale of a miniature to a very substantial single movement. Inevitably, the overall strategies of formal design and the proportions of contributory sections differ between these two extremes; in *Artikulation*, tiny discrete cells of activity alternate in a rapid interplay, whereas in *Visage* single textures are often remarkably prolonged, and processes of transition are correspondingly extended in proportion to the scale of the sections they articulate.

Except in the case of *Fontana Mix*, which eschews formal, progressive structure in the indeterminacy of its collage, the pieces display many of the traditional concerns of any composers, of this and earlier epochs, in shaping material into convincing aesthetic and expressive designs. Moments of catharsis or climax can be identified by listeners, strategically placed, as in so much other music, just before the works' closing sections; a range of introductory and closing gestures can be identified, somehow projecting these indefinable indications whether emphatic or subliminal in mode. Perhaps above all, the establishment of a balance between recapitulation or treatment of existing material and the introduction of contrasting elements is as clear a preoccupation in these works as in any music, and an infrastructure of the same, or very similar, written formal rules can be deduced.

The clearest example of an innovatory formal approach amongst this group is provided by *Telemusik*, with its Fibonacci-based structural plan. As in other moment-form compositions Stockhausen hoped to engender a new mode of listening, less concerned with cumulative, goal-orientated progression, and the abrupt dislocations of texture triggered by the punctuating percussion strokes contribute significantly to this new aesthetic principle. In some respects, the total scheme of deployment of material, with associated patterns of contrast, reappearance and evolution is perhaps not so far removed from principles implicit in much more familiar idioms. It is, after all, still overtly structured in accordance with discernibly intentional expressive and proportionate qualities. But the application of moment form principles very markedly had the effect of shifting the impact and incidence of detail from a 'micro' to a 'macro' level, and this is probably the most remarkable structural feature of the group of works, since fundamental aspects not only of form but also of interaction between hierarchic levels of structure are re-orientated.

A revolution even more epic in scale, if ultimately less productive, was made by *Fontana Mix*, with the quantum leap of its evident abandonment of structural intentionality making a massive shift to a qualitatively different philosophy of musical structure; the other formal innovations in the works involve new *methods* of structuring, but do not redefine the value and role of structure itself.

Even when not specifically intended so to do by their composers, works in a medium that encompasses categories of sound primarily associated with 'real-life' rather than 'artistic' activity are likely to suggest programmatic or descriptive analogy to listeners. In view of this, it is perhaps remarkable, even a tribute to their composers' handling of the medium, that these particular works did not seem to evoke stronger extra-musical images. Only *Visage*, with its overtly quasi-dramatic ambience, creates a consistent and persuasive sense of narrative, and, because of this, more abstract qualities of structure are somewhat eclipsed as the listener's attention is engaged by the episodic event-flow expected in an idiom akin to film or radio drama.

Although less formalised and symbolic than Le Corbusier's epic and grandiose scheme for the accompanying visual element, a very clear formal progression and overall design is evident in *Poème Electronique*, with the central appearance of the female voice and a number of strategically placed recurrences of significant material. The tolling bell at the start, and sirens at the end, are probably the most striking gestures in these key positions to be found in the group of works as a whole.

If, following Meyer (1973), it is accepted that a subtle tension between fulfilment and denial of expectations within a network of established and widely known parameters underlies much of music's expressive power, the inevitable lack of such a possibility in so radically innovatory a medium goes some way towards explaining the somewhat dubious and uncommitted response often noted in listeners. The problem is not that implicative relationships are impossible in these works, but that they operate largely with each work's particular terms of reference, unable to draw on a broad and complex pool of conventions (intrinsic at the level of 'medium' rather than 'message') in the creation of expressive ambiguity. Reflecting with hindsight on the whole process of comment and analysis involved in this project, it became apparent that the especially important roles in this music of various types of ambiguity and conjunction (both simultaneous and sequential) have somehow to be accommodated, classified and evaluated.

Discussing much the same problem, Henry (1970) suggests an underlying concept which he describes as 'valence', or the idea of sounds affecting each other in a kind of 'synergy', though he then goes on to give as examples a number of purely acoustic phenomena that delineate a more circumscribed area than I have in mind. If the notion of valence is opened out to include any interactive process between elements of this music, whether *audible* (sounds) or *conceptual* (associative references, extra-musical ideas), a factory is thereby identified that not only can be seen to operate in differing ways in each of these works, but, more importantly, that is central both to the structure *and* to the expressive thrust of each work.

With respect to *Poème Electronique*, for instance, the main elements in this relationship of valence are musical sounds, non-musical sounds and the human voice; the process by which they interact is largely one of overlapping, out-of-phase juxtaposition and superimposition. In other works, quite different elements can be seen to be interactively involved: a human voice and electronic sounds *opposed* in *Visage*, *related* in *Gesang der Jünglinge;* random snippets in *Fontana Mix;* electronic sounds, Japanese traditional instruments and various folk musics hierarchically intertwined in *Telemusik;* electronic sound and the phonetic surface of speech in *Artikulation*.

In other words, the most significant structural quality that all these works have in common (and it is a quality shared by many other works in the genre) is the exploration of what can conveniently be termed 'synergy' — an interaction in which whatever elements are involved become either *acoustically* or *expressively* changed and enhanced. The nature of this process can vary enormously; it may be to suggest a paradox, to assert a philosophical ideal, even (why not?) to make a joke.

A particularly wide-ranging exposition of a very similar concept is to be found in the writings of Koestler (1976), who brings explanations of the joke, scientific discovery and artistic expression within a unified theory based on 'matrices' of 'bisociative thinking'. Koestler himself does not explore ways in which these processes may be evident in music, dealing principally with literary and visual art. With a little ingenuity, such a broadening of the terms of reference to encompass the styles and processes of conventional music would not be difficult. But in the case of electro-acoustic music, the theory fits like a glove, being in effect a reformulation in different terms of the argument developed earlier. Thus, 'valence' may be seen as a parallel to the concept of 'matrices', 'synergy' as akin to 'bisociation'.

Listeners' response

Not unexpectedly, in view of the diversity of these works, listeners' reactions noted during the investigative part of this project varied considerably. On the negative side, occasionally at least, puzzlement, antipathy, even irritation; more positively, certain features tended to be noted with interest by listeners whenever they occurred, even in the very different sound worlds of these works:

(1) inclusion of the human voice, in particular its first appearance in a piece;
(2) inclusion of unexpected *concrète* sounds;
(3) inclusion of sounds of conventional musical instruments;
(4) sudden changes of texture or dynamics, often suggesting structural articulations within a formal scheme;
(5) recurrences of previously heard material, also tending to push the listening process towards longer-term, formal perceptions;
(6) movement of sound between channels, or contrasted spatial distribution of sound elements.

These were found to correspond to those qualities of this music identified at the outset as promising areas of enquiry and likened to Barthes' lexical codes, thus supporting the underlying principle of this project, which was to involve listeners in both the establishment and testing of analytical and evaluative hypotheses.

Bibliography

Barthes, R. (1975) *S/Z*. (tr. Richard Miller). London: Cape
Fennelly, B. (1967) A Descriptive Language for the Analysis of Electronic Music in *Perspectives of New Music*. 6 (Fall/Winter 1967) p79
Henry, O.W. (1970) *The Evolution of Idiomatic and Psychoacoustic Resources as a Basis for Unity in Electronic Music*, p. 256. PhD thesis, Tulane University
Koestler, A. (1976) *The Act of Creation*, London: Hutchinson
Meyer, L. (1973) *Explaining Music*. Berkeley: University of California Press
Schaeffer, P. (1952) *A la Recherche d'une Musique Concrète*. Paris: Editions du Seuil.
Smalley, D. (1981) *Problems of Material and Structure in Electro-acoustic Music*. International Electronic Music Conference, Stockholm (offprint). Stockholm: EMS
Wehinger, R. (1970) Gyorgy Ligeti: *Arikulation* (Aural Score). Mainz, Schott

Discography

Berio, L. (1961) *Visage*. Turnabout TV 34046 S
Cage, J. (1958) *Fontana Mix*. Turnabout TV 34046 S
Ligeti, G. (1958) *Artikulation*. Wergo 60059
Stockhausen, K. (1956) *Gesang der Jünglinge*. DGG 138 811
Stockhausen, K. (1966) *Telemusik*. DGG ST 643 546
Varèse, E. (1958) *Poème Electronique*. Columbia MS 6146

A real-time music-structure generating system for microcomputer

Michael Greenhough
Department of Physics, University College, Cardiff, UK

This paper describes the underlying philosophy and mode of operation of a computerised music-structure generating system. The system's principal object is to enable the user to search for and arrive at structures which are satisfactory for the task in hand, without needing to specify them explicitly.

We routinely elicit satisfactory timbres from conventional instruments without a knowledge of the mechanisms which map the physical input to the acoustical output space. The system described attempts to extend this intuitive kind of control to the higher levels of music structure. Essential features of the system are an extremely high degree of constraint on possible output structures, plus real-time operation.

The stochastic event-generating algorithm introduces context-free and context-sensitive redundancy into the pitch, rhythmic and other data. The user exercises indirect, overall control via joysticks and graphical displays. The devising of useful mappings between joystick positions and the controlling probability arrays is discussed.

KEYWORDS real-time, stochastic, intuitive, microcomputer, music-structure, MIDI (musical instrument digital interface).

Introduction

The system described in this paper has developed over a number of years from a melody-generating program running on a mini computer and driving an analogue synthesiser, to the present version which uses a personal computer to generate up to sixteen interdependent voices on a MIDI synthesiser. The detailed mechanics of the generating algorithm are given in Greenhough (1985). Here I propose to give a brief account of the underlying philosophy and organisation of the system, followed by illustrations of particular aspects of its operation.

At the heart of the system is a random number generator subject to various constraints. This determines pitches, durations and dynamic levels as well as the distribution of rests and sounded notes. It also controls the horizontal, vertical and diagonal relationships between these parameters, typically on a time scale extending up to a few seconds. The

161

user exerts a high-level, indirect kind of control over the output through the manipulation of joysticks and graphical displays.

The traditional way of generating musical structures on this level is, of course, to specify the distinctive features (pitches, durations etc.) in an explicit fashion. In contrast we normally control lower-level features such as timbre and vibrato indirectly via conventional instruments, with no explicit reference to, or indeed knowledge of, the physical variables (waveforms, spectra, envelope shapes etc.) underlying them.

There seem to be two principal reasons why we can control musical instruments in such an intuitive fashion.

(i) As real-time systems they provide immediate acoustic feedback to the player in response to any change in the controlling input (bow pressure, embouchure etc.).

(ii) They allow access to only an extremely limited region of the whole acoustic space. Moreover this region is characterised by a density of useful musical sounds which is incomparably higher than that for the space as a whole.

The system described here is an attempt to extend this technique of intuitive control, so clearly successful for timbre, to a higher level of musical structure. The approach taken was to design software with properties analogous to those in (i) and (ii) above.

Since real-time operation is essential, the degree of sophistication of the event-generating process and the number of voices it can handle are limited by the processing power available. For the purposes of this experiment the timbres available from a commercial MIDI synthesiser are considered quite acceptable. Since there are therefore no signal processing demands, a professional personal computer (currently, an IBM-PC) makes an adequate host for the structure-generating software.

The limitations in (ii) are translated as very tight constraints on access to 'musical-structure space'. The basic nature of the designed-in constraints should be such that the system has some natural tendency to produce 'musical' structures in the same way that, say, a guitar has a tendency to produce 'musical' sounds. It is instructive at this point to consider the kind and degree of acoustic constraints which characterise traditional instruments.

Let us take the guitar as representative of these. The sources of vibration (i.e. the strings) are uniform, one-dimensional to a good approximation, and have boundary conditions imposed by the bridge and nut which all but prevent movements at the ends. These are severe constraints indeed. Unless specially contrived or selected in this way vibrating objects will, of course, tend to be made of non-uniform materials and be three-dimensional, arbitrarily shaped affairs which produce correspondingly arbitrary acoustical signals when excited. Individual guitar sounds, however, consist of almost perfect harmonic series and occupy the minutest sub-region of the total sound space. Furthermore the string's fundamental frequency of vibration, potentially a continuous variable, is quantised by the fretting.

These constraints render the guitar's output very low in acoustic information. This is partly compensated for by involuntary variations in the direction and amplitude of the plucking action. In addition the player may add further information at will by varying the right-hand position, the amount of vibrato and other factors. By controlling the acoustic information rate around some moderate level the player ensures that the guitar's sound retains both interest and intelligibility. The micro-temporal features having thus been taken care of, to some extent, the player may concentrate on medium- and longer-term properties of the music.

Can we now device an analogous system which operates on the musical level of 'phrases' and 'sentences' and frees the user from needing to know and worry about organisation at this level?

Mechanics of the system

If the user does not specify the musical parameters of events explicitly then this information has to come from somewhere in the system. It derives, in fact, from a random generator which is constrained by a collection of probability distributions. These are best thought of as being of two types, which can be illustrated for the case of pitch as follows.

(i) Context-free distributions which determine the locally prevailing harmony. A programmed series of these can be used to form a chord progression which all voices can be made to follow.
(ii) Context-sensitive distributions representing the first- and higher-order differences between an event's pitch and that of a small number of context reference points chosen by the user.

Precisely the same scheme is used to generate data governing the duration, dynamic level and rest/sound attribute of the note events.

Choosing these simple but severe constraints results in a massive reduction in data and processing requirements and, necessarily, in the number of possible output structures. Simultaneously we acquire a dramatically reduced and, I maintain, enriched structure space to explore and select from.

In a typical operating configuration the pitch of a particular voice may be controlled by a context-free distribution, plus 1st- and 2nd-difference distributions which determine its relationship to each of two reference points. For example a series of context-free pitch distributions might lead the voice through a harmonic progression and the two pairs of fixed 1st- and 2nd-difference distributions might control each note's pitch in relation to, respectively, that of a note one beat back horizontally and that of a simultaneous note in, say, the bass voice. This would involve a total of 5 probability arrays each having potentially dozens of elements. These are displayed on the computer screen and can be modified at run time by a movable cursor. Thus the user has very fine control over the statistical properties of the output. The system configuration at the end of a successful session of refinement may be stored and called up subsequently as a starting point for further exploration. Such a set-up is suitable for assessment and development work involving leisurely, extensive explorations of the available structure space.

Often, however, we wish to further reduce and enrich the structure space. For example, for real-time performance using joysticks or other input devices we might want a space with just a few dimensions which enclose an anomalously high proportion of points of interest.

We could reduce the size of the space in some *ad hoc* way by limiting it to sub-regions which systematic exploration had shown were particularly rich in useful or appealing structures. Such empirically defined regions would most likely need to be represented in a piecewise fashion, which would be inelegant and involve a large quantity of data. The technique would have something in common with the implementation of collections of text-book rules. The resulting version of the system would be a move away from a structure generator and towards a kind of structure 'sampler', to borrow a term from current sound synthesis practice.

A space-limiting method more in keeping with the philosophy of the system would involve the application of some simple mathematical operation to modify a probability distribution according to the value of a single index. The operation should be chosen so as to produce a set of distributions related through this index to some significant musical property.

A linear scaling operation performed on the elements of a distribution will have no effect because they represent only relative probabilities. However, an exponentiation operation, whereby each element is raised to some power (the index mentioned above), shows some very interesting properties. We need not concern ourselves with normalisation here as this is taken care of implicitly at a later stage in the processing. What matters is how the relative probabilities, $[p(i)]^x$ change with the exponent x. It is convenient to regard each element $p(i)$ as variable between zero and unity. Since raising an element to the power of unity leaves it unchanged we can regard a distribution as exhibiting its standard form when $x = 1$.

Figure 1 shows the variation with x of a pitch distribution which in its standard form would generate notes typical of a major scale. It can be seen that x acts as a kind of contrast control. As x increases from 1, probable pitches become more probable and improbable ones less probable. For this distribution, only roots, 3rds and 5ths survive beyond $x = 3$, and eventually only the roots remain.

As x decreases from 1, so the differences in relative probabilities become less marked until we hit the equiprobable chromatic case at $x = 0$. As x goes negative the contrast reverses, formerly improbable pitches becoming increasingly probable and vice versa. In the region beyond $x = -2$, where former 'major' pitches fade out, we are left with a pentatonic

A real-time music-generating system 165

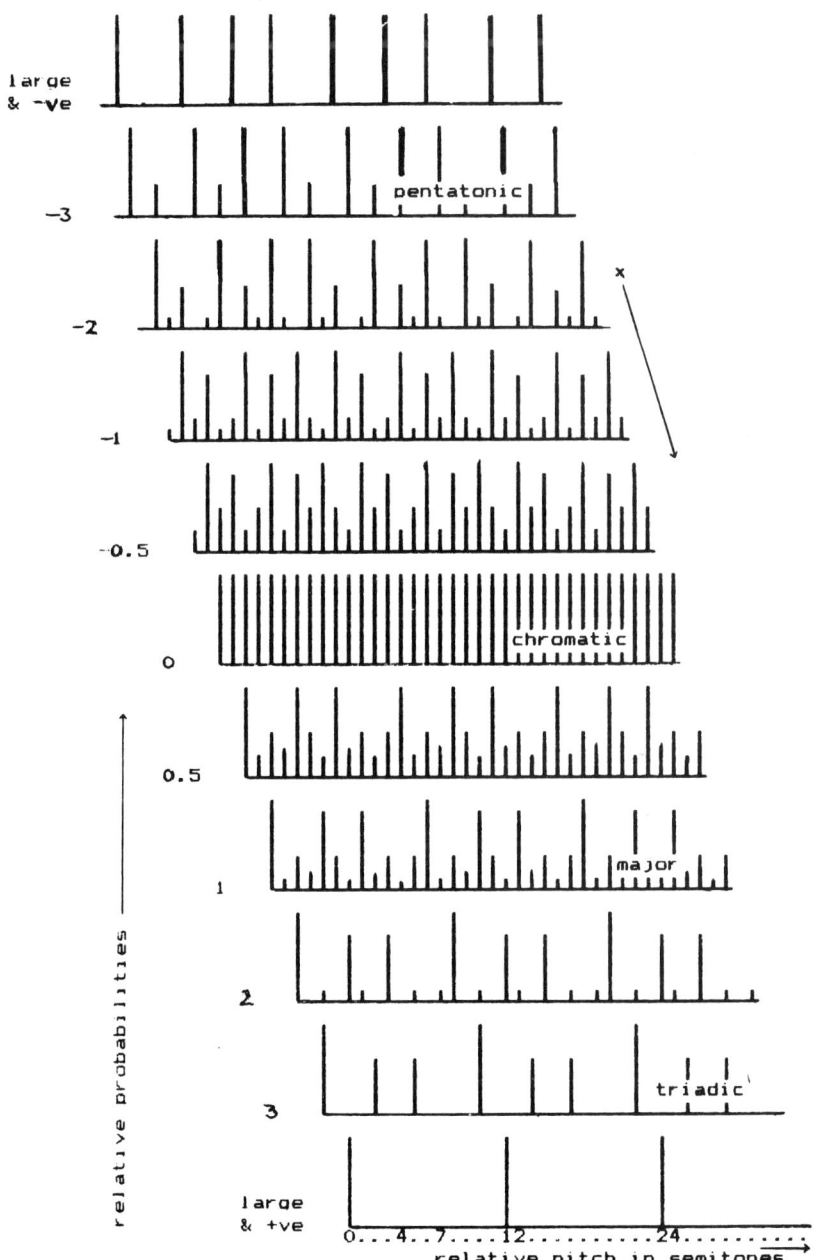

Figure 1 An exponentiation operation on elements of a pitch distribution enables gross control of tonality via the exponent x.

scale. Going further negative still, all that remains are the constituent notes of a major triad. These survive because at $x = 1$ they were given slightly lower probabilities than the other two 'black' notes.

We have thus acquired a single parameter, x, which functions as a kind of gross tonality control when applied to certain pitch distributions. The control is also useful when applied to distributions which govern other features of the output.

For example, a distribution of melodic intervals (i.e. first-order differences of pitch) which is characteristic of much traditional musical material would tend to have low probabilities for 'dissonant' intervals. If this is taken as the standard form (when $x = 1$) then at one end of the contrast control's range (x large and negative) the output will be dominated by, say, tritones and sevenths, and at the other end we will get only the remaining intervals, with a continuous interpolation possible between these extremes.

In a similar fashion we can exercise gross control of the rhythmic properties of the output. Figure 3(a) shows a distribution which gives, for each successive point in time, the probability that an event will start there. This gives us the possibility of imposing temporal patterns on the output with different degrees of regularity and of subtlety. If the exponential operation is applied to these time distributions then we can effect a continuous transition between two extreme cases representing complementary rhythms. This is a rhythmic analogue of the diatonic-pentatonic transition in Figure 1. The system always sees pitch as analogous to time and therefore, necessarily, pitch interval as analogous to duration.

It should be noted that the forms of higher-order distributions are also important here. If particular rhythmic features are to be evident in the output then it is necessary that the first-difference distribution (representing now the durations of events) contains appropriate non-zero probabilities. Similarly, all the pitches implied by, say, a chromatic distribution will actually appear in the output only if appropriate intervals are allowed in the 1st-difference distribution. For example, forbidding intervals comprising odd numbers of semitones would prevent half of the pitches from being expressed. In general the expression of a feature apparently encouraged by one distribution may be prevented because the context provided by higher- and lower-order distributions fails to allow it. This interdependence of distributions is a consequence of the difference-method simplification which has been adopted. It follows that an attractive (or obnoxious) feature may, as it were, lie dormant throughout extensive changes in the system parameters and then suddenly manifest itself as a result of some apparently unrelated change. It is tempting here to speak of "recessiveness" and, indeed, genetic analogies are proving to be generally fruitful in the further development of the system, as will be seen later.

Controlling the interrelationship of pitch and time

It is clear that the four parameters which the system controls (pitch, duration, dynamic level and the rest/sound attribute) are not generally considered as independent. There are many circumstances and many ways in which we might want them to interact. Perhaps the most important of these interactions, and the most susceptible to some kind of quantitative treatment, is that between pitch and time. As before, there are always *ad hoc* methods of ensuring that, for example, particular pitch or intervallic behaviour is associated with particular points in time. What would be appealing here, though, and consistent with the philosophy of the system, would be some simple mechanism which could be made to favour certain appropriate pitch-time relationships in a largely automatic fashion. Such a mechanism has been devised and implemented as described below.

The distribution in Figure 3(a), for example, gives the probability of an event starting, as a function of time. Generally speaking, events are more likely to start on stronger beats than on weaker ones. It follows that these time distributions contain ready-made measures of the metric importance of each point in time. Consider the case where the probabilities of Figure 3(a) are now applied (appropriately scaled) to a context-free pitch distribution as the exponent x, as described above. The result will be that on strong beats (x large and positive) principal pitches will become especially highly favoured and on weak beats (x large and negative) secondary pitches will predominate. Thus the rhythmic context automatically controls the distribution of pitches. If the scaling factor is carefully chosen the effect can be to add extra plausibility to traditional tonal output.

An example of system output

The system's rendering of a popular "standard", George Shearing's "Lullaby of Birdland", will be used to illustrate various features of its operation. A 32-bar chorus is shown in Figure 2. No melodic or rhythmic information from the original is involved here, only the chord sequence which influences the output in the following manner. A programmed series of context-free probability distributions, reflecting the harmonic progression which characterises the song, is used to control all six voices in parallel.

However, each voice is given a different perspective on these, appropriate to its function, by means of the pitch-time interaction mechanism described earlier.

Figure 2 Output resulting when the system is following the chord progression of George Shearing's "Lullaby of Birdland" and the voices are subject to a number of horizontal and vertical constraints, shown in subsequent figures.

Figure 2 *Cont'd.*

Bass line

Figure 3(a) shows the time distribution for the bass line. The particular effect of this on the pitch behaviour is that on strong beats the bass sees only the 'triadic' notes of the prevailing scale. (As there are no dynamic variations here a strong beat is simply a point in time where there is a high probability of an event starting.) On weaker beats it sees also 6ths and 7ths (as can be seen for example in bars 6 and 16).

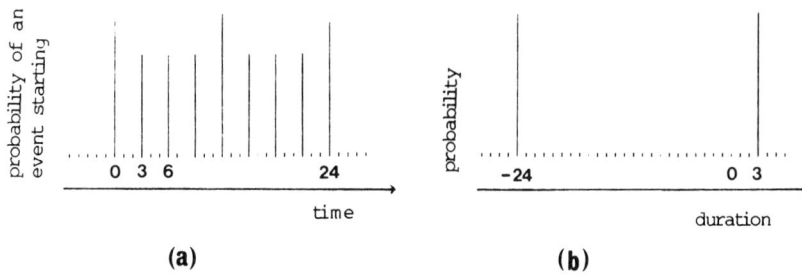

Figure 3 (a) Time distribution and (b) duration (1st-difference of time) distribution for the bass voice. The combined effect is to enforce quarter-notes (3 small time divisions) throughout. The time distribution extends only locally. Here two bars (24 divisions) are used. The duration of "–24" simply forces a continuous recycling through the time segment.

At all points in time it is the pitch of the bass note which is first to be generated. It has no vertical pitch reference points and therefore no knowledge of the behaviour of the other voices. It has just one horizontal reference point, one quarter-note back, through which its melodic movement is controlled. The distributions controlling the 1st and 2nd differences between the next note's pitch and this reference point are shown in Figure 4. It can be seen that the 1st-difference distribution forbids repeated notes but encourages movements by 1 and 2 semitones (2nds) and, to a lesser extent, 3, 4 and 5 semitones (3rds and 4ths). These latter simply allow movements between primary notes as long as a particular chord prevails (here, often only two beats), whereas the 2nds will tend to be taken across chord boundaries. This can be seen in the first two bars. The 2nd differences have a broad peak around the centre, that is, there are relatively high probabilities of small or zero changes in the 1st differences. This tends to maintain the direction of movement, whether ascending or descending, leading to a reasonable exploration of the voice's set range (A1 to E3) and preventing excessive short-term oscillations. In common with the others these distribution forms were simply set by ear and are clearly still far from optimal.

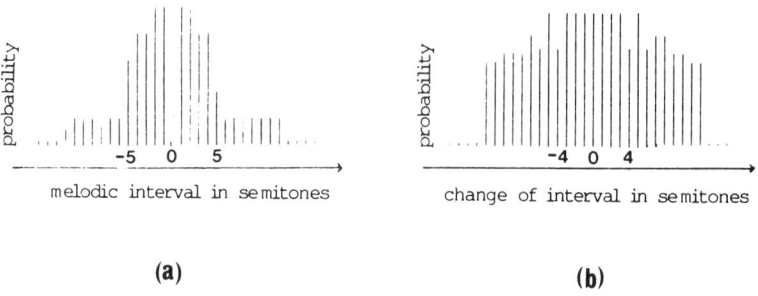

Figure 4 Horizontal control of pitch behaviour for bass. (a) moderates melodic movement through 1st-difference of pitch, (b) moderates turning behaviour of voice through 2nd-differences.

Accompaniment

This was engineered by means of chords made up of four notes with strong vertical interdependence.

Figure 5 shows the time probability distribution and its 1st difference which are shared by the four voices allocated to the accompaniment. These distributions are contrived to give a characteristic rhythmic pattern with only occasional variations which break up the chord. With respect to the bass the strong beats are placed a twelfth-note early to give a syncopation which the song seems to demand. However, pitch behaviour is, for obvious reasons, made to be dependent on the immediately succeeding bass note and harmony over which the notes are sustained.

The lowest of these four voices has two pitch reference points:
(i) horizontally, the pitch prevailing one quarter-note back in time. The related 1st-difference distribution (not shown) just moderates the melodic movement.
(ii) vertically, the pitch of the simultaneous note in the bass voice. The 1st-difference distribution (Figure 6(a)) maintains the vertical separation at intervals between 3 and 19 semitones (3rds and 12ths) with the emphasis on 7 through 16 semitones (5ths through 10ths).

Each of the three higher accompaniment voices has a single pitch reference point in its immediate lower neighbour and a typical 1st-

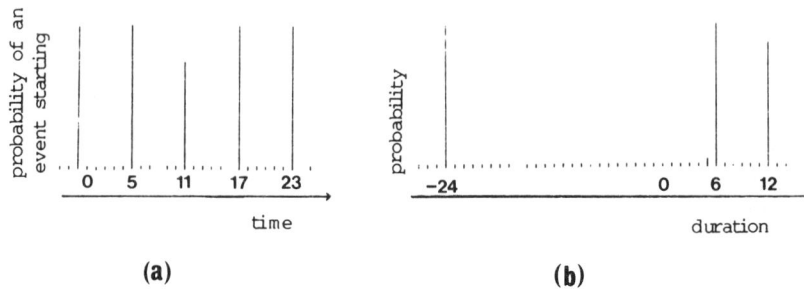

Figure 5 (a) Time distribution and (b) duration distribution for the four accompaniment voices. The combined effect is to force a repeated pattern with slight variations.

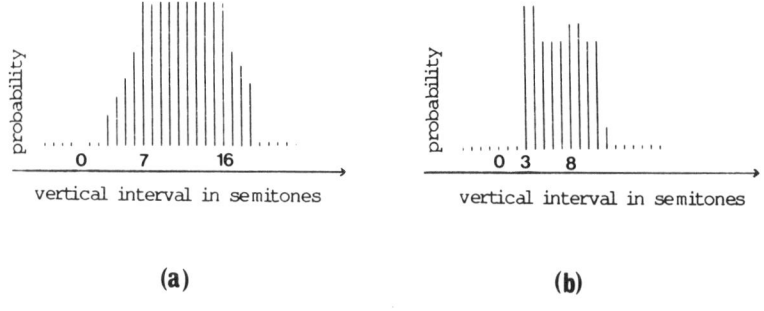

Figure 6 (a) 1st-difference of pitch distribution controlling vertical spacing of the lowest accompaniment voice above the bass. (b) as (a) but for vertical spacing between accompaniment voices.

difference distribution is given in Figure 6(b). The effect is to help keep the voicing fairly tight. More conventional constraints, such as the avoidance of certain repeated notes in the chord, are not easy to implement using the system's natural controlling mechanisms, though they could be contrived. The horizontal behaviour of these three higher voices is unconstrained, so they are completely dominated by the vertical constraints, which can therefore be made quite tight without the risk of 'impasse'. The time distribution (Figure 5) is such that the four voices are restricted to the constituent notes of the prevailing chord.

Solo voice

The time distribution and its 1st difference, given in Figure 7(a,b), are quite permissive here, and it can be seen that the voice has rather more adventurous rhythmic behaviour. As with the accompaniment the strong beats are set a twelfth-note ahead of the bass. The 1st differences allow note durations of twelfth, sixth, quarter and half-notes. A 2nd-difference distribution (not shown), which therefore controls the change of duration, has a sharp peak at zero. This will give any duration value which happens to occur a tendency to persist over consecutive notes. The effect of this can clearly be seen, for example, in bars 3,4 & 5.

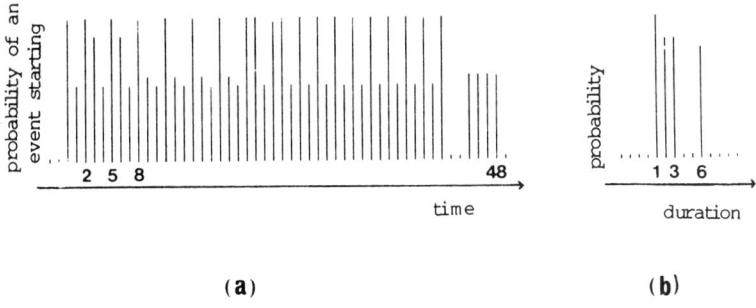

Figure 7 (a) Time distribution and (b) duration distribution for solo voice.

The pitch of the voice is controlled via two horizontal reference points.

(i) The pitch of the previous note. The associated difference distributions (not shown) are set only to moderate the melodic movement, though the second reference point, which has equal influence, will often force compromises.
(ii) The pitch of the note one bar back in time. The associated 1st-difference distribution has a peak around zero which encourages small intervals between pitches exactly a bar apart. The 2nd-differences have a peak at zero, which will encourage any such intervals to persist. This tends to generate fragments of tonal sequences, which are most evident where a note duration value persists for some time.

Since it has no vertical reference points this solo voice has no knowledge of the other voices and is kept in check only by its set range (G_4 to C_6) and the fact that it has to follow the chord sequence. In this latter respect, however, it has greater freedom than the other voices because many of its beats are weak (Figure 7) and so at these points its pitch can be any note of the related scale.

Conclusions

The particular performance shown in Figure 2 is typical of the raw output for the given settings of reference points, voice ranges and probability distributions and has not been specially selected or edited in any way. Given the extremely simple nature of the system's designed-in constraints the results are promising. Some parts of the example are musically very unsatisfactory. This is due to a number of factors including an unhealthy predominance of triadic notes and unfortunate voicings in the accompaniment. It is felt that considerable improvements could be made by more extensive listening and adjustments of the controlling probability data.

In general, changes in just a few data can result in output which is dramatically different yet retains its intelligibility. A wide variety of musical effects can be engineered in this way. The system could be used as an aid to the construction of large-scale pieces if comprehensive editing facilities were added. A commercial editing software package or a dedicated hardware MIDI sequencer would fit the bill quite well.

Recent developments

The generating algorithm which forms the core of the system naturally takes up a high proportion of the processing time in spite of being written in (8086) assembly language. We are currently implementing a version of the algorithm in the parallel-processing language, Occam, which will run on a network of transputers. The absolute speed of these devices alone would probably justify their use here but because music is such an eminently parallel phenomenon they seem a particularly appropriate choice for future developments. It will thus become possible to use more context reference points and higher-order differences for controlling the musical relationships. The number of voices could also be increased and the control of other parameters contemplated.

On a more fundamental level the user-system interaction is being enhanced by means of a new controlling procedure which operates in a manner similar to natural selection in the evolution of species. A sample musical structure is output which the user judges and responds to with "good", "bad" or "indifferent". The sample is then automatically analysed in terms of system parameters (the various order differences of pitch and time) and the probabilites making up the generating distributions are then adjusted positively, negatively or not at all, according to the user's response. This is analogous to the varying reproductive success of natural organisms automatically adjusting the frequency of their characterising genes in the species gene pool. Extremely complex and appropriate adaptations can arise in this way without the need for any explicit description or knowledge of the goals or processes involved. Evolutionary strategies have been used successfully (Rechenberg, 1973) for solving complex optimisation problems in engineering. Our preliminary results suggests that they could provide viable means for solving musical problems by virtue only of a user's passive knowledge (Gervais & Greenhough, 1987).

Acknowledgements

I am grateful to Jean-Philippe Gervais, Russell Payne and Margaret Shaw, all from the Physics Department, University College, Cardiff, for their contributions to the development of the system.

References

Gervais, J-Ph. & Greenhough, M. (1987) A Microcomputer Based System for Evolving Musical Structures, *Proceedings of the Institute of Acoustics (Reproduced Sound 3)*, 133–140
Greenhough, M. (1985) A Stochastic Algorithm for Real-Time Control of Musical Structures, *Proceedings of the Institute of Acoustics*, **7**, Part 3, 157–164
Rechenberg, Ingo. (1973) *Evolutionsstrategie* (Stuttgart: Frommann Verlag)

Generative models in computer-assisted musical composition

Kevin Jones
Music Division, Trent Polytechnic, Clifton Lane, Nottingham, UK

A number of generative models have been used to facilitate the handling of large amounts of data in computer assisted musical composition. Various modelling techniques are identified and compared. These include fractal (self-similar) models used in both stochastic and non-stochastic contexts.
   A technique is explained which makes use of recursive parallel production systems similar to those which have been used to devise effective models of biological growth. By applying a cyclic sequence of generative rules to divide up the pitch-time-timbre space, complex non-stochastic musical structures may be formed which exhibit multi-level self-similar features. Minor modifications of an initial seeding cycle may produce a variety of different outcomes as in each successive generation the controlling cycle moves in and out of phase with the number of nodes available for further growth.

KEYWORDS computer music, fractals, L-systems, automated composition, machine creativity, musical grammars.

1. Generative systems

It is possible to make use of a variety of generative models as practical tools in computer-assisted music composition. Not only do such models enable large amounts of data or note information to be handled more easily, but they may also open up unique access to new compositional styles and assist the composer's imagination in exploring the unrealized potential of machine creativity.
   A generative model enables a general method to be efficiently encoded in the form of a programmed algorithm which, when applied, will produce a structured set of note data values. Typically these may be defined in terms of parameters such as start time, duration, frequency and intensity. Determinants for various timbral indices may also be incorporated into the model. Alternatively a generative model may be applied over a micro-time scale to control the application of data appropriate to whatever synthesis model is being employed for a particular compositional application.

These techniques can be used in both stochastic contexts involving the targetted allocation of random values, and in non-stochastic contexts where, for example, incremental control of repeated loops or the systematic permutation of sets of sound data may be employed. This range of possible applications has been explored in a variety of compositional protocols.

Approaches concerned with the stochastic definition of overall trends in a large sound mass include the "tendency" masks of Barry Truax (1973) and Koenig (1971), Michael Hinton's IMPAC program (Hinton, 1979) and the granular synthesis techniques described by Roads (1978). This latter approach is a particularly interesting application which enables "clouds" built up from very short sounds to be defined and organized in terms where only definition of overall trends in the general sound shape is necessary, and where any attempt at detailed definition of individual sound-particles would be hopelessly cumbersome, impractical and, indeed, perceptually irrelevant.

A number of procedural music languages and more general generative systems designed for non-stochastic definition of score data have recently been proposed and developed. These enable structures which possess obvious hierarchical or nested relationships to be encoded more efficiently, often using grammatical constructs analogous to linguistic models. These include, for example, AMPLE (Jones, 1986) and Formes (Rodet & Duthen, 1984).

In addition to these practical aspects of sound data definition and control, generative models may be used to explore the compositional possibilities of geometric shapes and other types of natural structures which are capable of formal analysis and description. This classification includes the fractal models which are considered below. However, the area which holds the greatest potential interest to the author is in the construction of arbitrary structure-building models which may loosely relate to conventional musical forms but which are capable of breaking out of their constraints in order to produce a result which is genuinely unexpected. It is to this aspect of generative modelling that the present study is largely addressed.

2. Freedom and constraint

A straight line such as the one in Figure 1 may be used to represent a range of possibilities available for constructing a generative compositional model. The left-hand extreme represents a situation of maximum order where as many rules as are required can be imposed in order to define and realise a particular style.

By definition, the style model must be well-behaved, predictable, and non-creative. If it produces results that break outside the bounds of the original brief then the model is shown to be inadequate and must be modified. Consequently, music produced as a result of realising such a

Generative models 179

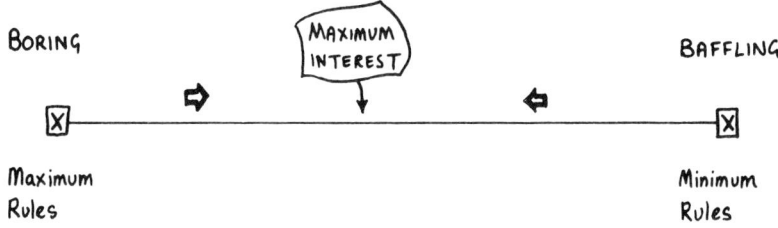

Figure 1 Rule delineation in the design of generative musical models.

model will be predictable and boring.

The other end of the line represents a situation with no rules; in other words totally random sounds. In theory they should hold maximum interest by virtue of their complete unpredictability. In practice, the unordered sounds are impossible for the mind to assimilate and the baffling chaos will soon produce the same effect as that of the opposite extreme: boredom.

Maximum interest occurs when a model is constructed which falls somewhere in between the two extremes. To be genuinely creative the model must needs be capricious and unpredictable, yet within the bounds of conceptually accessible musical reference points which will be perceived in the context of received cultural paradigms.

It is possible to devise models of conventional composition and subject them to progressive distortion by modifying or abandoning certain rules. This approach is typical of some earlier experiments such as those of Hiller and Isaacson (1959) in their "Illiac Suite". It is equivalent to proceeding from left to right along the line representation of Figure 1. Alternatively, an abstract starting model may be devised or appropriated from mathematical or scientific sources and then adapted to musical ends. This approach is equivalent to moving from right to left along the line representation and is closer to that which has been adopted in models described in this paper. An attempt is made to strip down the structuring logic to its barest bones in order to devise generative schemes which will optimise the balance between elegant simplicity of mechanism and structural complexity of generated output.

3. Fractal models

Fractal curves were first identified and named by the French Mathematician, Benoit Mandlebrot (1982). Their essential property is that they exhibit the phenomenon of self-similarity. This means that the overall characteristics of such a curve at a larger scale or macro-level are reflected in similar characteristics on the small scale or micro-level.

To explain this phenomenon Mandelbrot has used the example of a stretch of coastline which may be viewed from outerspace, in an atlas, from an aeroplane or directly on the ground. In each case the detail will be different, yet the same stretch of coastline will always maintain its own distinctly recognisable characteristics at each of these levels. For example one coastline may have a characteristically wavy shape, another may be bumpy, and yet another may be consistently rough and jagged.

A mathematically defined fractal curve will have the same property. Any section of the theoretical curve may be taken and magnified in successive stages and always produce an outline with the same characteristics. If the magnification process is repeated indefinitely, greater detail will constantly be revealed and it becomes apparent that the one dimensional line of the curve is turning into a two-dimensional plane-filling surface. This ambiguous trend, which implies a fractional dimension somewhere between one and two, gives rise to the term 'fractal'.

In practice, of course, when fractal curves are plotted or drawn the detail will be limited by the medium being used. Figure 2 shows a set of four computer-generated fractal curves whose general characteristics range from a moderately wavy shape (a) through to a curve with wilder, jagged characteristic (d). In each case characteristic features of an individual curve's shape are consistent at all perceptual levels, both in overall outline and in detail.

Mandelbrot has shown how such fractal shapes are characteristic of many natural phenomena including landscape features such as mountain outlines. Figure 3 is an example of a landscape generated by a fractal model. The program used to generate this figure, realised on a BBC microcomputer, is capable of producing an infinite number of different variations on the basic theme.

The examples considered so far exhibit statistical self-similarity where characteristic features are perceivable as being generally the same, but not identical. Mandelbrot has also identified families of curves which possess literal self-similarity, where the detail precisely models the shape-characteristics of the overall structure. Figure 4, for example, demonstrates how a straight line can be substituted by the thorn outline (b). Each individual straight line in (b) may then be replaced by a miniature copy of the whole object to produce (c). Each straight line in (c) can then again be replaced by the thorn outline . . . and so on, successively introducing further detail to arrive at (e). This is an example of a set of patterns known as "Koch curves". Many similar curves have

Generative models 181

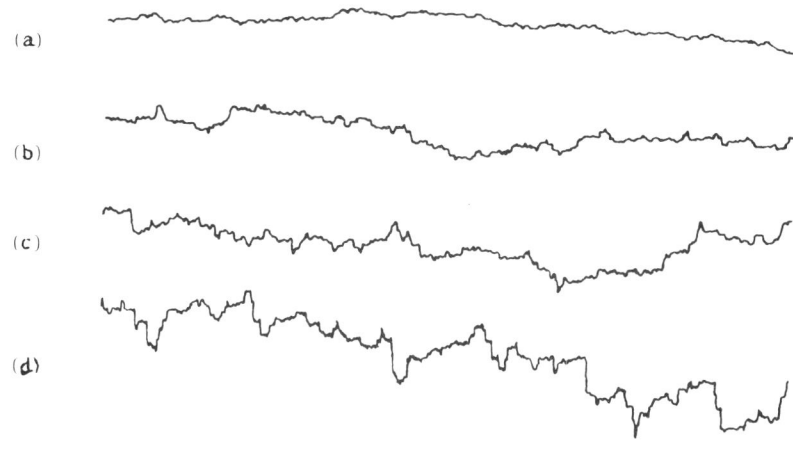

Figure 2 Statistical self-similarity: Four computer-generated fractal curves whose order of variability increases in stages from (a) through to (d).

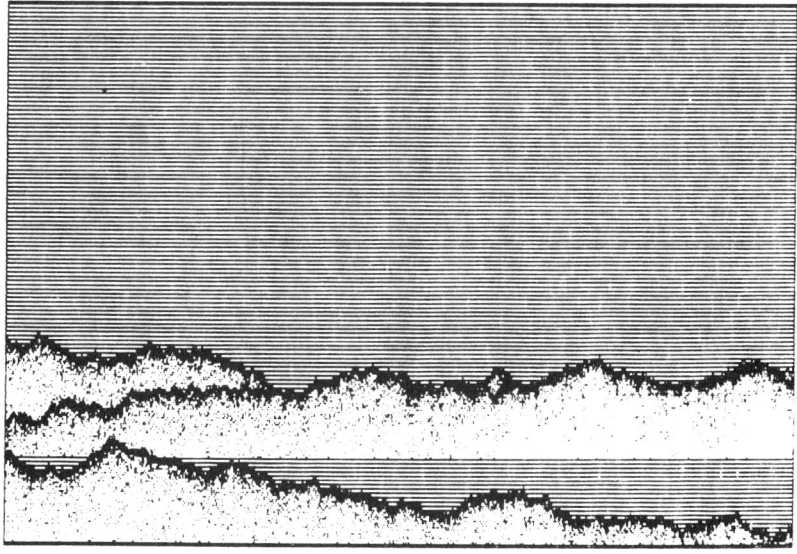

Figure 3 A fractal landscape.

been described and named in the literature (Mandelbrot, 1982).
Fascinated by the properties and potential of fractals a number of authors and composers have suggested ways in which they may be applied musically and have sometimes used them in their own compositions. These include examples of statistical self-similarity (Voss and Clarke, 1978; Bolognesi, 1983; Degazio, 1986; McNabb, 1986) and literal self-similarity (Ames, 1982; Prusinkiewiz, 1986).

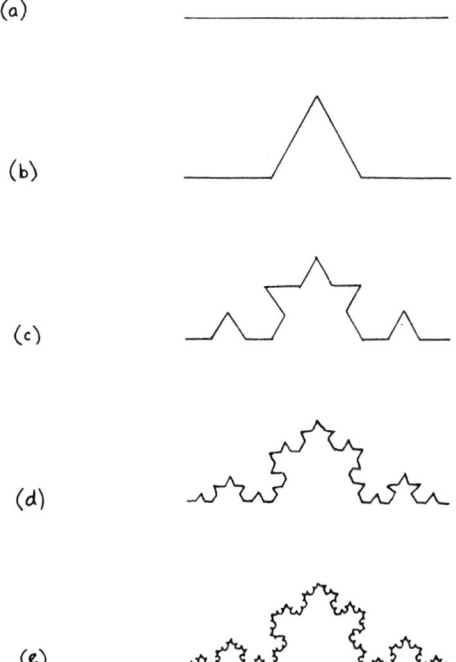

Figure 4 Literal self-similarity in the derivation of a Koch curve.

In contrast to the first example, here the abstract fractal model is applied in a musical context in a rather different way which in the author's opinion produces a distinctive and aesthetically satisfying result.

5. Recursive techniques: space grammars and L-systems

Recursive definition is a powerful technique useful for generating self-similar structures. It means that a computational procedure is defined in terms of itself. An example of a recursive phenomenon likely to be familiar is a style of picture occasionally encountered which shows a man holding a picture which shows himself holding the same picture, which shows himself holding the same picture . . . and so on *ad infinitum*.

The method described in building up the Koch curve of Figure 4 made use of a recursive definition where a "line" was replaced by the "thorn" which itself consisted of four "lines" each of which could be replaced by a "thorn" . . . and so on, until the process had been repeated for a specified number of generations or until the required detail had been reached.

5.1 Line textures, rhythms and trees: space grammars in one dimension

I have used this form of recursive definition in order to generate rhythm patterns where a random choice has been applied to decide at each stage whether a particular length of time may be split up into smaller units, or otherwise stay unsplit and have a single note occupy that duration.

The coding used to define a procedure called rhythm(D), which will fill a duration D with a randomly-generated rhythm pattern, will typically have this outline structure:

rhythm(D) [
 IF randchoice THEN makenote(D)
 ELSE rhythm(D/2) rhythm(D/2)]

To fill a duration D a random choice is made equivalent to tossing a coin. If it is "true" then a note is made (i.e. played or notated) with that duration. Otherwise the same rhythm procedure is called again twice but each time with the duration halved. Clearly, it is likely that in running the procedure in a computer program the duration could keep splitting up indefinitely as the "rhythm" procedure repeatedly calls itself in never-ending loop. To avoid this a test needs to be added to check if the duration value D has fallen below a lower limit at any point, in which case it would have to stick with making a note with that limiting duration and would not be able to split any further. The amended general procedure definition will then look like this:[1]

rhythm(D) [
 IF randchoice OR D < limit
 THEN makenote(D)
 ELSE rhythm(D/2) rhythm(D/2)]

Figure 7 shows a derivation tree for a typical realisation of this procedure, which splits up an initial duration value of 96, with a lower-limit value of 6.

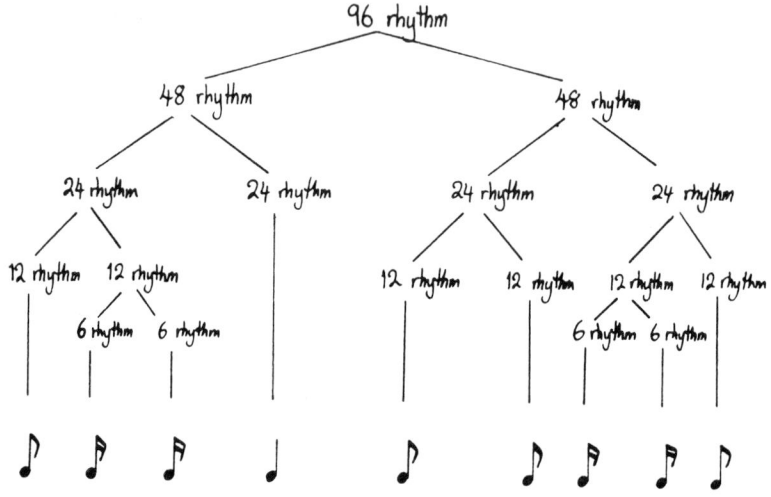

Figure 7 A typical realisation of the recursive rhythm algorithm.

Even though a rhythm has been generated randomly this way, it will always be characterised by a strict metrical format, and as is demonstrated below can give rise to some fascinating self-similar properties.

The random decision which chooses whether to split or make a note does not have to have an even outcome. It can be weighted in favour of greater splitting for busy movement where there is a bias towards semiquavers, or alternatively it may be weighted towards less splitting for a prevalence of longer durations. Similarly the split need not be binary or exactly in half. A one-third/two-thirds split, or a split at the golden section might be interesting alternatives. It is also a simple matter to add provision for the generation of rests.

This generative model is an example of what I have termed a "space grammar", which is described more fully in Jones (1981). However, rather than being a grammar in the strict sense, it turns out that the model is, in fact, closer to a mathematical construct devised for modelling biological growth, known as an L-system, which originates from the work of Lindenmayer (Herman & Rozenburg, 1975).

In general, a grammar contains a set of re-write or production rules which describe a generative process where the symbol on the left hand side of a production rule is replaced by a set of symbols on the right hand side of the rule. The set of symbols used will include "tokens" and "terminals". Tokens represent syntactic categories, or nodes, and will always be replaced by further symbols. Terminals are not replaced and form the items in the terminal string, that is, an utterance or musical phrase generated by the grammar. In consequence grammars are not particularly good at handling the recursive structures which are so useful in defining self-similar relationships.

In contrast, an L-system does not distinguish between tokens and terminals. Repeated generation by the application of recursive re-write rules may continue indefinitely until some terminating condition is reached. This may take the form of a fixed number of generations (as with the Koch curve) or alternatively, as in the rhythm example above, a test to see whether a lower limit of divisibility has been reached which corresponds to a limit of perceptual detail.

The generative hierarchy of Figure 7 produces a parsing-tree network familiar from grammatical representations of structural relationships. I have used a similar patterning process which makes use of recursive procedures in order to generate literal tree representation such as those of Figure 8. This highlights the biological parallels of the generative system and, like the landscape and melody examples above, demonstrates the deeper underlying level at which the fractal model works and which can be expressed through a variety of corresponding forms. As with the other examples above, this is just one of a vast number of similar structures which the program is capable of generating.

5.2 Plane textures: space grammars in two dimensions

This recursive process can be extended into two dimensions to determine the way in which a plane may be divided up. Instead of deciding whether to 'stay put' or to 'split' the horizontal time space into two parts, an additional option is added which permits the plane to split vertically, representing a division of the pitch space. The process is considered in more detail in Jones (1981) from which Figure 9 is reproduced to demonstrate a typical sequence of plane splitting operations.

It is only recently that I have realised the quite startling parallel that exists between this particular structure building device and a similar two-dimensional extension of L-systems described by Lindenmeyer (Herman & Rozenburg, 1975; Mayoh, 1974). In describing a developmental growth model of the leaf *Phascum Cuspidatum* he rotates the plane through forty five degrees to assume a diamond shape, in which subdivisions of the plane may be described in terms of left-hand and right-hand divisions

188 Kevin Jones

Figure 8 Tree-like structures generated using a one-dimensional recursive algorithm.

rather than in terms of horizontal and vertical. In other respects the growth model is remarkably similar to that illustrated by Figure 9. Jones (1981) suggests a way of applying this type of protoscore outline with a specific mapping into traditional musical notation (see also Figure 13 below).

Figure 10 is an alternative realisation of the same plane splitting algorithm which demonstrates the sort of result which may be obtained when extended to deeper levels of detail to produce the type of textural score required for application in granular synthesis models. Two-dimensional statistical self-similarity should be evident in the general pattern relationships at all levels from fine detail in the micro-structure and equivalent shapes at the medium level through to the overall macro-structure.

5.3 Solid textures: space grammars in three dimensions

The same process can be extended to any number of dimensions. Three dimensional application, for example, may be used to generate scores where a number of notional instruments, each with its own pitch-time

Generative models 189

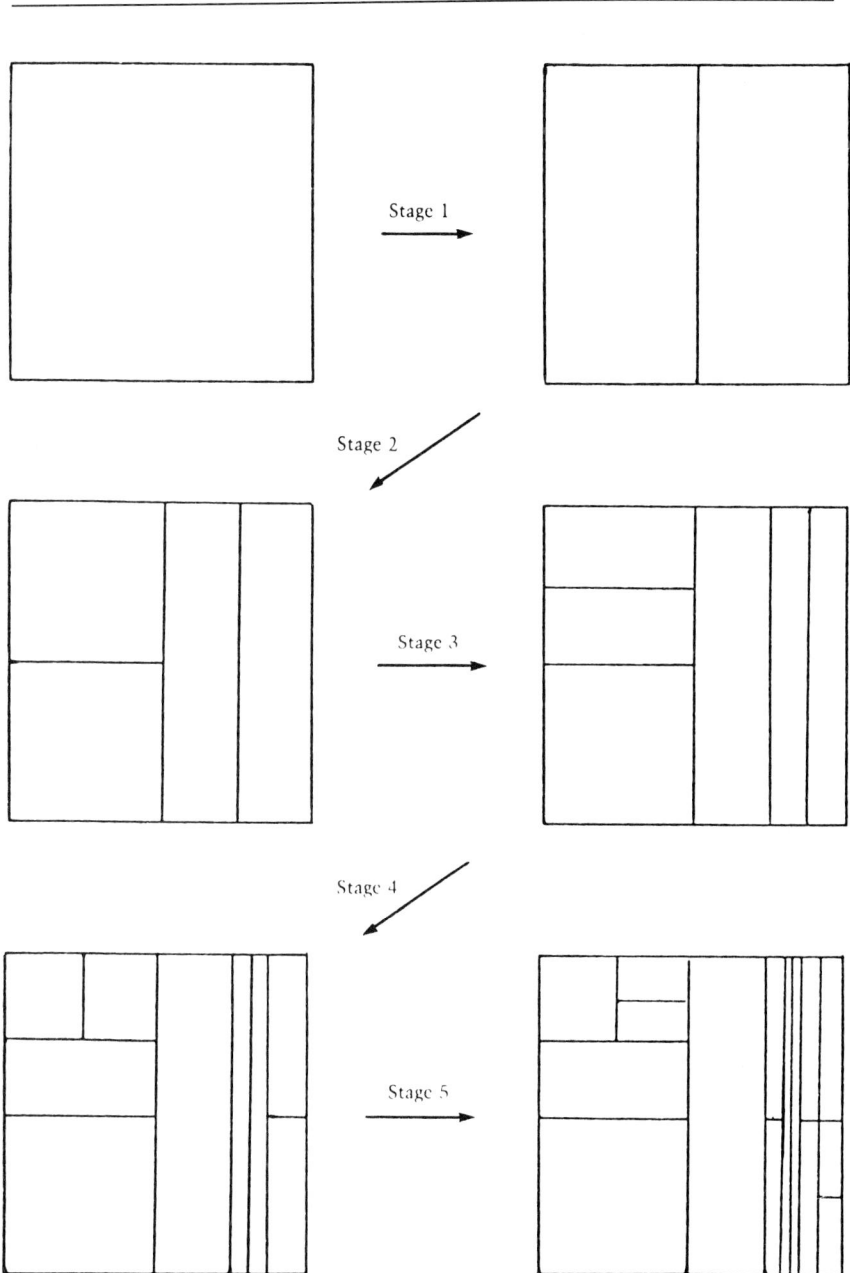

Figure 9 Application of a two-dimensional space grammar to partition a plane vertically and horizontally.

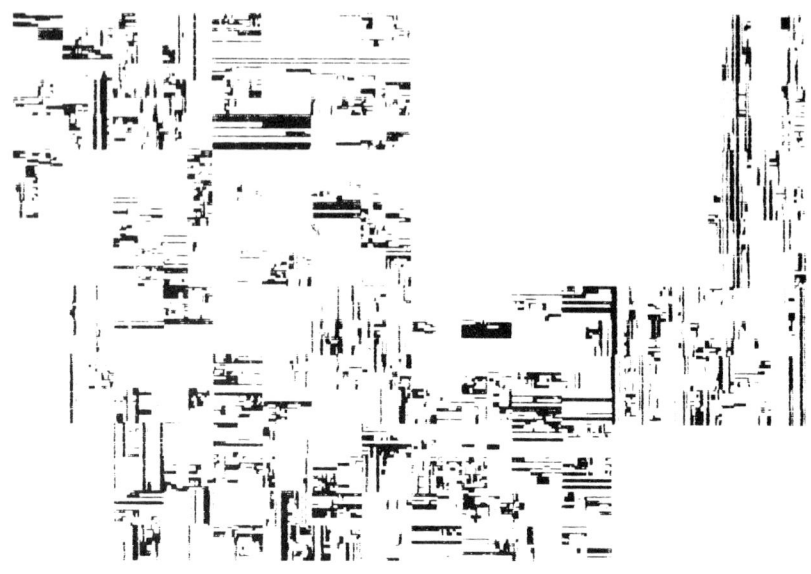

Figure 10 Textural score generated by a two-dimensional stochastic space grammar.

plane, can be represented along an additional timbre axis so that each of a set of instrumental-plane slices line up in sequence, one behind another. Again, this is explained in Jones (1981). The way in which the three-dimensional space is divided up generates self-similar relationships which not only link pitch and time patterns but also the arrangement and balance which links different instrumental timbres. The very simple pattern-generating process can exercise sophisticated control in the growth and correlation of textural homogeneity or textural contrast.

Figure 11(a), for example, could represent moderate activity over a small group of fairly high-pitched timbres at the start, which is followed by a group of sustained notes. This leads into a section of much denser activity across all timbres, with timbral planes at the "back" of the score being characterised by generally higher pitches, and those at the "front" by generally lower-pitched activity. The section then concludes with a brief extension of sustained "chords" similar to those featured at the start.

It is a very simple matter to vary the bias in a space grammar definition to influence the overall character of the generated output.

Generative models 191

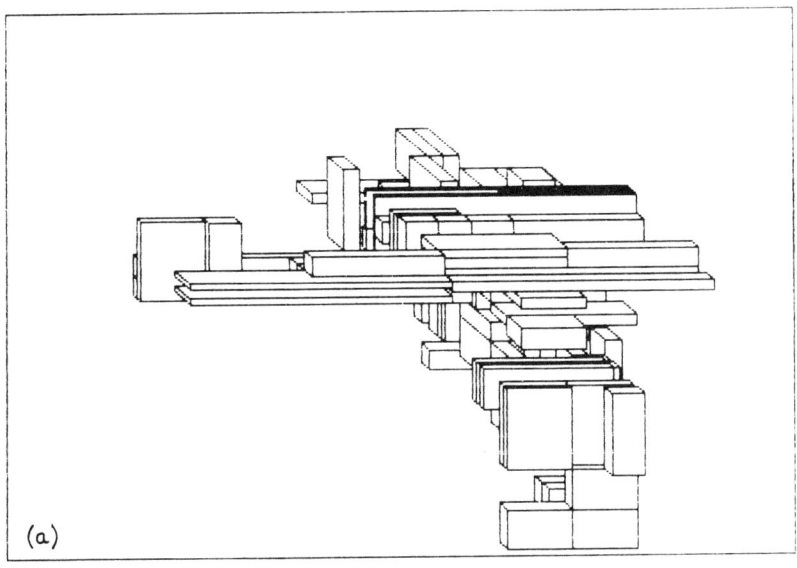

(a)

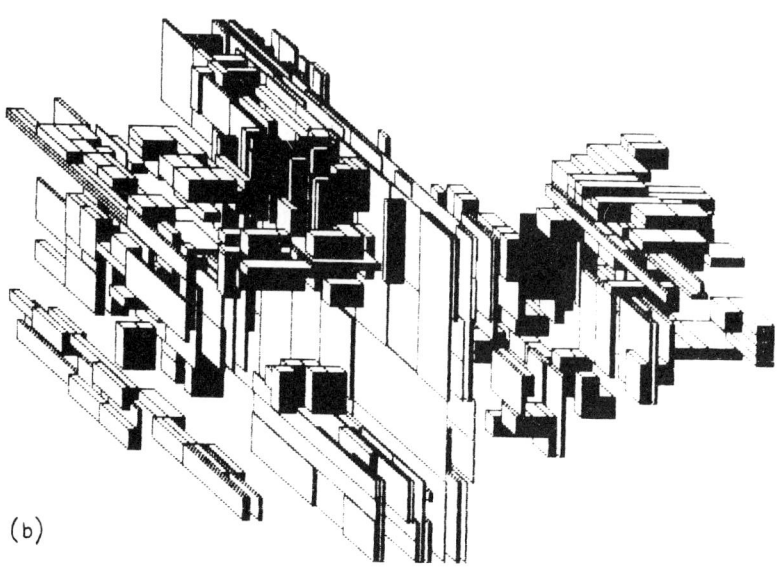

(b)

Figure 11 Solid figures generated by a three-dimensional stochastic space grammar.

6. Cyclic generation

The statistical self-similarity which results from applying the space-grammar model with random decision making may be extended to produce results which exhibit literal self-similar characteristics. A repeated cycle of operations stored as a fixed sequence may be used to determine the order in which splits or terminations are to occur.

6.1 Cyclic generation in one dimension

This can be demonstrated by considering the sequence of operations shown in Figure 12 which divide up the time space to generate a rhythmic pattern. Here a five-fold cycle of operations has been employed, consisting of four splits followed by a termination.

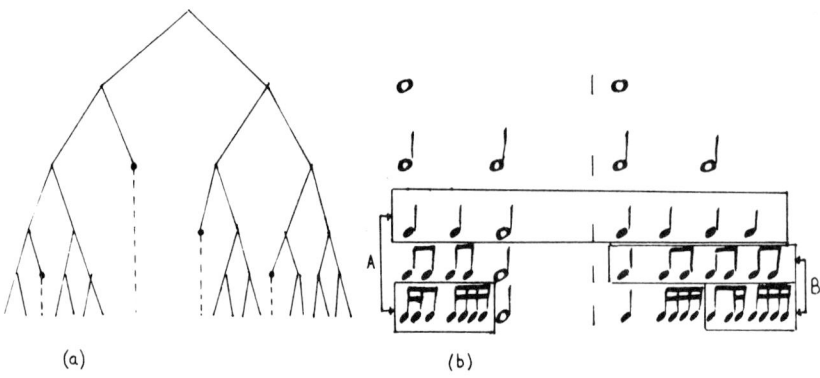

Figure 12 Cyclic application of a space grammar to generate a self-similar rhythmic pattern.

The way in which this sequence has been applied can be read from the top of the splitting diagram and then from left to right across the nodes working down through each generation:

split
split > split
split > terminate > split > split
. . . .
and so on

The corresponding durations in traditional musical notation are shown in Figure 12(b) where the duration of a note in the final rhythmic pattern is determined by its terminal status in the parsing tree.

The inevitable self-similar relationships formed as the controlling cycle moves in and out of phase with the number of nodes available for potential regeneration should be evident. Two examples are highlighted at A and B. They demonstrate the presence of expanded or augmented versions of rhythmic cells in the terminal string which are observable higher up the parsing tree. This results in a high degree of structural integrity.

6.2 Cyclic generation in two dimensions

It is possible to experiment with different ways of using a seeding cycle to control the generative process. One possibility is to define an *a priori* sequence of operations. This sequence can be stored in an array through which a pointer will move step by step returning to the beginning of the cycle array after the last entry has been reached. Another possibility is to generate this controlling sequence at random, so making the result less predictable.

If such an initial random source is being employed by the model, as an alternative to storing a randomly generated control sequence in an array, a single constant can be used to seed the computer's random number generator at the beginning. Then every time a fixed number of random values has been used, say seven for example, the generator can be re-seeded with the same constant so that an identical sequence of pseudo-random numbers will be generated once again. As the random number cycle moves in and out of phase with the decision pattern resulting from the recursive programming logic which the cycle itself is controlling, essentially the same effect will be produced as would occur if an arbitrary fixed set of operations had been set up.

Not only is this approach more straightforward to program, but it also makes the internal generative logic more convoluted, less accessible and therefore more opaque and potentially capable of delivering greater surprises!

Figure 13 is an example of cyclic generation in two dimensions where the precise splitting sequence employed is known only to the computer. Self-similar features can be identified which link both pitch and rhythm in a tightly integrated structure. The highlighted note groups identify just one of a number of similar relationships where augmentation is apparent both pitch-wise and time-wise.

6.3 Cyclic generation in three dimensions

Extending the idea to three dimensions gives even more scope for the generation of complex structures which are full of fascinating multi-level

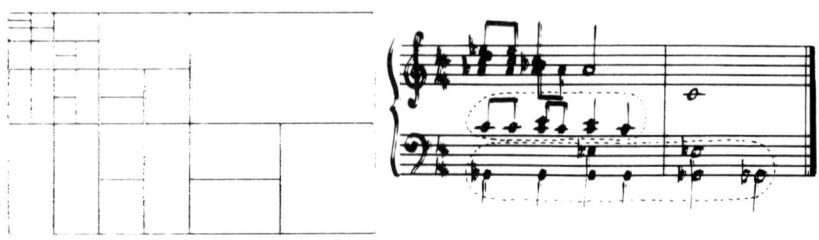

Figure 13 Two-dimensional application of a cyclic space grammar with score mapping.

self similar relationships. Examples of typical structures are given in Figure 14, some of which could be almost be termed "solid fugues"!

Each piece of music generated by the application of such models has an individual character. It may contain *ostinati*, split-chord patterns, textural variations where the same pitch pattern is passed through a variety of timbral combinations, and so on. A tiny variation in the order or content of an initial seeding cycle may result in the generation of significantly different structures.

7. Conclusions

The use of fractal models, L-systems and space grammars in the generation of musical scores offers exciting prospects for computer-assisted composition in both stochastic and non-stochastic contexts. A genuinely unexpected and creative result may be produced in both types of application. A neat recursive algorithm combined with a simple initial seeding idea is capable of generating musical material which possesses a sophisticated complexity combined with a high degree of structural integrity. The techniques may be applied successfully both in the definition of note-based scores and in the generation of granular textures.

Not only do such structures possess interesting musical characteristics, but their intrinsic symmetry and order strikes a deep resonance with intuitive feelings about the nature of pattern in the wider quest to understand the creative process.

Generative models 195

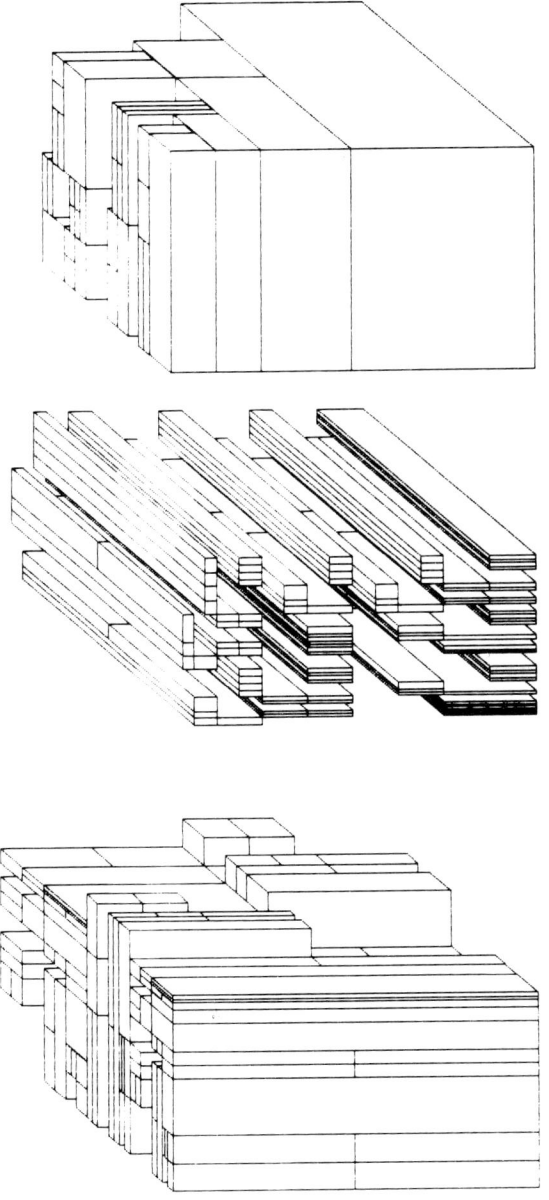

Figure 14 "Solid fugues" generated from a three-dimensional cyclic space grammar.

Notes

1. A practical quirk which may occur if attempting an implementation in some computer languages (such as AMPLE, see Jones (1984)) is that recursive definition of a procedure (or "word" in AMPLE parlance) has to make use of its as yet undefined self, which may confuse the language's interpreter or compiler and make definition theoretically impossible! This rather interesting Catch 22-type logical paradox can be easily dealt with by initially deceiving the computer into a false sense of security with an empty dummy definition of the procedure, in effect just registering its name, which can then be replaced by the genuine definition.

References

Ames, C. (1982) Crystals: recursive structures in automated composition. *Computer Music Journal* 6(3) pp. 46-64
Bolognesi, T. (1983) Automatic composition: experiments with self-similar music. *Computer Music Journal* 7(1) pp. 25-36
Degazio, B. (1986) Musical aspects of fractal geometry. *Proceedings of the International Computer Music Conference 1986* Computer Music Association, California pp. 435-442
Dodge, C. & Bahn, C. (1986) Musical fractals. *Byte* 11(6) pp. 185-196
Herman, G.T. & Rozenburg, G. (1975) *Developmental Systems and Languages* Amsterdam: North-Holland
Hiller, L.A. & Isaacson, L. (1959) *Experimental Music* New York: McGraw Hill
Hinton, M. (1979) *Interactive Music Performance and Composition (IMPAC)* EMS: Stockholm
Jones, K.J. (1981) Compositional applications of stochastic processes. *Computer Music Journal* 5(2) pp. 45-61
Jones, K.J. (1984) *Exploring Music with the BBC Micro and Electron* London: Pitman
Jones, K.J. (1986) Real-time stochastic composition and performance with AMPLE. *Proceedings of the International Computer Music Conference 1986* Computer Music Association, California pp. 309-311
Koenig, G.M. (1971) *Project One* Utrecht, Institute of Sonology
McNabb, M. (1986) Computer music: some aesthetic considerations. In *The Language of Electroacoustic Music* S. Emmerson (ed.) Basingstoke: MacMillan pp. 141-154
Mandelbrot, B.B. (1982) *The Fractal Geometry of Nature* San Francisco: Freeman
Mayoh, B.H. (1974) Multidimensional Lindenmayer organisms. In *L-Systems* G. Rozenburg & A. Salomaa (eds.) New York: Springer-Verlag
Prusinkiewicz, P. (1986) Score generation with L-systems. *Proceedings of the International Computer Music Conference 1986* Computer Music Association, California pp. 455-457
Roads, C. (1978) Automated granular synthesis of sound. *Computer Music Journal* 2(2) pp. 61-62
Rodet, X. & Cointe, P. (1984) FORMES: Composition and scheduling of processes. *Computer Music Journal* 8(3) pp. 32-50
Truax, B.D. (1973) The computer composition — sound synthesis programs POD4, POD5 and POD6. *Sonological Report no. 2* Utrecht, Institute of Sonology
Voss, R. & Clarke, C. (1978) 1/f noise in music: Music from 1/f noise. *Journal Acoust. Soc. America* 63(1)

Reflections on the poetics of time in electroacoustic music

Julio D'Escrivan
Music Department, City University, London, UK

The perception of music is conditioned by the listener's ability to remember and recognize the material he has been presented with and its transformations. The nature of aural perception is linear in that music unfolds gradually, this unfolding distorts the listener's perception of real time creating moments of stasis and change alternatively. The electroacoustic medium allows the exact reproduction of the sound-event and therefore of its unfolding. The manipulation of these factors and the *virtual time* to which this gives rise are the means of shaping the listener's memory and his perception of musical pace. Through the use of *mimesis* and *quotation* the composer may determine the flow of time in his work, while recording allows him to reproduce time itself as borne by the sound object.

KEYWORDS   poetics, time, refrain, quotation, texture, electroacoustic.

In his book *Art and Scholasticism*, the French philosopher Jacques Maritain comments that no matter how purely intelligible in itself, beauty is perceived in the senses and through the senses. The intuition of artistic beauty is opposite to the abstraction of scientific truth. In the latter the task of the intellect is speculation in order to bring the mind to conform to reality: it is the pursuit of truth (Maritain, 1974, p. 34). Our subject is musical composition, and our basic premise is that composition is an Art and not a Science, its commitment is to producing works not concepts. Even when a scientific discourse is invited by the technical depth and complexity of a piece of music, the most important quality of the work is its appeal to the *ear*; for music posing as scientific research makes poor science. The converse is also true. Because of all this it may be concluded that our speculation is that of the composer who relies more on his ears than on extramusical ideas in order to create his sound-world.

The composition of electroacoustic music is articulated through the manipulation of *time* perceived. *Time* is therefore a *poetic* element ('Poetics' understood as the theory of artistic production as opposed to 'aesthetics', the theory of the beautiful in artistic production).

The history of music creation, which together with its political, social and economic circumstances generates the history of music, has been a constant struggle to master the properties of sound, in a search for beauty heard. From the earliest times, man has tried to infuse his ideas with permanence. At its most basic level he has transmitted his knowledge orally, from one generation to the next. At a higher level he has recorded his thought in symbols. The development of writing and consequently of literacy is the fruit of this on-going communicational effort.

The latter part of the 20th century has seen the advent of recording devices capable of literally duplicating "the message". The recording of sound and light has seen the dawn of a new "audio-visual" tradition, that in which we actually preserve the spoken word, the image seen. A kind of oral tradition of the second order, one heightened by the visual, is the hallmark of our century. We may say that, with regard to the past, when words and 'frozen' images were the means to record events there is a difference in kind: *in our time we are able to record time itself*. Not the plot of a novel, but an actual unfolding of that plot –one of many possible– in real time, together with its suggestion of time imagined: virtual time (as in the case of the cinema). Not the score of a piece of music but the *actual interpretation* of the music, and in the case of an electroacoustic piece of tape music, not an interpretation, but the music *itself*[1].

Thus the *course* of time is being recorded, both in the inexorability of time passing and in the poetic subtlety of time suggested. Let us make an analogy with the cinema. Andrey Tarkovsky, the Russian film director, in his book *'Sculpting in Time'*, comments "The dominant, all-powerful factor of the film image is rhythm, expressing the course of time within the frame" (Tarkovsky, 1986, p. 113), which is to say that the rate at which the different audio-visual images succeed each other gives rise to a 'virtual' time.

Working in the electroacoustic medium today, a composer has at his disposal the resources to record and process sounds, as well as the means to synthesize them. For the purpose of our discussion, we shall concentrate on recorded sounds and its implication for the composer. Because we are dealing with *recordings of sound* and not the *sounds themselves*, we find that the basic untreated material *is already imbued with time*.

To borrow Trevor Wishart's terminology (Wishart, 1985), the *gestural-structure of the sound-object* is fixed; The imprint which the sound bears in its spectrum and envelope, as a consequence of the manner in which it was produced and *shaped in time*, is fixed. When we playback a sample[2] at a different rate to the one at which it was recorded, the corresponding *gestural-structure* is proportional to the original one, never different in kind[3]. Commenting on gesture, Denis Smalley writes: "If we do not know

---

[1] Some composers hold the view that a given sound diffusion is an interpretation of the taped piece. However, with the advent of digital MIDI controller instruments, for real time interpretation, merely controlling the amplitude of the music pales in comparison as an interpretative device.

what caused the gesture, at least we can surmise from its energetic profile that it could have been caused, and its spectromorphology will provide evidence of the nature of such a cause. Causality, actual or surmised, is related not only to the physical intervention of breath, hand, or fingers, but also to natural and engineered events, visual analogies, psychological experiences felt or mediated through language and paralanguage, indeed any occurrence which seems to provoke a consequence, or consequence which seems to have been provoked by an occurrence" (Smalley, 1986, p. 82).

Preserving the gestural structure is important because it preserves the time imprint of the sound event, it "freezes" time. In Tarkovsky's words: "Editing brings together shots which are already filled with time, and organises the unified, living structure inherent in the film and the time that pulsates through the blood vessels of the film, making it alive, is of varying rhythmic pressure", (Tarkovsky, 1986, p. 114). He also points out that time flows through the film not because, but in spite of the editing.

The task of the composer is to give order to his "shots"/samples, and the way in which he groups them and tailors them gives rise to the musical argument: the way in which he emphasizes or contradicts the *inherent time* in them determines the flow of musical time.

The recording of a sound event may be fragmented into segments. According to their length they may or may not show kinship to the original sample. This is a common technique in electroacoustic music. If the fragments of a sample are tailored as sudden onsets with an immediate decay so as to make possible their rapid iteration, this will lead, according to the speed of the iteration, to a continuum between the fragment of the gesture and a texture with more or less differentiated grain[4]; this *attack-effluvium continuum* generates *texture* (using terminology from Smalley, 1986).

We may think of texture as being the simultaneous unfolding of *many* separate musical actions perceived as *one* complex musical action. In his article Smalley refers to texture as follows: "Texture . . . is concerned with internal behaviour patterning, energy directed inwards or reinjected, self-propagating; once instigated it is seeming left to its own devices; instead of being provoked it merely continues behaving . . . Where gesture is occupied with growth and progress, texture is rapt in contemplation" (Smalley, 1986, p. 82). The more fragmented the sample, the less its inherent time is perceived.

The consequences of iterating fragments is therefore twofold: the first one, the generation of texture, is evident. The second, is a corollary of

---

[2] A portion of sound recording as opposed to the individual instantaneous amplitude reading of an analog to digital conversion.
[3] Even when a sample has been played at a lower frequency, therefore lasting longer in real time on playback, its implication of virtual time may remain constant, in the same way as a slow motion film sequence may be perceived as the slowing down of an event, but not as a different event.

this: the suspension of time. Here lies *the inner rhythm of texture* which *is* its living fabric. Texture does not refer beyond *itself* if each moment presents a unique state within the attack-effluvium continuum. It refers to the *piece as a whole* when the fragments are recognizable from previous occurrences; this gives rise, partially, to the poetic resource of *refrain*. To the extent that texture refers to itself by virtue of the sample fragments being sufficiently unrecognizable, we perceive a kind of stasis, a *rallentando* of time. If, on the other hand, the fragments lengthen and it is possible to recognize previous material, an element of partial refrain is introduced and the music is propelled forward by the sense of change. Finally if the refrain is too literal then time appears to come to a halt, and the *virtual* time of memory is introduced: the flashback. A refrain which is not literal implies variation, and variation in turn implies development, which embodies the passage of time. A literal refrain implies stasis, it belies development. Tarkovsky, again: "I find music in film most acceptable when it is used like a refrain. When we come across a refrain in poetry, we return, already in possession of what we have read, to the first cause which prompted the poet to write the lines originally. The refrain brings us back our first experience of entering that poetic world, making it immediate and at the same time renewing it. We return, as it were, to its sources . . . Plunging into the musical element which the refrain brings into being, we return again and again to the emotions the film has given us, with our experience deepened each time by new impressions" (Tarkovsky, 1986, p. 158).

Sampling, that is to say the recording medium used to capture sound events or to create sound objects, allows us great flexibility in the use of borrowed material (quotation) and in recreating extraneous sound events (mimesis). In the same way as the refrain points back to the first poetic principles, quotation and mimesis point to the poetic references outside the work proper. They are clues to the compositional world from which the piece has emerged, or simply to the everyday life of the composer. Quotation and mimesis interrupt the flow of time in proportion to the length of the reminiscence they may elicit. Every listener will have a different perception of these since the key to recognizing them is extraneous to the piece of music, whilst the kind of interruption in the flow of time caused by a refrain depends on the clarity of the reference within the piece and the familiarity with the work.

The course of time is therefore imposed on the musical argument by a combination of arbitrary decisions and the discovery of relationships amongst the *time-imbued* samples. Refrain, mimesis and quotation are the instruments that allow us to shape the musical narrative through the articulation of time; they are its poetic principles. The narrative of music is like a narrative of the aural imagination, of the sensitive experience of sound. This is what it *is* in the first place, but being a narrative it also

---

[4] ". . . where the once individual impulses have lost any vestiges of separate identity" (Smalley, 1986, p. 72).

brings with its unfolding the definition of causal relationships between its elements, or of simultaneity, or simply of succession. Although the key to understanding its poetics lies here, the secret of its beauty is always beyond us. We only know it by intuition, when the intellect "finds its joy without abstraction, effort or discourse" (Maritain, 1974, p. 34).

References

Maritain, J. (1974) *Arte y Escolastica*, Club de Lectores, Avenida de Mayo 624, Buenos Aires. Translated from the 3rd French edition of 'Art et Scolastique', 1920, Louis Rouart et Fils, Editeurs, Paris
Smalley, Denis (1986) Spectro-morphology and structuring processes. In *The Language of Electroacoustic Music* edited by S. Emmerson, Basingstoke: Macmillan Pres
Tarkovsky, A. (1986) *Sculpting In Time*, London: The Bodley Head
Wishart, T. (1985) *On Sonic Art*, York: Imagineering Press

Rhythm as motion discovered

Javier Alvarez
Department of Music, The City University, London, UK

"Rhythm as motion discovered" is divided into three parts that discuss some of the author's current compositional ideas. The first part has two themes: firstly, the relation between language and material and the privileged position of the electroacoustic composer in his dealings with musical material as a sonic craftsman. Secondly, that meaning in musical language is in fact a 'discovery' of satisfactory relations between the motion of musical structures and physical human experience and suggests that by 'discovering' this relation the listener engaged in the apprehension of musical form. The second part of this paper describes how the author's compositional work has stemmed from the perspective of rhythm proposing that rhythmic structures are perhaps the strongest and most crucial references in music. Concepts such as repetition, rhythmic objects, and their transformation in the context of recent works (namely *Caracteristicas* and *Temazcal*) are analysed. In the third and final section musical time, structure and rhythmic objects are discussed in terms of the techniques and procedures described previously and in the context of the work *Papalotl*. Finally, it is proposed that motion can be thought of as a *rhythm of rhythms*, and that by shaping motion in the aural experience the composer can in fact articulate musical time and form in a way that has a poetic meaning to the listener.

KEYWORDS composition, language, materials, motion, musical time, rhythm, repetition, structure.

Materials, language and musical behaviour

> . . . it will in Time be that he will discover the path, disentangle his face, speak and vomit what he has swallowed and free himself from his dreams.
> The Book of Chilam-Balam

Since my first incursion into the field of electroacoustic music, I have been thrilled to discover in the method of work immense similarities with Origami, the Japanese art of paper folding which I have been practicing now for nearly fifteen years. This similarity is relevant to my work: here I have two activities in which language and materials are magically bound together, where invention is *experienced as it is being produced*, and language unfolds *as it is invented*. As someone who is highly suspicious of recipes, I have found working in electroacoustics and with computers a liberating experience in my musical explorations. No doubt, all sorts of

203

composers bear witness to the difficulties in articulating a musical language, particularly in a time of great stylistic diversity, but I believe that the electroacoustic composer is specially privileged in that he gets immediate aural feedback on his work. In a similar way to a concert performer, one is here in a position where one's "technique" and "sound" are constantly reformulated as a result of what one hears coming out of one's "instrument". But in the private world of the electroacoustic music composer, this has a more far reaching effect. It is not only the act of subjecting a given technique to aural judgement, but more important, questioning one's own thought processes, preconceptions and materials as they impinge on one's perception. Furthermore, perception itself is gradually broadened as a result of this active way of listening. Anyone who has worked with computers will recognize the effectiveness of this feedback/feedforward loop. This, I propose, undoubtedly reflects on the rigour with which one chooses and organizes one's material.

I therefore believe that the nature of this working method –the composer's "musical behaviour"– determines to a large extent how he articulates large structures and musical form. Any discussion on the structuring of art is virtually impossible without constantly referring to the interplay between the composer's methodology and perception, his material and language[1]. In Origami, to come back to my opening suggestion, each fold on the square piece of paper brings out a number of consequences, both in relation to the original material itself, to the way in which new folds are suggested or could be executed and to the predicted overall formal result. As in music the material is not necessarily so restricted, the consequences of manipulating material and the continuity of *how* this is precisely done are even more crucial in articulating form.

The writer Jorge Luis Borges has pointed out that *'a language is a tradition, a way of feeling reality, not and arbitrary repertoire of symbols'*. (Borges, 1972, p. 1081). If one imagines for a moment that a working method is like a tool box then language can be thought of as being what we construct with the those tools. Language does not possess a fixed identity, it changes as we change. Language in art is something essentially personal, founded on a collection of images of the world around us, on our idiosyncracies, ideologies, rituals, and on the dreams and projections of what we repress. Through these we discover the world and reveal ourselves to others. Musical language emerges when these external and internal images are lured into sonic specificity by the utensils that one acquires in one's musical experience. To draw an onology with Borges's words, the *reality* for the electroacoustic music composer is that of the studio environment, and the *symbols* are the sound objects chosen from the sonic continuum. Musical *language* is both the sound and the sense which the composer intuitively sculpts out of this multidimensional environment. Musical language in sonic terms is invented as one 'feels' one's way through this reality. In saying this I am not implying the supremacy of intuition or a rejection of a rationale behind the act of composition. I am rather suggesting that for me a meaningful musical language cannot rely on its *conventional* aspects, that it cannot simply be constructed from an arbitrary choice of materials (pre-*reality*), as in most European formalist and notational traditions (with respect to which I have always felt a foreigner) but on the *discovery* of how 'possible' and even unrelated sound objects actually behave in space and time and how forces can be articulated with them in music. In Origami, folds play a similar role; they are the source and the instigators of form. In sound, however, this is only verifiable as an aural experience. This is why, in this sense, for me, composition is a practice; the *praxis* of discovering the musicality inherent in any sonic experience. If meaning is a result of communication, then language is not about discovering a way to invention but about inventing a way to discovery.

Rhythm as a starting point

In opposition perhaps to many approaches to composition mine has always been focused around one of the more basic aspects of music: rhythm. My earliest musical experience was through dance. Since then I have been fascinated by motion in music; in later practice this has become the starting point of most of my explorations into musical dimensions, just as the blank piece of paper is to the practice of Origami. This has obviously had a bearing on my attitude towards formal design in that in many of my works the organization of formal elements stems from the articulation of initial rhythmic ideas. Pitch and timbre end up being organized as the 'collide' with rhythmic structures. But before I describe my approach to dynamic musical forces and form I will begin with some general observations that illustrate my point of departure.

In most Western art the articulation of form has been rooted in the concepts of symmetry and balance. Western music too, has in many ways inherited this conceptual framework. Historically this has been operative mainly in the realm of pitch organization models, from medieval modality through tonality up to the twelve tone and total serial systems. As far as rhythm is concerned the implications have been more a consequence of the organization of pitch. I am specifically thinking of instances like the 'rules of thumb' of classical counterpoint and harmony (where rhythm follows the contour of harmonic functionality) or the abstracted hierarchisation of rhythm in terms of durations^2 and avoidance of literal repetition in the compositional strategies of recent years. But we must not forget that in listening to any music, as in the appreciation of other discursive arts, form is gradually apprehended as time passes and not as a 'one shot' experience as in the static visual arts or architecture. Musical form is in fact shaped within the dynamic perceptual process of our psychological state and memory. What we hear and forget and what we project in the unknown future is only meaningful in experiental time. It is from this viewpoint that abstracted notions such as symmetry in composition seem so foreign: how can symmetry be perceived objectively when measurable chronometric time and unmeasurable experiental time cannot be simultaneously experienced? As far as rhythm is concerned, the concept of form based on notions of duration suffers from the same weakness in that durations can only be experienced comparatively, that is in relation to preceding and successive durations. It might all be notationally sensible (and indeed marketable from a publisher's point of view!). But it would be naive to pretend that our perception processes all durations in a complex piece of music and that we are able to trace the formal symmetries which such music is supposed to articulate. Our appreciation of temporal structures is determined by the limits of what we can represent in memory and what we can physically "resonate" to. As far as purely temporal structures are concerned, 'time durations' apply to long (in a chronometrical sense as well) events. Because of this characteristic, they are not immediately quantifiable items: even the educated listener has a hard time relating durations adjacent to the one he is currently perceiving! Notions such as symmetry and balance, while clearly seen on the printed page, are not aurally operative in music where elements are not able to serve each other element as context. This referential aspect is a crucial factor for any network to be semantically "meaningful". I tend to believe that other formal/temporal references such as pulse, repetition, and *rhythmic objects* (discussed below) must be reconsidered if we are to free our esthetical experience from the tyranny of the worn-out formalist and abstracted norms of Western music. Furthermore, the formidable potential of the electroacoustic music medium is a clear invitation to do so especially when many non- Western musical sources and ideas still remain un-examined. In this article, I shall discuss some of my approaches to the use of such references hoping that these may serve as suggestive alternatives.

Rhythm, discovery, motion and meaning

In conventional textbook definitions (for example Cooper & Meyer 1966, or Apel, 1972) rhythm has been typically described in terms of 'beats', 'regular patterns', 'meter' etc. Again, the challenge comes when we consider that these neat definitions apply to musical time *as notated* and not as the *actual sound experience*. The limitation of this approach becomes more evident when, in working with computers, one realizes that sound objects very often embody time periods other than simple ratios, or metrical and chronometric measurements. Such conceptions tend to reinforce a lattice based idea of temporal relations rather than dealing with motion in terms of shape, behaviour and physical response as in dance. Although I shall not discuss it here, this is just one of the problems brought by Western musical notation, most particularly in the last twenty years[3].

I mentioned before that rhythmic motion has been the starting point in my musical experience and I would like now to qualify this. This notion is closely related to the idea of *discovery* outlined above in relation to musical language. I will suggest here that rhythmic structures constitute perhaps the strongest temporal references by which *motion* is *discovered* by the listener, and by which dynamic musical gestures can be constructed. Motion *is* the meaning of rhythm. Motion can after all be understood as an emergent property of physical gesture. In this sense, my notion of 'rhythm' is holistic. By 'rhythm' I am implying the collection of all such discrete, aurally identifiable gestures. In this collection-continuum which I shall call the *rhythm palette*, I include all temporal structures ranging from simple pulses to complex statistical structures. (See Figure 1).

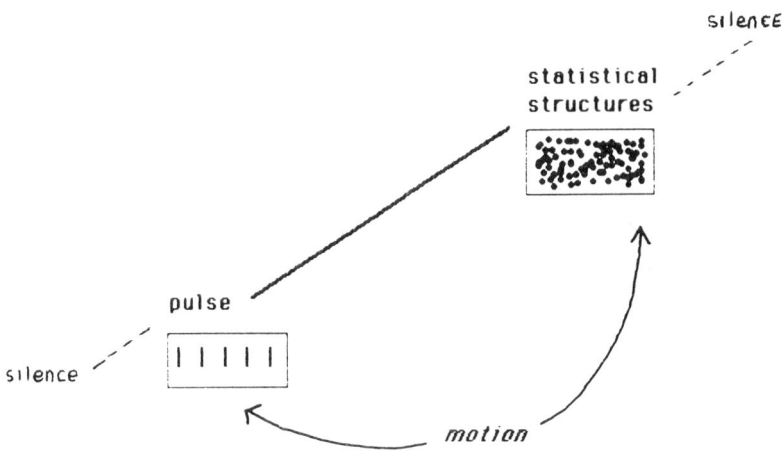

Figure 1 The Rhythm pallette.

The rhythmic object

Within this rhythm palette, my interest has been drawn to experiment with *rhythmic objects*. As with the concept of *sound object* (well known to electroacoustic music) so the idea of rhythmic object here implies a short entity with very clear characteristics, such that at subsequent hearing, the object can still be recognized as being the same. Because of the mobility inherent in any sound object, rhythmic objects can only be grasped in terms of the correlative elements that inhabit them. As such rhythmic objects are usually the synthesis of two global aspects. Firstly, they are made up of the relations between accented and unaccented parts.

'Accent' here has not a speculative meaning: accent is in itself an objective phenomenon and has an organizing function which is aurally verifiable through differentiation of timbre, length or dynamics. Secondly, there is a timbral character and spectral trajectory inherent in all rhythmic objects. The interaction of these two global aspects determines the shape and behaviour of a rhythmic object and its implied motion. Depending on which of these two aspects predominate, the rhythmic object will either be closer to a purely pulsed rhythmic cell pattern or to the more familiar idea of a sound object[4] (see Figure 2).

It has always seemed to me that sound objects behave in a way very similar to natural events. Repetition is an essential part of nature and life in its cyclic eventualities: photosynthesis, day and night, sex, work, sleep, life and death . . . etc. Within the framework of all such natural-to-cosmic repetitions we apprehend and differentiate the uniqueness and singularity of the events in our life. In Gilles Deleuze's words:

'if repetition exists, it expresses a singularity against the general, an extraordinary against the ordinary, an instantaneity against variation, an eternity against permanence. In all aspects, repetition is transgression. It questions the law, denounces its nominal and general character in search of a deeper and more artistic reality.

(Deleuze, 1986 pp. 9–10)

Since my first experiences with rhythmic objects, it has seemed very natural, if sound objects were short, self contained events, to articulate them into larger phrases and up to a large structural status by means of repetition. Whilst the uniqueness of the object is preserved, the larger structures (objects of objects) are imbued with its original characteristics. This always provides a great number of choices and possibilities which I have explored in my recent works.

Repetition and pulse

One of the most important consequences of using repetition in sound is the generation of the most basic grouping of events: pulse. A pulse can be thought of as a chain of events or 'points' that are perceived as being equally spaced in (musical) time. The features of pulse are its *period*, or the perceived interval between the events and *phase*, or the actual time at which any particular event is perceived relative to some reference time. All pulses are potentially infinite series, but in the limited context of a rhythmic object, pulse is inferred within the boundaries of the object. In the case of repeated rhythmic objects, which already contain a strong pulsating energy, the results can be extremely rich and compositionally suggestive. When a rhythmic object is repeated two sorts of pulse start emerging together: a global pulse related to the pulse and period of the repetition and a local pulse manifest in the phase and period of the object itself (Figure 3); I shall come back to this.

Rhythm as motion discovered 209

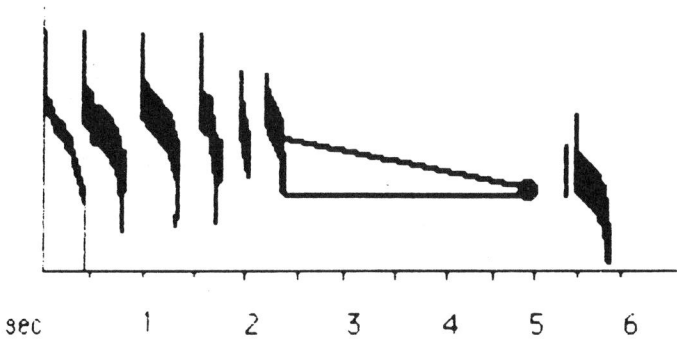

rhythmic object with discontinuous accented shape saliences and internal pattern grouping predominant over timbral features

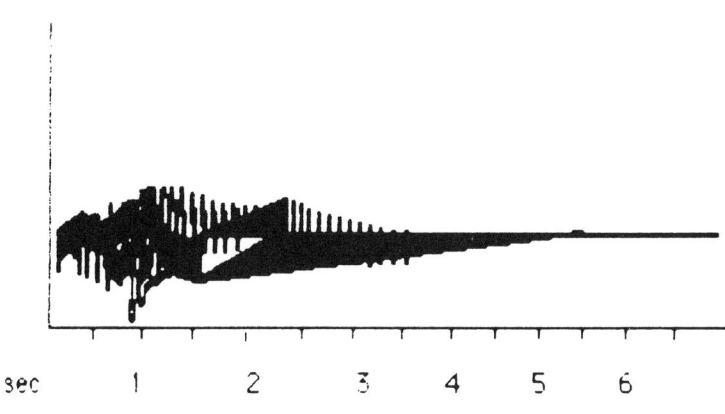

rhythmic / sound object with continuous un-accented shape timbral chracteristics and spectral trajectory predominant over salient features.

Figure 2 The sound and rhythmic objects.

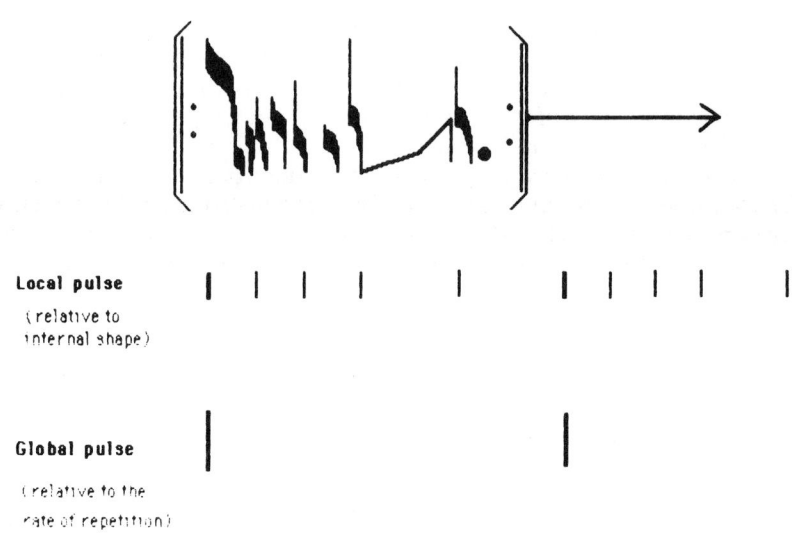

Figure 3   Repetition of a rhythmic object: global and local pulse.

Just precisely how the phenomenon of pulse is inferred has been discussed in some detail by psychoacousticians and psychologists[5]. From my practical experience I have come to the conclusion that a pulse 'point' emerges by the existence of two accented events. The period and phase of the successive pulse points is determined by the temporal position of the accented events. This is assumed in this article. Pulse is invariably meaningful for the listener in that it serves him as a reference onto which motion is mapped. I therefore like to think of pulse as a sort of reflection of repetition. In dealing with repetition we are implicitly articulating pulse and motion.

Rhythmic objects and variation

Among my first attempts to use repetition to articulate larger musical structures was my work *Caracteristicas* (1982) for flute, oboe, cello and piano. In this work, I initially started by pairing each instrument with specific rhythm objects of different characteristics (hence the title). I also established a meeting point – an axis – between the repetition of selected rhythmic objects and the 'breaking up' of the inner design of the objects. In this particular case I wanted to elucidate motion in the music by moving between periodic and aperiodic gestures, so simple additive repetition preceded or followed by segments of free variation (or 'breaking up') seemed effectively appropriate. (See Figure 4). To digress slightly, I like to think of this opposition as an analogy (in terms of timbre) to harmonicity and inharmonicity. The repeated object corresponds to a harmonic area, its breaking up to an inharmonic one. In fact, in *Caracteristicas*, repetition was frequently paired instrumentally with clear harmonic contours, while departures from repetition were paired either to harmonic ambiguity or to inharmonic instrumental sounds, such as multiphonics. The opposite pairing is also present in the piece. At the level of motion the results were meaningful: when the harmonic/inharmonic axis was paired with repetition/variation, pulse (which was easily inferred from repetition) acted as a stable rhythmic state close to pure pulse, but as soon as the object was broken up the movement became thrust forward in search of a new "harmonic" area of repetition. When the opposite pairing up was effected, inferred pulses were unstable and any variation would deflate the expected sense of motion. This general principle was made operative both at the level of each single line and of the ensemble as a whole, so, to an extent, the motion of the piece is the result of a polyphony of pulses and of their harmonic shapes. But, in terms of timbral and harmonic motion, these become primarily organized as they 'encounter' repetition. The dynamic between these dimensions and repetition, relative to their interaction, is what was described before as 'collision'.

The use of this pairing up of dimensions, and the 'collision' between the two or more distinct elements gives repetition an entirely new meaning. Its role becomes strongly referential as the listener is able to apprehend changes that occur within the objects themselves. This is in preference to its more familiar literal role. Precisely because repetition provides us with *schemeta* onto which our memory latches (through pattern and grouping) the smallest inner variation or transformation of a rhythmic object within it becomes highly significant in our perception of how musical time passes. But the relation is dialectical in that change in the objects also give us a reference to the internal dynamism of the repetition itself. When the objects change gradually, repetition ceases to be mere re-articulation, approaching more and more a continuous stream analogous to a succession of frames in film. Another analogy which might be useful in further clarifying this idea can be found in the perception of movement under stroboscopic lights. When watching an actor under a stroboscopic light, for example, an unchanged and predictable action on his part will end up centering our attention on the strobe itself and its rate of change. But when the action is varied, we cease to focus on the on/off framework and focus on the action itself. We attempt to reconstruct the action as we watch intently: a sense of motion emerges, relative to the rate

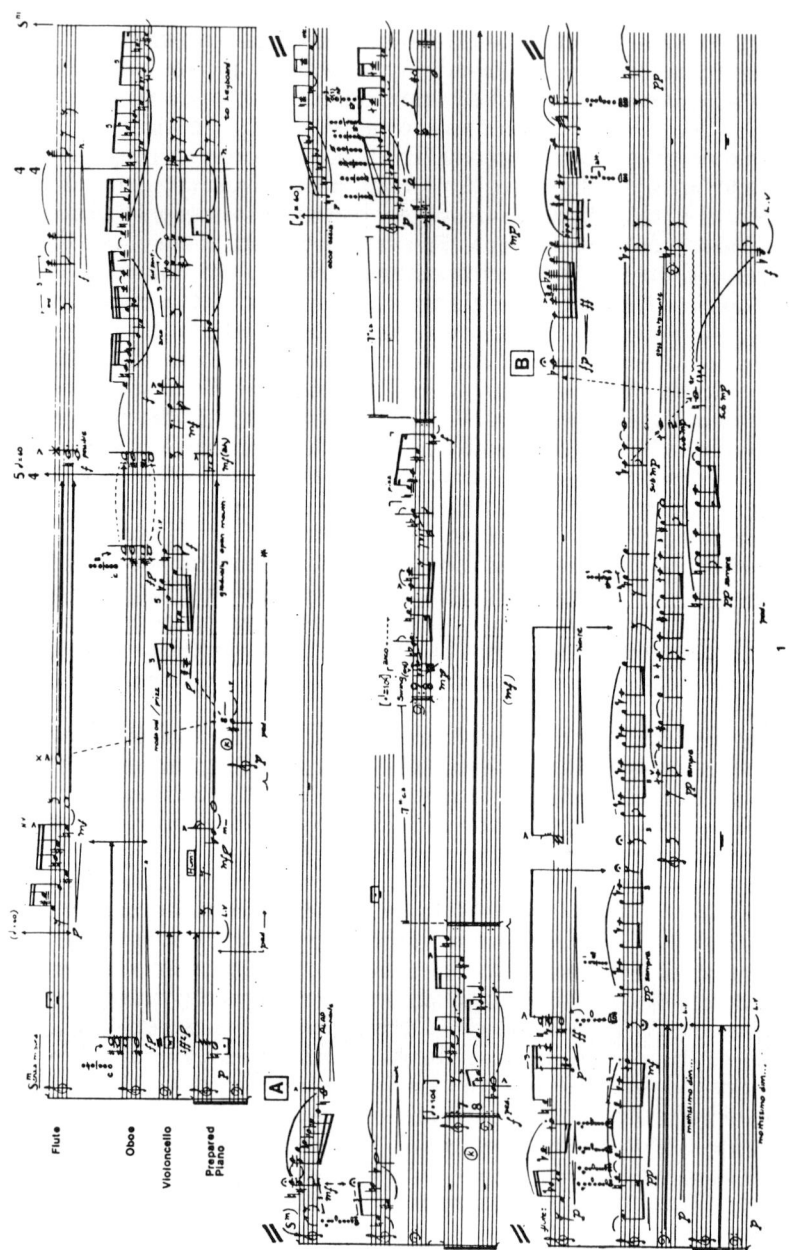

Figure 4 *Caracteristicas* (1982).

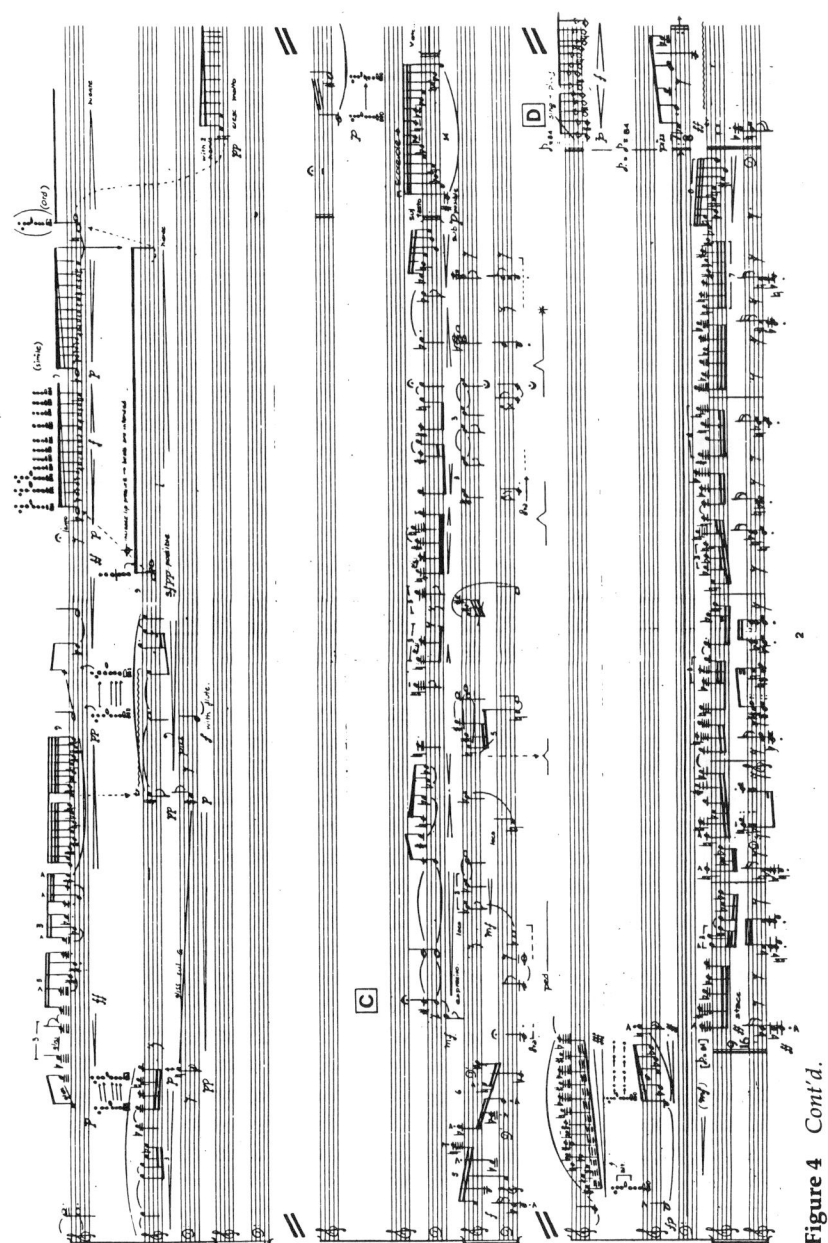

Figure 4 Cont'd.

of the stroboscopic light. In fact, when watching actors under strobes, slow movements will seem even slower, and fast ones will actually seem a lot faster. Under these conditions, our whole sense of speed is easily led in one way or another, and most significant to our discussion, our temporal and spatial perception is modified.

In sound these changes can happen, in respect to repetition, in any musical dimension with similar dynamic effect. For instance, as an unchanging short object is repeated, our interest in its timbre is minimal and we will eventually be drawn towards the globality of the repetition itself. In any case, only if the repetition becomes fast enough (above 18–20Hz) will its timbre contour fuse into a harmonic 'field' related to the frequency of the repetition. But if its timbre contour changes as the object is being repeated, then repetition itself moves into the background and the timbral trajectory is discerned as such. If the frequency of the repetition is fast then the change will be perceived as a gesture. Similar processes operate in the area of harmonic content or the accent contour of the objects. This is basically an expansion of the local/global pulse idea, but for timbral and harmonic processes to be operative, repetition must have a frequency in the audio range. For objects with salient accented features repetition above about 16Hz will produce partial frequencies related both to the period and phase of the accents (or other salient features) in the original object and to the frequency of the repetition itself. This was the principle used in *Papalotl* (1987) for piano and tape to generate gestures and rhytmic objects from short percussive pitched sounds which I will describe in more detail later. At this scale of audio change and repetition, it is therefore possible to think of dynamic morphologies based on interpolations between rhythmic objects and timbre, between timbre and rhythmic objects, between rhythmic objects and harmonic fields etc., as 'collisons' between dimensions of the sonic continuum. I shall presently examine some of my attempts at variation and transformation of rhytmic objects under repetition in the context of purely traditional (non-digital) studio techniques in my work *Temazcal* (1984) for amplified maracas and tape.

In *Temazcal* most of the material of the maracas is drawn from traditional rhythmic ideas found in a large number of Latin American folk musics (Figure 5). Because the maracas have a limited timbre (basically noise-based), its objects are primarily rhythmic cell patterns (according to the terminology outlined above) which are juxtaposed against the rhythmic/sound objects on tape and utilized timbrally to supply the high frequencies of the total spectrum of the work. Variation in the maracas part is mainly achieved by a process which works in the following way. Each short section in the work is headed with a main pattern, which contains two or three secondary patterns (see Figure 6). The player responds to the pulse and objects on tape by repeating and/or chaining these cells and repeated patterns together in any order, thus obtaining larger pattern strands. Different performers have come up with diverse strategies to put these together — the solutions have been very suggestive

Figure 5 Traditional Latin American rhythmic cells.

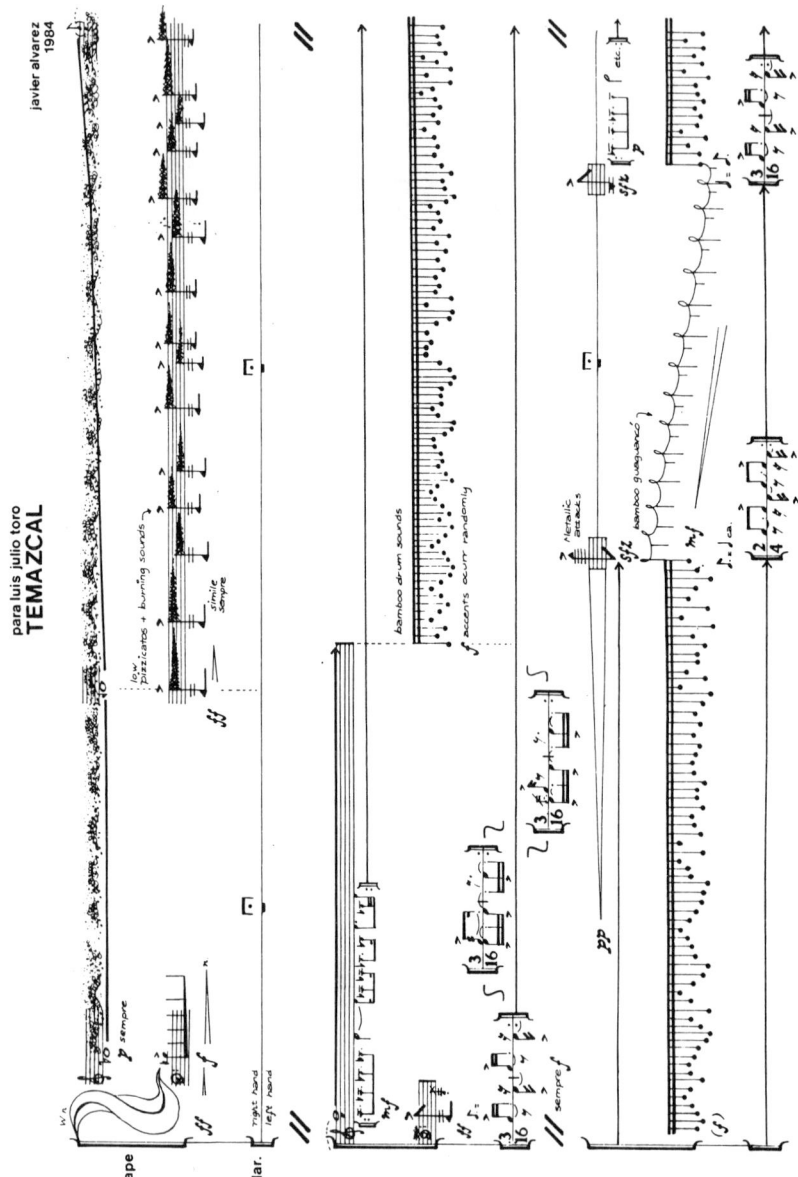

Figure 6 *Temazcal* (1984).

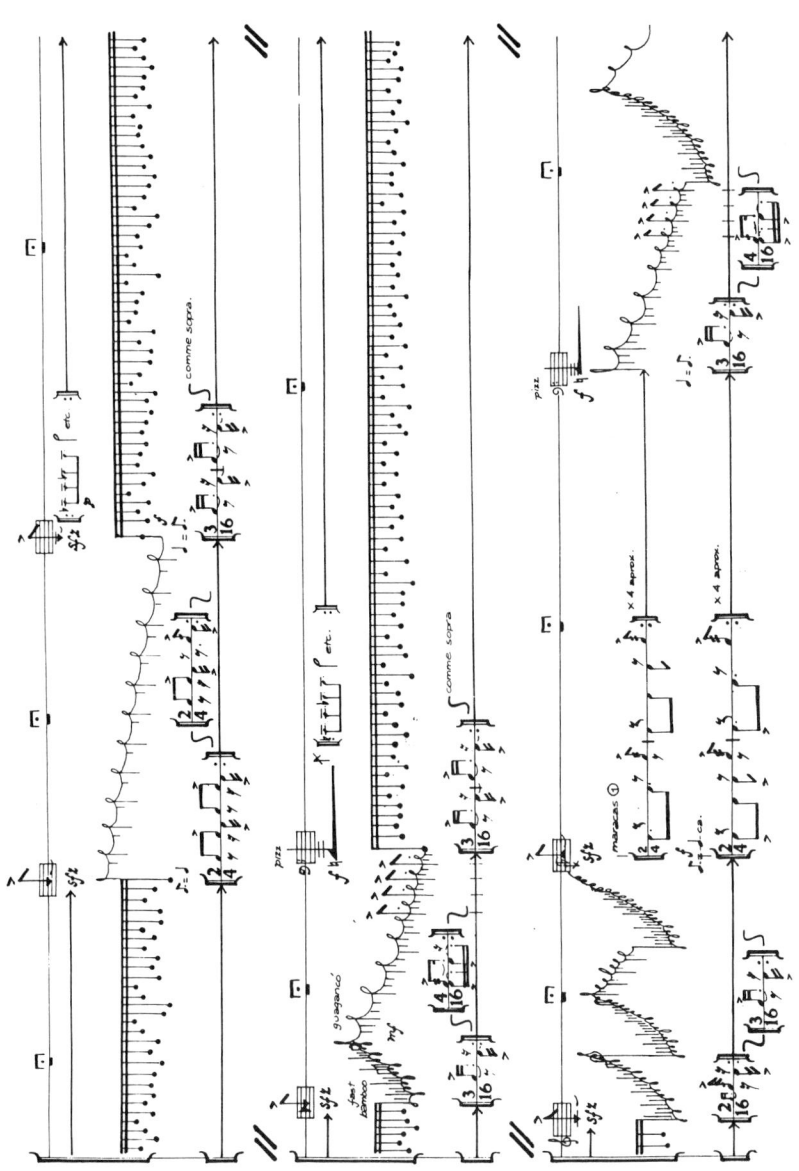

Figure 6 Cont'd.

Figure 7 Example of resultant patterns in performance of Temazcal.

in regards to how this kind of material can be developed (see Figure 7). In each section, the complexity of the strands is thereafter left to the player and result from his reactions to the motions suggested to him by the pulses on tape. This is æsthetically very attractive to me, in two senses. Firstly, in that the performer must, by the very nature of the work, engage in active listening, and almost dance in order to pull the piece together. Secondly, this simple approach breaks away from the concept of the tape as a straight-jacket: in *Temazcal* it is possible to interpret freely the suggested material, but, even under these apparently loose conditions, synchronisation points invariably remain extremely accurate while the response to the material on tape remains seemingly personal.

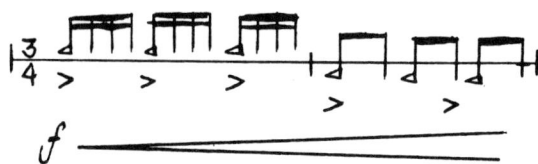

Figure 8 Seminal rhythmic object in *Temazcal* (tape part).

With regards to the rhythmic objects on tape, the variations and transformations deal with similar but more complex ideas. The first is concerned with the concept of rhythmic transformation of a basic rhythmic object (Figure 8). The sound object itself was physically produced with two bamboo wooden rods and recorded in the studio. The transformational process it underwent is based on the concept of 'collision' outlined above between a) the local pulse of the rhythmic object b) the global pulse emergent from its continuous repetition against c) the frequency of an amplitude modulating square wave (a type of repetition at sub-audio frequency). The whole process is described below. In the first place, extended material was generated by repeating (looping in *musique concrète* terms) the basic rhythmic object. The phase trajectory of the object's local pulse points was approximately 1.75 to 2.0Hz (MM ♩ = 80 to 120 in the notated score). The global pulse points (repetition rate) ocurred with a period of 0.33Hz (or every 3 seconds approximately). By amplitude modulating this material with a square wave whose frequency evolved from 12Hz to 20Hz (this was simultaneously frequency-modulated by a very slow 0.33Hz sine wave) a great amount of new material rich in saliences emerged. By varying the frequency of the slow sine wave (analogous to the rate of the stroboscopic light) or the speed of the repeated material (analogous to the speed and shape of the action of the actor) further inner motions and resultant rhythmic objects were sculpted. (Figure 9). In this sense, many of the objects present in *Temazcal* can be thought of as contracted versions of the kind of process described above, and the rhythmic processes as expanded versions of the objects themselves.

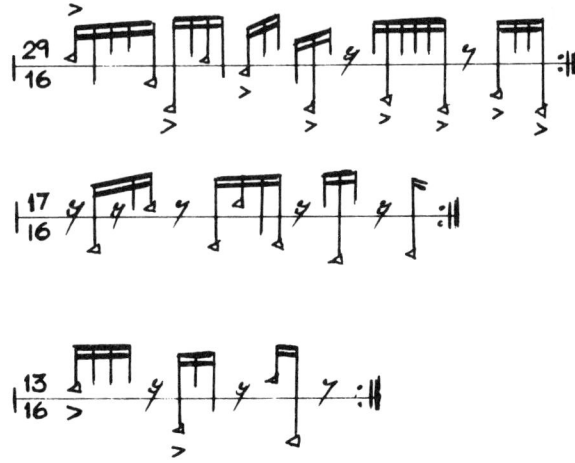

Figure 9 Resulting patterns after transformations.

Rhythmic objects and rhythmic processes

The second idea stems colaterally from the relation between object and process. If process is thought of as an expanded version of the object, then we can generally speculate that the rhythmic object can be revealed to us in different ways by its scale. In zooming in and out of scale (achieved by 'speeding' up or down, in tape transposition terms, for example) it is possible to perceive the same event as an instantaneous gesture by the effect of great contraction or as a vast sonic landscape by the effect of extraordinary magnification. This is something that stems from well known sound recording techniques and which has enormous implications in articulating the dynamic structures typically found in electroacoustic music and cinema. Moreover, it is only from this large scale perspective that the concept of time duration acquires syntactic significance for me. In other words, durations serve only to describe the larger perceptual dimension of sonic landscapes, but they themselves do not articulate the singularity of rhythmic structures other than as chronometrical quantifiers of discrete events. Durations in this sense are comparable to sub-audio frequencies, far too large to have perceptual significance. As far as *Temazcal* is concerned, the spatial magnitude idea is used consistently in instances such as the appearance of material generated from the harp as a source, both as a texture (repeated and 'speeded up' to six times of the original) and as the real object-harp at the end with all its anecdotal and extra-musical connotations. But in a more global and poetic way, the piece is permeated with the idea that the tape part enacts the life of some kind of 'gigantic maraca' inside which the listener sits and feels the movement and resonance of the beads as they hit the inner walls of the magnified instrument. The concept of spatial magnitude has great poetic potential and is particularly idiomatic to electroacoustic materials. For this reason extremely mobile structures such as sound objects offer a quasi-organic physical and perceptual environment from which entire works and indeed musical architectures can be constructed. At the compositional level, it suggests multiple possibilities — within this continuum of contraction and dilation of sound objects — of creating clear dynamic forces which effectively shape motion and help further to articulate musical time.

Musical time and structure

Musical time is irreversible. In listening to music, our experience has a clear cut phenomenological frame: a beginning and an end. Trevor Wishart has clearly expressed this uni-directionality of the musical experience:

> '*In sound, the musical experience begins at the beginning and must be taken in the (irreversible) order and at the rate at which it comes to the listener. Furthermore, our experience of what arrives later is modified by our (perhaps*

inaccurate) memories of what has passed, and in this sense there can never be a clear cut "recapitulation" '.

(Wishart, 1985 p. 23).

I have always felt that to invent music is to a great extent to invent some kind of living organism. In inventing music, the composer is also creating a temporal entity which reflects in the listener. Just as pulse is a reflection of repetition, so is musical time a poetic reflection of an objective musical sonic experience. In fact, one could say that musical time if the life-span of such an invention. In this sense, the clearer the referential framework of a piece of music received by the listener, the fuller will be his apprehension of its musical time. Although the composer cannot control how the listener will react and modify his perception, he is in a position to alter the flow of referential 'clues' presented to the listener and by that token modify the listener's engagement in the discovery of musical meaning. This, I believe, is crucial in articulating structure in musical discourse.

The relationship between rhythm and structure: the *rhythm of rhythms*

So far, I have spoken of rhythm as a local structure, in terms of rhythmic objects, pulse, and repetition. But perception is a chain of information, built of synthesis, memory, comparison and premonition. In terms of dynamic structures, as listeners we travel, going back to my earlier analogy, between the stroboscopic light itself and the result of applying the stroboscopic light onto other actions, establishing relations between the details and the globality of motion and shapes. If I am attracted by simple rhythmic entities such as rhythmic objects it is because they provide the possibility of constantly establishing links between events which are in themselves complex, and thus establishing a flow of information which will guide the listeners' sense of musical temporality. In this respect I dream of pieces that will (chronometrically) last, say, 3 hours, but will 'feel' (perceptually) like 3 minutes . . . And because I believe that communication is a pre-condition of musical language, I find it absolutely necessary for the composer to control the flow of information by creating motion between events of great complexity (where only the globality of the discourse is important) and those of great simplicity (where the discourse is stripped down to its bare essentials). This travelling between '*entropy*' and 'primeval pulse' is what I see as the basis of dynamic musical structure. Both modernist 'complexity' or minimalist styles, regardless of their philosophical justifications, suffer from a lack of structural dynamism precisely because they rely, at the extreme, on one basic undifferentiated flow of information. In these instances, the educated listener will limit himself either to a statistical perception of generalities, or to the foreseeable predictability of local events. It is ironic, that in both cases, although for apparently different reasons, the listener's perception is reduced to an unengaged simplistic level. As musical structure can only be evaluated in the aural experience, it is not surprising that musics fabricated on paper calculations can often result in structurally bland and often shapeless entities, incapable of projecting a clear temporal identity in the ears of the listener. As has been pointed out, in dealing with complexity and simplicity in music, temporal *contexts* cannot be ignored[6].

For this reason, dynamic musical structures only emerge when the music engages in motion between the complex and the simple, precisely because motion defines a perceptual framework for the apprehension of timbre, shape, dynamics and musical time. Therefore, in a more global sense than I have spoken before, motion at this level can be thought of as the essence of dynamic structure, *a rhythm of rhythms* of poetical content.

In my work *Papalotl* (1987) for piano and tape, I have attempted to put into practice some of the ideas that I have outlined above, particularly with regards to creating an ever moving organism. The idea that permeates the work is that of a sort of rhythmic *trompe l'oeil*, effected by a constant shift between the periodic and aperiodic pulses implied by the rhythmic cell patterns used. It was my idea to create a work where the listener was constantly struggling to understand simple pulses, yet never entirely fulfilling his desire. Imagine for a moment that you are trying to dance a waltz and as soon as you are in step, the music is changed to a polka, and as soon as you've readjusted a faster waltz appears, and so on . . . This, in dance, is an exhilarating experience, one in which you're always about to loose your balance, one in which listening becomes of vital importance, one where keeping your balance *is* the poetics of movement. In *Papalotl*, it is the incessant shifting of the pulses which constitute the piece's most important structural identity (see Figure 10).

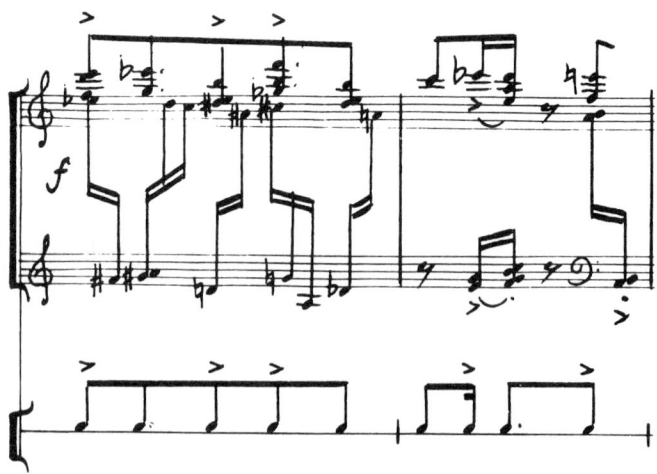

Figure 11 Typical rhythmic object in *Papalotl*.

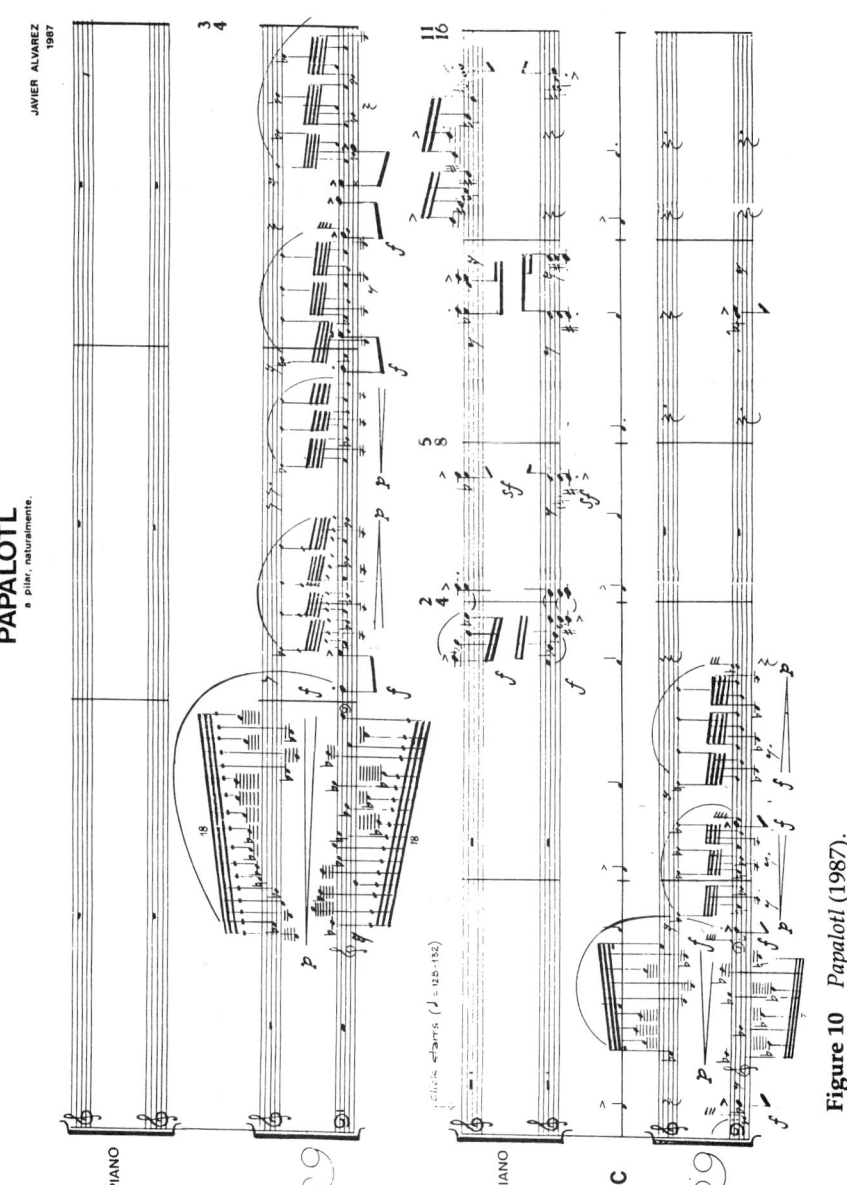

Figure 10 *Papalotl* (1987).

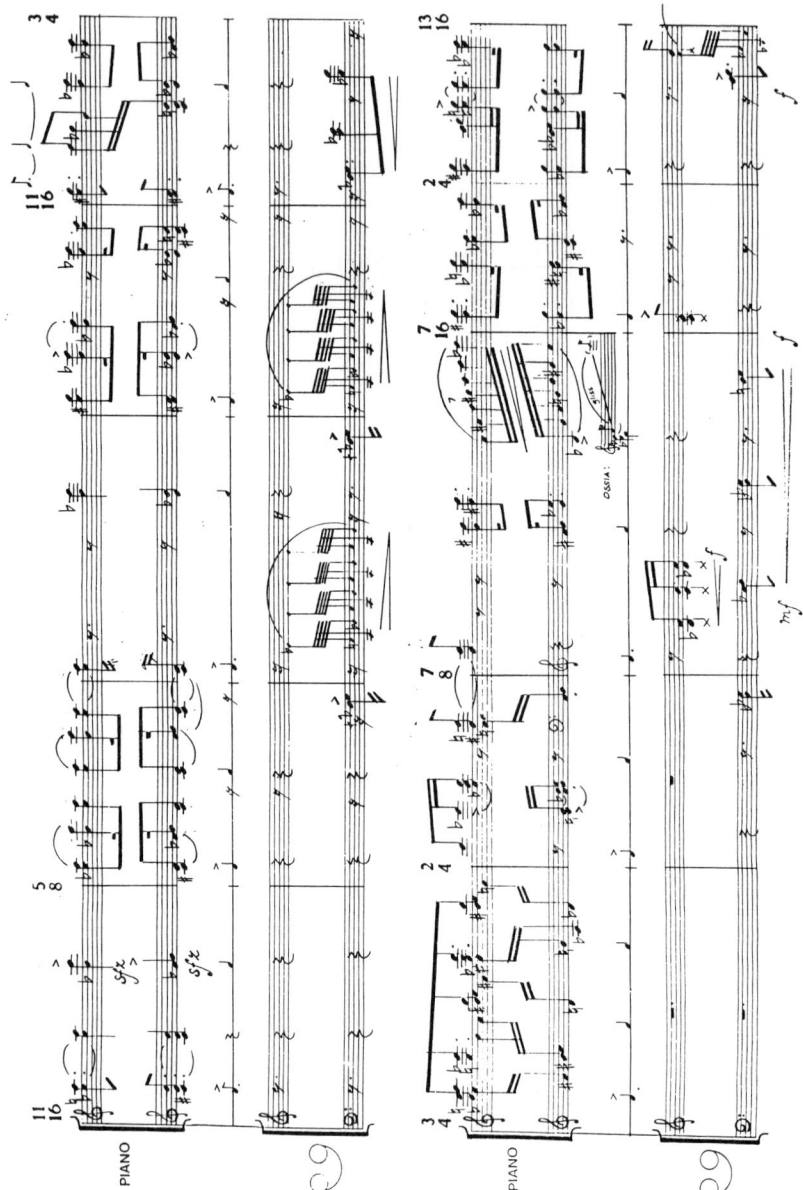

Figure 10 Cont'd.

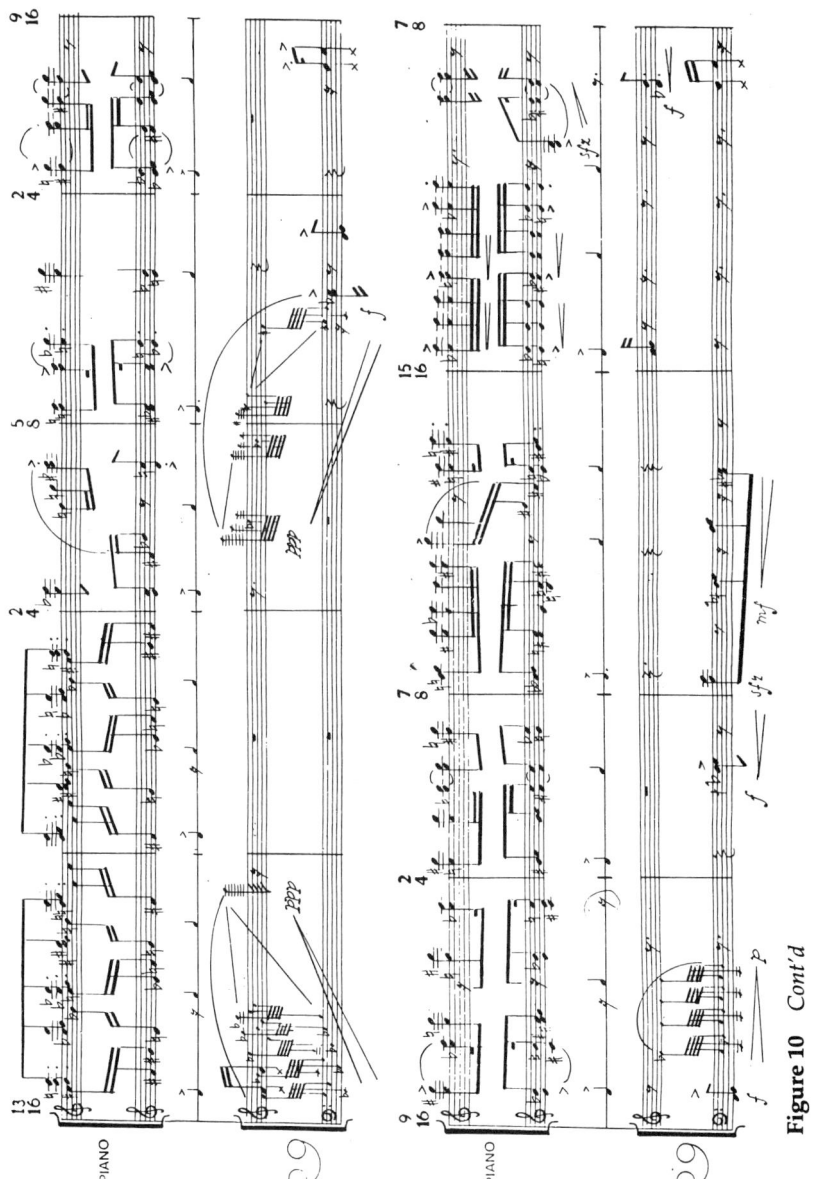

Figure 10 Cont'd

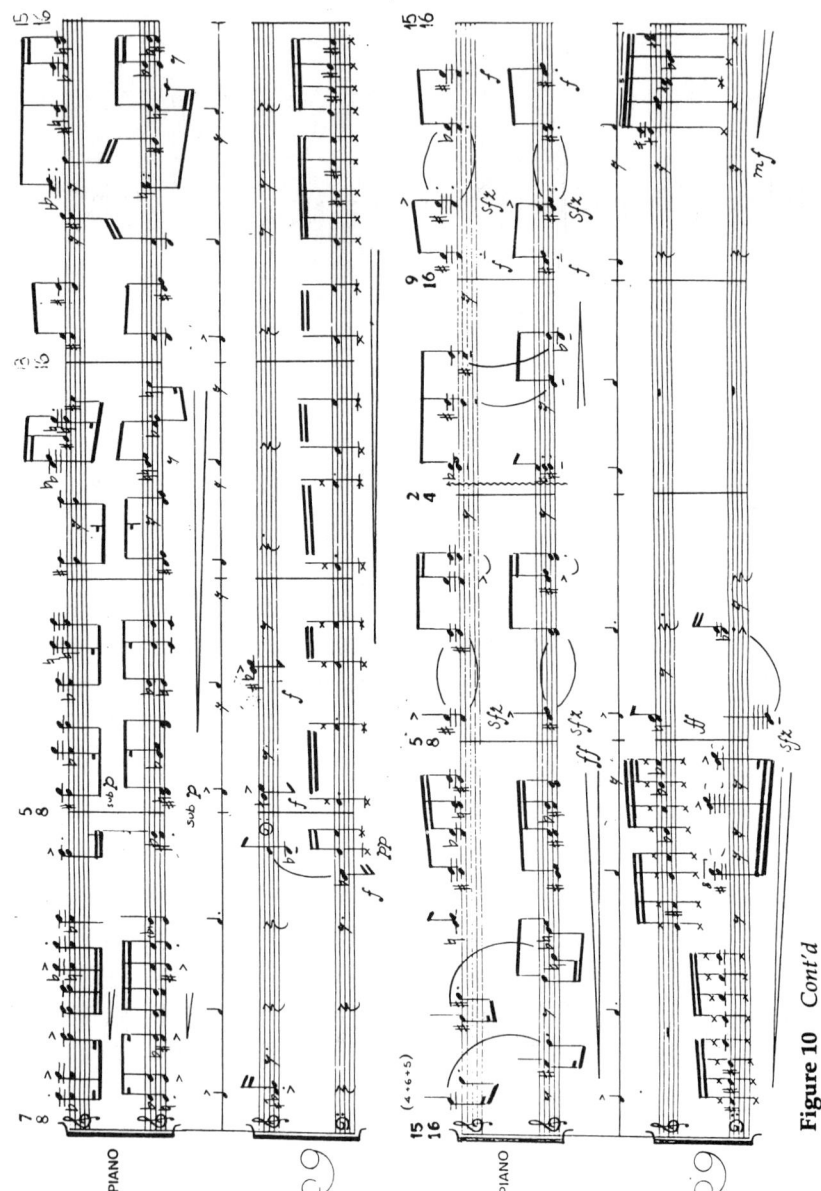

Figure 10 Cont'd

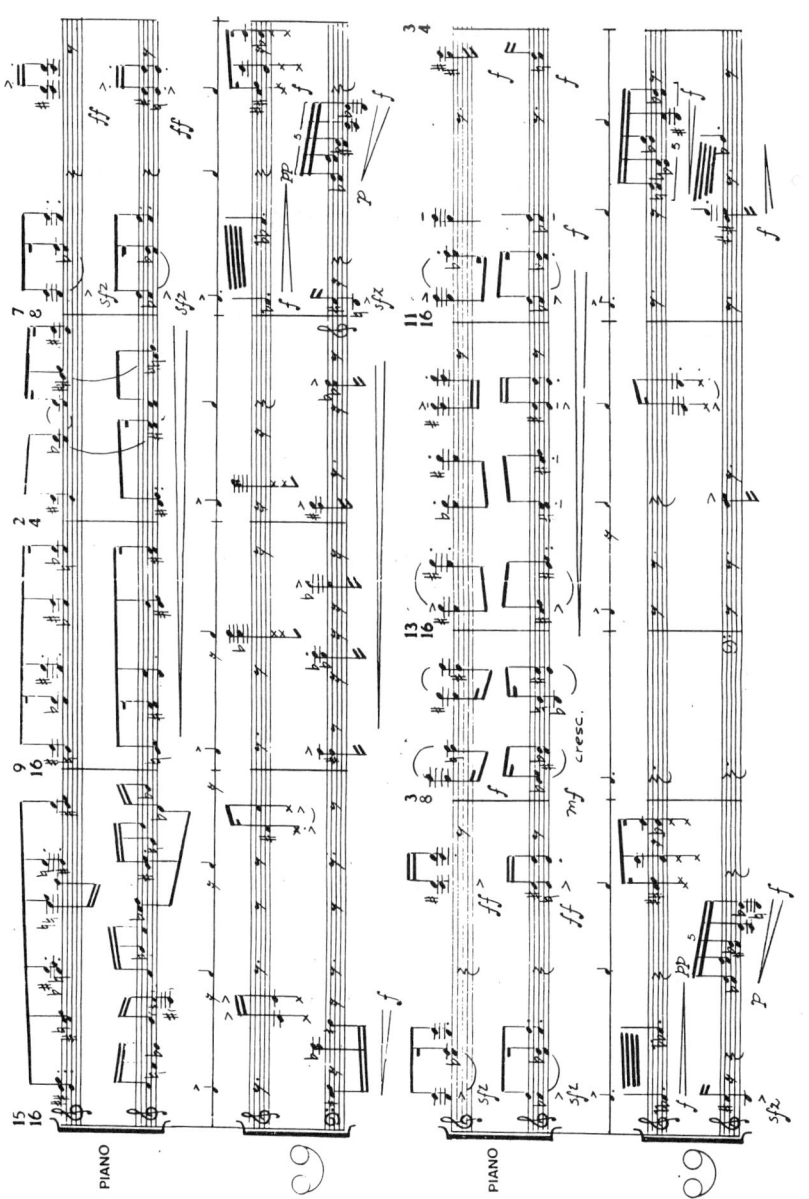

Figure 10 Cont'd

More to the point, however, in *Papalotl* I have used nearly two hundred rhythmic objects (see Figure 11 for a typical example) which are used as the building blocks for the piano and the computer parts. These have been combined and added to construct larger strands of music. The piano part consists mainly of chords playing the patterns. As far as these are concerned, their transformation results mainly from simple operations. These include the following: a) simple addition b) addition of a cell to half of its preceding one c) alternation of these two procedures d) repetition of the above and e) prolations (see Figure 12). Whilst the basic time unit (MM ♩= 528) nearly always remains constant, the pulses implied by the known medieval principle of *talea* and *color*. By the additional operations on the rhythmic patterns, new *talea* are generated, and out of their varying relation with the actual pitches in the piano part, pulse points are made to emerge at harmonically significant points. Chord sequences are also subjected to the processes of addition described above for the rhythmic cells, so both the *talea* and the *color* are changing incessantly throughout the work. Furthermore, pulse variation is achieved by rhythmic modulation applied to the resultant *color*, while the resultant *talea* are left unaltered.

The computer part of *Papalotl* was built of note type sounds from the inside resonances of a piano which were sampled on a Fairlight Computer Music Instrument Series II. Because the samples were short, repetition became the basic procedure to extend them into full-bodied objects. The choice of material, however, was not haphazard: through it the computer becomes a sort of disembodied piano which, in spite of its abstracted presence, retains a perceptual link with the listener. The relation between this material and the piano's was further elaborated by using the same patterns in both parts to determine their transformations. (ie. rate of repetitions, movements of the filter, length of resonances, speed of the attack, etc.). In the computer part, all the control parameters, including phasing, echoes and reverberation were entirely programmed maintaining the same pattern shapes but activated at much higher speeds, in frequencies usually related to the main harmonic centre of the piano part at that particular moment. So for instance, when the piano part is centered at around a c# region, the note objects and/or control parameters were activated to repeat and resonate at harmonic frequencies of 17.32Hz (c#0), 25.96Hz (g#0); 30.87Hz (b0) or 34.65Hz (c#1), etc. Again, as in *Caracteristicas*, periodic repetition in the piano part was paired with harmonic frequencies and aperiodic repetition with inharmonic frequencies operating the control files and rates of repetition of the sampled sounds. In spite of the fact that the piano and computer parts are constantly being juxtaposed, this pairing up gives the work a coherent resonance, and shapes the movement in both parts in a characteristic way. Also, by this means, the piano provides the upper partials of the entire spectral composition of the work, while the tape part constantly touches upon fundamentals.

Finally in *Papalotl*, my most important goal was to compose a work where motion could become structure, where movement was always present, yet never grasped. It seemed to me that the only possible way to achieve this *rhythm of rhythms* was to be able to zoom in and out of the immediacy of its rhythmic percussive surface by creating a landscape, a sort of magnification of all the minute processes which I have described above. The tape 'solos' were therefore composed with this transition of scale in mind. In this sense this work shares with my previous *Temazcal* the idea of recreating a 'giant' instrument inside of which the performer and listener alike experience the resonance, in this case, of the strings'

Figure 12 Pattern transformations in *Papalotl*. Process of simple addition. 1. Pattern a and b added together. 2. Addition of the first half of a to b (ab). 3. Pattern ab and c added together. 4. Addition of the second half of ab to c (abc). 5. Addition of a and b to abc.

motion, becoming an ordinary piano of extraordinary power. As I said before, what is important to me, as a composer, about this motion within an invented landscape is its poetic content, the compositional techniques and procedures being mere devices to communicate it.

To reinvent the aural tradition

The actual techniques employed were very much dictated by the idiosyncracies of the Fairlight instrument. *Papalotl* is, in its entirety, the result of composing in the studio, at the computer, piano part included. The music was later transcribed into standard notation from the computer files after the piece had been completed.

This brings me back to my opening thoughts. *Papalotl* is essentially the result of an aural compositional practice and as such, it corresponds exactly to the ideas abstracted from the actual process of composition itself. Indeed, as I look forward into the future, I believe that the aural process available through electroacoustic techniques is of paramount importance to musical composition, for its tools allow musical thought to acquire higher levels of abstraction and imaginative power which unveil previously unimagined schemes, strategies and images. This, I am certain, will lead us to the discovery of untried ways of listening and to the invention of a new aural tradition.

Notes

1. This statement obviously implies the adoption of an aesthetic position. There is a large amount of music produced today which assumes that structure is only elucidated at the pre-compositional stage. This article assumes that structure is mainly apprehended in the sonic experience. For further discussion of this point see Simon Emmerson's *The Relation of Language to Materials* in *The Language of Electroacoustic Music*. ed. S. Emmerson. London 1986. MacMillan Press. pp. 17–40.
2. I am questioning here the abstracted notion of rhythm in terms of durations, abstracted from (timbral and dynamic) shape: "Pitch and duration seem to me to form the basis of a compositional dialectic, while intensity and timbre belong to secondary categories". Pierre Boulez in *Boulez on Music Today*. Trans. S. Bradshaw and R. Rodney Bennett. London 1971, Faber and Faber. p. 37.
3. The limitations of notation vis-à-vis the multi-layered experience of music is far more pronounced than this argument indicates. For a detailed discussion of this matter see Trevor Wishart's *Beyond the Pitch/Duration Paradigm* in *On Sonic Art*. York 1985. pp 7–27.
4. For a detailed account of the morphology of sound objects see Denis Smalley's *Spectro-Morphology and Structuring Processes* in *The Language of Electroacoustic Music*. Ed. S. Emmerson, London 1986, MacMillan Press. pp. 61–97.
5. See, for instance, recent writings such as Richard Parncutt's *The Perception of*

Pulse in Musical Rhythm in *Action and Perception in Rhythm and Music*, ed. A. Gabrielsson. Sweden 1987. The Royal Swedish Academy of Music, No. 55. pp. 127-137 and Stephen McAdams' *Music: a science of the Mind?* in *Contemporary Music Review*, vol 2. London 1987. Harwood Academic Publishers.

References

(anonymous-Mayan) *El Libro del Chilam Balam*. Mexico. Fondo de Cultura Economica, 1957
Alvarez, Javier (1982) *Caracteristicas*. London 1982. Published by the composer on Black Dog Editions, 23 Barrington Rd. London N8 8QT
Alvarez, Javier (1982) *Temazcal*. London 1984. Black Dog Editions
Alvarez, (1987) *Papalotl*. London 1987. Black Dog Editions
Borges, Jorge Luis. (1972) *El Oro de los Tigres*. In *Obra Completas*, Buenos Aires, 1974, Emece Editores. (reference trans. by J. Alvarez)
Cooper, Grovesnor W. and Meyer, Leonard (1960) *The Rhythmic Structure of Music*. Chicago and London, 1960. The University of Chicago Press
Deleuze, Gilles. (1986) *Difference et Repetition*. Paris, France. Presses Universitaires de France 1968. (Reference trans. by J. Alvarez)
Wishart, Trevor (1985) *On Sonic Art*. York. 1985. Published by the composer on Imagineering Press, 83 Heslington Rd. York YO1 5AX, UK.

Index

Alvarez, J.
   Caracteristicas 210–214
   Papalotl 214, 224
   Temezcal 214, 224
AMPLE 178, 196
Analogies (genetic) 166, 174–175
Analysis (research) 139
Analysis-by-synthesis 72, 90
Anderson, J. R. 70, 79
Associative relations 123–24
   (see also Paradigmatic relations).
Attention 111, 118, 123

Bach, J. S.
   Aus meines Herzens Grunde
   (chorale setting) 36–38, 40
   C major prelude 21
Barthes, R. 145
Berio, L.
   Visage 150, 158
Berwald, F.
   String quartet no. 5 in C major 100
Biological growth 177, 187
Blackboard architectures 47
Brownian motion 184

Cage, J.
   Fontana Mix 152, 157
   Music of Changes 134
Chaos 179
Chomsky, N 16, 26, 29–30
Chopin, F.
   Prelude in F-sharp minor 78, 86–87
Circle of fifths 18, 94, 107
Closure 117, 118, 121, 128
Codes 31, 118, 119, 121, 145–149
Color (and Talea) 228
Comprehensibility 141
Concrete sound sources 153–154
Connectionism 40, 47
Consciousness 111, 113, 120, 121, 128
Consonance
   as flexible concept 32, 38–39
   and constraint system 34–39
Constraint systems 34–40
Context-spaces 56, 62
Culture 2, 111, 114, 118, 124
Cyclic generation 192–195

Diachronic 126, 127
Discrimination net 60, 61

Electroacoustic music 203, 220, 230
   harmonic processes 153
   human voice 150
   language 151
   listeners' response 159–160
   melodic processes 152
   music quotation 151
   scores 147
   spatial organisation 155–156
   structural organisation 157–159
Ensemble 90, 99
Environment 2, 12
Experts, community of 41
Expression 69–79, 90, 99, 106
   note timing 79
   phrase-final lengthening 69
   rubato 69–78
   stress lengthening 79

Fibonacci 138–139
Flexibility in cognition 30–31
Form and process 60, 61, 116–117, 128, 203, 205, 230
FORMES 178
Forte, A. 32
Fractals 177, 180–184
Frames 121, 125, 127, 129

Geometric shapes 178
Gestalt 10, 118
Gesture 198, 199
Golden Section 186
Grammar 17, 18, 20, 30–31, 44, 54, 57, 58, 63, 177, 187
Granular synthesis 178, 184
Grouping
   analysis 43, 45
   boundary 69, 73, 116, 118, 123
   boundary strength 69–70, 74–78
   preference rules 46, 53, 62

Harmonic charge 96, 97
Harmonic processes 153
Harmonic spectrum 184
Harmonisation 50
Haydn, F. J.
   Sonata no. 59 in B-flat major 77, 86

Heuristics 53
Hiller, L. and Isaacson, L.
  Illiac Suite 179
Hierarchic
  clustering 76
  embedding of cognitive
    units 70
  timing components 70
Human voice 150
Hypothesis-testing 136–143
I Ching 134, 142
IMPAC 178
Implication (musical) 113, 123,
  129
Interpretation 76, 89

Jackendoff, R. see Lerdahl, F.

Koch curve 180, 182, 185, 187
Koenig, G. M. 178
Koestler, A. 159
Kunst, J. 30–31

Language 15, 16, 20, 31, 112,
  114–115, 129, 151, 178, 203,
  204, 205
Learning in AI models 39
Leman, M. 30, 40
Lerdahl, F. (and Jackendoff, R.)
  10, 16, 22, 27, 29–30, 40, 43, 44,
  46, 51, 53, 59, 62, 69, 70, 73, 79,
  114, 118, 119
Ligeti, G.
  Atmosphères 139
  Artikulation 147, 151
Lindenmayer 187
Linguistics 123, 125, 126, 130, 178
  (See also Language)
LISP 30, 69, 80, 93
Listeners' response 159–160
Look-ahead 70
L-system 185, 187–194

Machine creativity 177
Mandelbrot, B. 180, 182
Maritain, J. 197, 201
Marr, D. 71–72
Matrices of bisociation 159
Melodic charge 94–96, 107
Melodic processes 152
Memory 70, 71, 79, 113,
  118–122, 125, 127, 129, 130n2
Metre 20, 24, 116, 119
Meyer, L. B. 7–8, 158
Moment form 114, 130n4, 157
Motion 205, 207, 211, 221, 222, 229
Mozart, W. A.

Sonata in A major, K. 331 3, 7–8
Music analysis
  and psycholinguistics
    29–30
  and psychology 1–12
  of transitional music 31–33
Music theory
  and cognition 1–12, 30
  flexibility in 30–32
  scope of individual theories
    30
  synthesis in 32

Nattiez, J.-J. 135
Normal forms 49
"Now" 113, 116, 119, 121, 125

OCCAM 174

Paradigmatic relations 124, 126,
  128, 130n3 (See also Associative
  relations)
Parallelism 46, 51
Parallel processing 174
Parallel production systems
  177
Parmegiani, B.
  Dedans–Dehors 139
Parsing 24, 50–55, 61, 187, 193
Perceived present 111,
  113–119, 121, 122, 125, 129,
  130n2
Performance
  algorithm 74, 80–85
  analytic theory of 7, 76
  expression 7, 23, 24, 69–79, 90
  indeterminism of 71, 76
  process of 70–71
  reproducibility of 69
  rules 107
Phenomenology 111, 113, 117
PI system (Thagard and Holyoak)
  41
Pitch reduction 22
Pitch-time-timbre space 177
Poetics 197
Production systems 177
PROLOG 30, 34, 36
Prolongation 22, 119–120, 130n1,
  n2
Pulse 208, 210, 220
Psychological present
  see Perceived present
Psychophysics 5, 18

Random number applications 178,
  179, 184, 185, 193

Recursive techniques 185–196
Referent 128–129
Refrain 200
Repetition 208, 211, 214, 219, 228
Rhythm 20, 24, 205, 221
Rhythmic cells 193
Rhythmic object 207, 214, 219, 220, 228
Ring modulation 150
Roads, C. 178
Rule-based composition systems 178, 183
Rumelhart, D. (and McLelland, J.) 40 (See also Connectionism)

Saussure, F. de 111, 123–126, 130
Schaeffer, P. 136
Schemata 54
Schenker, H. 8–9, 22, 30, 32, 111, 119–121, 129, 130n2
Seeding cycle 177, 193–194
Segment 113, 118, 119, 121
Self-similarity 177, 180–191
Semiotics 111, 112, 114, 123, 126, 130
Shaffer, L. H. 25, 69, 76, 78, 90
Shearing, G. 167
Signification 111, 112, 123–129
Skryabin, A.
   Feuillet d'Album, Op.58 32–33, 38–39
   Prometheus 32
   'mystic chord' 32
Smalley, D. 140, 141, 199
Solid fugues 194–195
Space grammar 185, 186, 190–91, 195
Spatial organisation 155–156
Steels, L. 34, 40
Stochastic music 177, 178
Stockhausen, K.
   Carré 135
   Gesang der Jünglinge 150, 152
   Telemusik 139, 147, 151, 152, 154, 157
Structuralism 122
Symmetry 194
Synchronic see Diachronic
Synchronisation 99, 105
Syntactic categories 187
Syntagmatic relations 123, 124, 126, 128–129, 130n3

Talea 228
Tarkovsky, A. 198, 199, 200
Tempo 23, 25, 74
Texture 199
   score 190
   line (one dimensional) 185
   plane (two dimensional) 187, 190
   solid (three dimensional) 188
Timbral indices 177
Time 111, 112–113, 117, 119, 123, 125, 205, 220, 221
Time-span reduction 48, 51, 69
Timing 79, 105
Tonality 5, 15, 17, 24, 97, 114, 118, 119, 166
Trees 186, 187–188
Triad 19, 20
Truax, B. 178
Tuning 91, 101–106

Uncertainty 47

Varèse, E.
   Poème Electronique 153, 158

Winograd, T. 29–30
Wishart, T. 198

Xenakis, I.
   Pithoprakta 139

ARS MUSICA '89

THE SPRING OF CONTEMPORARY MUSIC
March 3rd – March 24th 1989

This exciting new annual festival of contemporary music, based principally in Brussels but with centres in other major Belgian cities, aims to discuss 'modernity' and the philosophical and aesthetic questions raised during the last 15 years. Presenting a panorama of Belgian and European contemporary music, the festival will focus on composers and compositions from the last 15 years, and is aimed both at the general public as well as those with a specialist interest.

The first and last weeks are devoted exclusively to concerts, while the second week, and focal point of the festival, will be a series of seminars and masterclasses culminating in a colloquium. The colloquium, attended by composers, performers and representatives of important musical reviews, including **'Contemporary Music Review'**, will consider the concept of 'modernism' and the place of the media and the public in the creation, interpretation and perception of contemporary music.

The centre of all these activities will be the old Belgian Radio building, Place Flageyplein, built in the thirties in Art Deco style.

For further information:

ARS MUSICA
18 Place Eugène Flageyplein
B – 1050 Brussels
Belgium
Tel: 32/2/647 10 49
Telex: 62 193 BRTBRA B
Fax: 32/2/640 39 76